7

This is the Prophets and it's a good one. I hope you enjoy it as much as I do. All my love to you,

Charles

Bear Valley Lectureship
September 2015
Denver

Majoring In The Minors

A Study of The Minor Prophets – Part Two

Publication of Bear Valley Bible Institute International

Edited By

Neal Pollard and Donnie Bates

HOPKINS publishing inc.

P.O. Box 3687
Cleburne, TX 76033
HopkinsPublishing.com

Copyright © 2015 Bear Valley Bible Institute International
ISBN-10: 1-62080-047-0
ISBN-13: 978-1-62080-047-8
Library of Congress Control Number: 2015947058
Version 1.0

eBook:
ISBN-10: 1-62080-048-9
ISBN-13: 978-1-62080-048-5

**Discover Other Titles By
Hopkins Publishing
HopkinsPublishing.com**

Dedication

This year's Lectureship has continued looking at the great prophetic books of the Old Testament. Every Bible student has appreciated the work of God's men seen in these books. They were truly men of God. They handled the difficult and unpopular task of delivering messages of punishment and judgment. Yet their love for God was the foundation of their lives. They wanted to be difference makers. They wanted to see God's people return to Him and enjoy all of His wonderful blessings. This year's lectureship book is dedicated to a man who embodies the spirit of these Old Testament prophets. He has duplicated their love for God's people, their work ethic and their life-long commitment to spiritual causes. This man is **Dave Chamberlin.**

At the age of 18, Dave began his work with the United States Air Force. He was a military instructor (both tactical and technical) in basic training as well as doing aircraft maintenance in Amarillo, Texas. During this time he met and married Barbara Ann. They have now been married for 58 years. The year they were married (1957) is also the year that Dave was converted to Christ.

For the next six years, Dave worked in both the New York area as well as in Amarillo. He worked for General Electric from 1959-1963, then opened his own automotive repair business in Amarillo in 1963. However, it wasn't long before Dave's heart turned toward ministry. So, in 1965 he enrolled in the Sunset School of Preaching. Upon graduating, he accepted a job preaching in Minot, North Dakota.

In 1969 Dave and Barbara Ann decided to take on a mission work, and they went to Tauranga, New Zealand. Dave was a preacher for a local congregation but also was a teacher and director for a local preacher school. They worked in New Zealand until 1975.

In 1976 Dave was the Educational Minister for the Lakewood (CO) church of Christ and a part-time instructor for the Bear Valley School of Preaching.

In 1977, Dave became a full-time instructor at Bear Valley. He also took the position of Dean of Students, a position he still fills today.

In 1997 Dave took a position as full-time minister for the Twin Peaks congregation in Longmont, CO. He worked with them until 2003, serving as both a minister and one of her elders. He drove down weekly to continue teaching for Bear Valley.

In 2004, Dave and Barbara Ann returned to work with Bear Valley full time. He reassumed the role of both instructor and Dean of Students. For the past four years Dave has served as one of the elders of the Bear Valley Church of Christ.

Dave is the 'senior member' of the Bible Institute. This year makes 39 years (1976-2015). His expertise in the Old Testament, plus his love for history brings an important and needed element to the curriculum of the Bible Institute. Dave, thank you for your love for the Lord, your love for training preachers and your many years of faithful service.

It is most fitting, in view of a lifetime of sacrificial service to the Lord's church and to the Bible Institute, that we dedicate this Lectureship volume to **Dave Chamberlin**.

For the Faculty and Lectureship committee,
Denny Petrillo
President
Bear Valley Bible Institute International
2015 Bear Valley Lectures

Table of Contents

SECTION I

Special Studies

CHAPTER 1

Seeing The Church
In The Minor Prophets

Jim Dearman

There are many in the religious world today who would consider this writer's assignment impossible. Their conclusion would be based upon their belief in one of the most pervasive, yet perverted, teachings in denominationalism—the doctrine of premillennialism. It denies the possibility of seeing the church in any of the prophets.

The premillennial premise contends the church was never in the mind of God until after the Christ was rejected by the Jews and crucified. Before that time, according to this perverted teaching, Jesus came initially to establish an earthly kingdom. However, when the Jews refused to accept him as the awaited Messiah, this thwarted the Lord's plan. The Lord then established the church as a temporary institution, ushering in a parenthetical period, the church age. According to the theory, when the Lord comes again, He will succeed in establishing an earthly kingdom and reigning for a literal one thousand years in Jerusalem on the literal throne of David.

The fanciful theory purports to draw most, if not all, of its key points from one passage in the Revelation letter—Revelation 20:6. Yet, this text contains no hint of an earthly reign of Christ, a rapture, a tribulation of several years between a first and second resurrection, or any of the other major tenets of premillennialism. The thousand-year reign is, obviously, figurative; and there is not a scintilla of evidence to support the premillennial conclusions. In fact, their premise will crumble under the weight of prophecies in the Old Testament, which clearly predict the establishment of the church. If one definitive predictive statement about the church exists in any of the Old Testament books, the premillennial theory is nullified. In truth, not one, but many unmistakable predictive statements among the prophetic books point clearly to the establishment of the church. The scope of this study will be confined to those pertinent prophecies in the Minor Prophets, particularly those among the last six books.

IMPORTANT PRELIMINARY CONSIDERATIONS

Before examining specific prophecies, it is important to establish two very important facts. The first is that the church and the kingdom are one and the same. This is crucial in order to prove that, when the prophets refer to the coming kingdom, they are referring to the church rather than a still future earthly reign. Premillennialists seek to distinguish between the church and the kingdom to suit their theory, but Jesus demonstrates otherwise.

In Matthew 16:18-19, in His exchange with Peter, the Lord uses the terms "church" and "kingdom" interchangeably: "And I also say to you that you are Peter, and on this rock I will build My church, and the gates of Hades shall not prevail against it. And I will give you the keys of the kingdom of heaven, and whatever you bind on earth will be bound in heaven, and whatever you loose on earth will be loosed in heaven." These words followed Peter's confession that Jesus is the Christ. The Lord commended Peter for the confession and then uttered the promise to build His church.

Notice the interchangeable use of the words "church" and "kingdom" in verses 18 and 19. The Lord's use of the two words clearly demonstrates a dual description of one institution. Therefore, when the prophets of old predict anything about the nature of the coming kingdom, they are speaking of the church. The Lord's synonymous use of the two terms proves this to be the case.

A second important preliminary consideration involves Old Testament prophecies concerning the crucifixion of Christ. If premillennialism is true, the cross was not anticipated by the prophets, and their writings should contain no Messianic material relating to the Lord's betrayal and death. Remember the premise of premillennialism is that the Lord intended to establish an earthly kingdom in His first appearance. However, that effort was supposedly thwarted by the Jews when they rejected and crucified Him. However, if there are predictive statements about this matter in the prophets, how could the Lord have been surprised by the rejection?

We are certain He was not surprised by the Jews' rejection of Him. He spoke of His impending suffering on more than one occasion. Matthew 17:22-23 records: "Now while they were staying in Galilee, Jesus said to them, 'The Son of Man is about to be betrayed into the hands of men, and they will kill Him, and the third day He will be raised up.' And they were exceedingly sorrowful." Then, as the betrayal was near at hand, the Lord spoke these words to the twelve: "The Son of Man indeed goes just as it is written of Him, but woe to that man by whom the Son of Man is betrayed! It would have been good for that man if he had not been born" (Mat. 26:24).

In the passage just noted, Jesus declares that His betrayal and crucifixion had been written beforehand. But where had it been written? It had been written in the prophets that the Son of God, the Messiah, would suffer and die for the sins of mankind. Therefore, His rejection was predicted, anticipated by the Christ as He lived among men, and accomplished in accordance with the writings of the prophets.

In Matthew 16:18-19, the passage cited earlier, Jesus not only uses the words "church" and "kingdom" interchangeably, He also assures His apostles that the gates of Hades would not prevent its establishment. This is an obvious reference to His death, at which time His spirit would reside for a short time in the Hadean realm, specifically in Paradise. Therefore, the Lord knew His death was imminent and essential to the accomplishment of His mission—the building of His church—the establishment of His kingdom. It is difficult to imagine how any objective observer could conclude the Lord's initial purpose in coming to earth was to establish an earthly kingdom and that He did not anticipate His rejection by the Jews.

We now examine a few key prophetic statements from the Minor Prophets that clearly refer to the Messiah's mission to give His life a ransom for many. In doing so, He fulfilled the many prophecies in the Old Testament pointing to the crucifixion and to the church as the institution in which the manifold wisdom of God finally is made known. Indeed, one can see the church in the Minor Prophets.

SEEING THE CHURCH IN HABAKKUK

The first of the prophecies in which we see the church is Habakkuk 2:14. There the prophet declares: "For the earth will be filled with the knowledge of the glory of the Lord, as the waters cover the sea." While the initial thrust of Habakkuk's words relate to Babylon, the ultimate fulfillment is in the latter days, the Christian age. Certainly, the glory of God would be seen in the fall of Babylon, as well as in the destruction of other nations in that time. However, the greater glory of God is seen in the salvation through the "Anointed," who is mentioned in another of Habakkuk's prophecies: "You went forth for the salvation of Your people, for salvation with Your Anointed. You struck the head from the house of the wicked, by laying bare from foundation to neck." These words in Habakkuk 3:13 bring to mind the prophecy of Daniel in Chapter two of his book, where he looked ahead by inspiration to the kingdom that would break in pieces all other kingdoms and abide forever. Both these prophets wrote of the eternal kingdom, the church of Christ. One sees the church in Habakkuk's prophecy.

SEEING THE CHURCH IN ZEPHANIAH

Zephaniah prophesied during the reign of Josiah, the young king of Judah who instituted positive reforms in a land that had become corrupted through the idolatrous influences of the Canaanite pagans. However, since Zephaniah cries against the nation of Judah itself with unmistakable condemnation, it appears his prophecies must have come in the early part of Josiah's reign, before the implementation of the righteous king's reforms. In the final verses of Zephaniah's prophecy, there is a clear Messianic utterance, which offers the hope of redemption to the remnant of Israel:

For then I will restore to the peoples a pure language, that they all may call on the name of the Lord, to serve Him with one accord. From beyond the rivers of Ethiopia My worshipers, the daughter of My dispersed ones, shall bring My offering. In that day you shall not be shamed for any of your deeds in which you transgress against Me; for then I will take away from your midst those who rejoice in your pride, and you shall no longer be haughty in My holy mountain. I will leave in your midst a meek and humble people, and they shall trust in the name of the Lord. The remnant of Israel shall do no unrighteousness and speak no lies, nor shall a deceitful tongue be found in their mouth; for they shall feed *their* flocks and lie down, and no one shall make *them* afraid.

Sing, O daughter of Zion! Shout, O Israel! Be glad and rejoice with all *your* heart, O daughter of Jerusalem! The Lord has taken away your judgments, He has cast out your enemy. The King of Israel, the Lord, *is* in your midst; you shall see disaster no more.

In that day it shall be said to Jerusalem: "Do not fear; Zion, let not your hands be weak. The Lord your God in your midst, the Mighty One, will save; He will rejoice over you with gladness, He will quiet *you* with His love, He will rejoice over you with singing."

I will gather those who sorrow over the appointed assembly, who are among you, *to whom* its reproach *is* a burden. Behold, at that time I will deal with all who afflict you; I will save the lame, and gather those who were driven out; I will appoint them for praise and fame in every land where they were put to shame. At that time I will bring you back, even at the time I gather you; for I will give you fame and praise among all the peoples of the earth, when I return your captives before your eyes, says the Lord (Zeph. 3:9-20).

Zephaniah depicts the "remnant of Israel" in terms reminiscent of Micah's clear Messianic prophecy in Micah 4:7: "I will make the lame a remnant, and the outcast a strong nation; so the Lord will reign over them in Mount Zion." Zephaniah describes the redeemed remnant as humble and meek, characteristics of those under the rule of the Christ, the perfect standard of meekness and humility (Mat. 11:28-30).

Zephaniah's call for song and shouting in verse 14 pictures the praise that would pour forth from hearts filled with gratitude for the blessings in the church under the New Covenant. The Hebrews writer reinforces this thought in Hebrews 13:15-16: "Therefore by Him let us continually offer the sacrifice of praise to God, that is, the fruit of *our* lips, giving thanks to His name. But do not forget to do good and to share, for with such sacrifices God is well pleased." One truly sees the church in the prophecies of Zephaniah.

SEEING THE CHURCH IN HAGGAI

Haggai, one of three post-exilic prophets, utters words in Chapter 2:6-9 that have their fulfillment in the kingdom which cannot be shaken, the church of Christ:

> For thus says the Lord of hosts: "Once more (it *is* a little while) I will shake heaven and earth, the sea and dry land; and I will shake all nations, and they shall come to the Desire of All Nations, and I will fill this temple with glory," says the Lord of hosts. "The silver *is* Mine, and the gold *is* Mine," says the Lord of hosts. "The glory of this latter temple shall be greater than the former," says the Lord of hosts. "And in this place I will give peace," says the Lord of hosts.

There can be no question as to the ultimate application of this prophecy to the church; the Hebrews writer removes all doubt in Hebrews 12:25-28:

> See that you do not refuse Him who speaks. For if they did not escape who refused Him who spoke on earth, much more *shall we not escape* if we turn away from Him who *speaks* from heaven, whose voice then shook the earth; but now He has promised, saying, *"Yet once more I shake not only the earth, but also heaven."* Now this, *"Yet once more,"* indicates the removal of those things that are being shaken, as of things that are made, that the things which cannot be shaken may remain. Therefore, since we

> are receiving a kingdom which cannot be shaken, let us have grace, by
> which we may serve God acceptably with reverence and godly fear.

When the Scripture provides its own interpretation of an Old Testament prophecy,

can any honest student of the Word deny it? The Hebrews writer applies Haggai's prophecy to the dissolution of the Old Covenant and the initiation of the New, in which the kingdom, the church, is the undeniable and unending institution in the writer's mind.

The words of Haggai 2:23 also find their ultimate fulfillment in the Christ, the chosen of the Lord, of whom Zerubbabel was merely a type: "In that day, says the Lord of hosts, I will take you, Zerubbabel My servant, the son of Shealtiel, says the Lord, and will make you like a signet *ring;* for I have chosen you, says the Lord of hosts." The phrase, "in that day," is a reference to the Christian age, the final dispensation, which began with the establishment of the church on Pentecost following the resurrection and ascension of Christ.

SEEING THE CHURCH IN ZECHARIAH

It is indisputable that Zechariah is the most Messianic of all the Minor Prophets. As noted earlier, prophecy concerning the Christ, His crucifixion, and His coronation cannot exclude the church. The blood Christ shed in His death is the purchase price of the church, according to Paul's statement in Acts 20:28. Therefore, one cannot accept the cross without acknowledging the church. With this truth in mind, we examine two of Zechariah's prophecies concerning Christ and the church. The first reference is Zechariah 3:7-10:

> Thus says the Lord of hosts: "Hear, O Joshua, the high priest, you and
> your companions who sit before you, for they are a wondrous sign; for
> behold, I am bringing forth My Servant the BRANCH. For behold, the
> stone that I have laid before Joshua: upon the stone *are* seven eyes. Behold,
> I will engrave its inscription," says the Lord of hosts, "And I will remove
> the iniquity of that land in one day. In that day," says the Lord of hosts,
> "Everyone will invite his neighbor under his vine and under his fig tree."

Here Zechariah describes the "BRANCH," an undeniable reference to the Christ and the redemptive work He would accomplish though His sacrifice. The references to the removal of iniquity in one day in verse nine is reminiscent of Jeremiah's prophecy in Jeremiah 31:31-34. The Hebrews writer, in Hebrews 8:8-12, applies Jeremiah's prediction to the church. Zechariah's words must also apply to the kingdom now in existence, the church of our Lord.

A familiar text regarding the church is in Zechariah chapter six. In this passage, as in the text in chapter three, verse eight, Zechariah identifies the BRANCH, the Messiah, as the one who would build the temple of the Lord (verse 12). In verse 13, the prophet repeats the prediction for emphasis and adds information that becomes the death blow to the premillennial premise that the kingdom and the church are not synonymous.

The prophet points out that the Messiah will rule in glory on His throne and that, during that same time period, He will be priest on His throne. Therefore, if one can find Scriptural proof that Jesus is priest now, then He must also be king now; otherwise, the prophecy of Zechariah is false. The Hebrews writer provides proof of the prophet's accuracy in Hebrews 4:14-5:6:

> Seeing then that we have a great High Priest who has passed through the heavens, Jesus the Son of God, let us hold fast *our* confession. For we do not have a High Priest who cannot sympathize with our weaknesses, but was in all points tempted as *we are, yet* without sin. Let us therefore come boldly to the throne of grace, that we may obtain mercy and find grace to help in time of need. For every high priest taken from among men is appointed for men in things *pertaining* to God, that he may offer both gifts and sacrifices for sins. He can have compassion on those who are ignorant and going astray, since he himself is also subject to weakness. Because of this he is required as for the people, so also for himself, to offer *sacrifices* for sins. And no man takes this honor to himself, but he who is called by God, just as Aaron *was*. So also Christ did not glorify Himself to become High Priest, *but it* was He who said to Him: *"You are My Son, Today I have begotten You."* As *He* also *says* in another *place:* *"You are a priest forever according to the order of Melchizedek."*

There is no doubt that, at the time Hebrews was written, Jesus had become High Priest in the heavens at the right hand of the Father. Therefore, Zechariah's prophecy in Chapter 6:12-13 had been fulfilled. This demands that Jesus is reigning over His kingdom now; He is both King and High Priest now.

The Hebrews writer returns to a discussion of the Lord's priestly office in Hebrews 6: 19-20: "This *hope* we have as an anchor of the soul, both sure and steadfast, and which enters the Presence *behind* the veil, where the forerunner has entered for us, *even* Jesus, having become High Priest forever according to the order of Melchizedek." In chapter 7, the writer continues his analogy between Christ and Melchizedek, identifying the ancient ruler as both king and priest of Salem. Throughout the chapter, the writer contrasts the priesthood of Melchizedek with the Levitical priesthood. In so doing, he makes clear that Christ could never be a priest on earth because He was of the tribe of Judah, not the priestly tribe of Levi (Heb. 7:14)

In Hebrews eight, the writer summarizes his compelling arguments on the priesthood:

> Now *this is* the main point of the things we are saying: We have such a High Priest, who is seated at the right hand of the throne of the Majesty in the heavens, a Minister of the sanctuary and of the true tabernacle which the Lord erected, and not man. For every high priest is appointed to offer both gifts and sacrifices. Therefore *it is* necessary that this One also have something to offer. For if He were on earth, He would not be a priest, since there are priests who offer the gifts according to the law: (8:1-4).

Thus, the prophecy of Zechariah 6:12-13 and the Hebrews passages cited combine to produce an irrefutable argument that Christ is reigning both as King and High Priest over His kingdom, the church. We not only see the church in this powerful prophecy, we see how the prophecy and its fulfillment forevermore defeat the false premise of premillennialism. Therefore, the whole system falls under the weight of this testimony.

SEEING THE CHURCH IN MALACHI

Malachi, the last of the Old Testament prophets, presents undeniable proof that the church was in the writer's mind as he closed out the revelation of God to man for some 400 years. In Malachi 3:1, the prophet echoes the prediction of the Messianic prophet Isaiah from Isaiah 40:3. He points to John the baptizer as the forerunner of the Christ: "Behold, I send My messenger, and he will prepare the way before Me. And the Lord, whom you seek, will suddenly come to His temple, even the Messenger of the covenant, in whom you delight. Behold, He is coming, says the Lord of hosts."

In Matthew 3:1-3, the inspired writer specifically applies the words of Isaiah to the baptizer and, in so doing, ties in Malachi's prophetic utterance as well: "In those days John the Baptist came preaching in the wilderness of Judea, and saying, repent, for the kingdom of heaven is at hand! For this is he who was spoken of by the prophet Isaiah, saying: the voice of one crying in the wilderness: prepare the way of the Lord; make His paths straight."

It is especially important to note that John's message was one of repentance, in view of the kingdom at hand. The phrase "at hand" in this context must refer to something about to occur; therefore, the church was about to be established. Jesus also preached the same message: "From that time Jesus began to preach and to say, repent, for the kingdom of heaven is at hand" (Mat. 4:17). Therefore, the kingdom, the church, was about to be established as both John and Jesus were predicting. Malachi's prophecy, as did Isaiah's, clearly had the church in view hundreds of years before its establishment.

CONCLUSION

The church of Christ is not an afterthought—not "Plan B" that had to be implemented because Christ was initially rejected by the Jews in His effort to establish a kingdom here on earth. Even while on the earth, "Jesus answered, 'My kingdom is not of this world. If My kingdom were of this world, My servants would fight, so that I should not be delivered to the Jews; but now My kingdom is not from here'" (John 18:36). This declaration from the Lord before Pilate should settle the matter. Yet, despite the Lord's denial that His kingdom is of this world, the premillennialists say, "But it is!"

The church was planned by God (Eph. 3:8-11); it was prophesied (as seen in this study); it was promised by the Lord (Mat. 16:18-19); it was prepared by John and Jesus (Mat. 3:1-2; Mat. 4:17); it was presented with power on Pentecost by the apostles (Acts 2:1ff.); and the New Testament reveals its inspired pattern that must be followed until time is no more (Acts 2:42). Then, the Lord will return to take home to the Father all those who have followed that pattern (1 Cor. 15:24). The church is the manifestation of God's manifold wisdom (Eph. 3:21), and it is precious beyond description.

WORKS CITED

The Holy Bible: New King James Version. WORD*search* Electronic Software, Version 8.0.2.71

Chapter 2

The Minor Prophets
And The Post-Exilic Period

Tim Lewis

Re-read the familiar; read the unfamiliar. That appeal is everlastingly relevant. It always applies and never expires. Dedicated and conscientious Bible students always benefit from reviewing familiar material in scripture. Much can be gained by diligently testing comfortable conclusions, especially unexamined conclusions that have been adopted as the by-product of someone else's study, but as we continue to re-examine familiar passages we also must challenge ourselves to dig a little deeper into the hidden treasures of God's inspired word. For instance, how much do New Testament Christians know about some of the more obscure books of the Old Testament? How much do they know about the post-exilic period and the prophets who served God so faithfully during that important time in history?

Remember, it is not enough to re-examine the familiar, we need to read and study the unfamiliar too. However, some Christians are reluctant to study books like Haggai, Zechariah and Malachi, because, at first glance much of the material presented by these post-exilic prophets seems confusing, murky and more than a little mysterious. In fact, first time readers tend to be intimidated by some of the apocalyptic and eschatological language of Zechariah, but as is often the case with other scripture the more you read the last three books of the Old Testament the better you will understand the mission and message of these three men.

The best place to begin a study of the Minor Prophets and the post-exilic period is to carefully consider how they fit into the historical picture of the Old Testament. It is an exciting time in Bible history filled with challenges and opportunities. Jeremiah set the stage for these events when he prophesied against the people of Judah telling them that God was going to "summon all the peoples of the north" and "Nebuchadnezzar King of Babylon" and he was going to bring them against the land of Judah and its inhabitants (Jer. 25:9, All references taken from NIV84). In no uncertain terms, Jeremiah declared, "All Judah will be carried into exile, carried completely away" (Jer. 13:19).

God's declaration of judgment was decisive and devastating, but he did not leave his people without hope. He made it clear to them that "when seventy years are completed for Babylon, I will come to you and fulfill my gracious promise to bring you back to this place" (Jer. 29:10) and that is exactly what happened! The final destruction of Judah by Babylon occurred in 586 B.C. After Nebuchadnezzar's death, Cyrus the King of Persia "entered Babylon almost without a struggle in 539 B.C." (Lewis 146) and after capturing that city he promptly issued the following decree:

> This is what Cyrus king of Persia says: "The LORD, the God of heaven, has given me all the kingdoms of the earth and he has appointed me to build a temple for him at Jerusalem in Judah. Anyone of his people among you--may his God be with him, and let him go up to Jerusalem in Judah and build the temple of the LORD, the God of Israel, the God who is in Jerusalem" (Ezra 1:2-3).

Under the decree of Cyrus the people of God were allowed to return to Jerusalem to rebuild the temple. Zerubbabel led the first group of exiles back to Jerusalem in 536 B.C. Ezra led a second group in 457 B.C. and Nehemiah led the third and final group in 445 B.C. Upon their return from captivity, the people of Judah discovered that the temple of God had been destroyed (Ezra 5:12), the wall of Jerusalem had been broken down and its gates had been burned with fire (Neh. 1:3). The people who had survived Babylonian exile were now back in the province of their homeland, but they were "in great trouble and disgrace" (Neh. 1:3).

With that historical context in mind, let us now consider some of the goals and tasks that were given to post-exilic prophets. The book of Ezra is an indispensable resource when it comes to providing vital background material about Haggai and Zechariah. According to Ezra, after "the Israelites had settled in their towns, the people assembled as one man in Jerusalem" (Ezra 3:1). Under the leadership of the priests, they "began to build the altar of the God of Israel to sacrifice burnt offerings on it" (Ezra 3:2) and "despite their fear of the peoples around them, they built the altar on its foundation and sacrificed burnt offerings on it to the Lord, both the morning and evening sacrifices" (Ezra 3:3). The builders even managed to lay the foundation of the temple (3:10) but then opposition arose from "the enemies of Judah and Benjamin" (Ezra 4:1).

The people of the land sought to help with the rebuilding project, but Zerubbabel refused to let them join in the work. His response was firm and uncompromising, "You have no part with us in building a temple to our God.

We alone will build it for the LORD, the God of Israel, as King Cyrus, the king of Persia, commanded us" (Ezra 4:3). From that point on the inhabitants of the land "set out to discourage the people of Judah and make them afraid to go on building" (Ezra 4:4). When the Samaritans complained to the Persian authorities about what the people of Israel were doing, the work came to a stand-still (Ezra 4:6-24) and it remained unfinished and neglected for the next sixteen years.

What started out as a form of social and political intimidation eventually grew into a spirit of indifference and inactivity. The people continued to procrastinate and even started making senseless excuses and saying things like "The time has not yet come for the LORD's house to be built" (Hag. 1:2). It was at this point that God sent his prophets to confront Israel and to re-ignite the building project. Working in tandem, Haggai and Zechariah "prophesied to the Jews in Judah and Jerusalem in the name of the God of Israel" (Ezra 5:1).

In fact, Haggai leveled this scathing rebuke at the people, "Is it a time for you yourselves to be living in your paneled houses, while this house remains a ruin?" (Hag. 1:4). He challenged them to "give careful thought" to their ways (Hag, 1:5, 7; 2:15, 18), encouraged them to "be strong" (Hag. 2:4), reminded them of God's abiding presence (Hag. 1:13; 2:4) and by referring to God as the "LORD Almighty" fourteen times in thirty-eight verses, Haggai also reassured the people that any work they performed for God would be energized by God's infinite power.

Haggai also pointed out that human effort is pointless and ineffective without divine approval. He made it clear that God would not bless the work of their hands while they continued to pursue selfish interests and neglected God's greater purpose for their lives. In fact, Haggai explained that God had actually thwarted their self-centered efforts; he said, "You have planted much, but have harvested little. You eat, but never have enough. You drink, but never have your fill. You put on clothes, but are not warm. You earn wages, only to put them in a purse with holes in it" (Hag. 1:6).

Speaking for the LORD, Haggai said, "You expected much, but see, it turned out to be little. What you brought home, I blew away…because of my house, which remains a ruin, while each of you is busy with his own house" (Hag. 1:9). Haggai, once more speaking for the Lord, commanded the people to "Go up into the mountains and bring down timber and build the house, so that I may take pleasure in it and be honored" (Hag. 1:8).

In his book, *The 12 Minor Prophets*, George Robinson who referred to Zechariah as Haggai's junior colleague concluded with regard to Haggai's ministry that "No prophet ever preached more directly or earnestly to his own contemporaries and no prophet was ever more successful" (138). Ezra's inspired record of these events seems to support that conclusion. According to Ezra, "the elders of the Jews continued to build and prosper under the preaching of Haggai the prophet and Zechariah…they finished building the temple according to the command of the God of Israel and the decrees of Cyrus, Darius and Artaxerxes, kings of Persia" (Ezra 6:14). Working closely with Zechariah, Haggai "was able to produce the spark that set the Jewish people to work" (Yates 199) and the results were phenomenal – "the temple was completed" (Ezra 6:15).

While the work of Haggai and Zechariah was closely linked with that of Ezra, Malachi most likely worked during or just after the time of Nehemiah. As Roy H. Lanier Jr. insightfully observed, "The mention of the temple (Mal. 1:10; 3:1, 10), the sacrifices (Mal. 1:14), the altar (Mal. 1:7), the tithes (Mal. 3:8), and the incense (Mal. 1:11) indicates the worship at the temple had been restored but was now being done negligently, carelessly, and only as a ritual" (Lanier 44). Haggai and Zechariah were builders; Malachi, on the other hand, "was a fearless reformer who spoke directly to the sinners of his day without hesitation or embarrassment" (Yates 215). From the content of Malachi's four chapter book, it seems as though the people of Judah had somehow forgotten that their God was a "great king" (Mal. 1:14). They became lackadaisical and lazy and started cutting corners in their worship. They were not only guilty of robbing God in tithes and offerings (Mal. 3:8) but they were actually placing "defiled food" on God's altar (Mal. 1:7). The people were bringing blind, crippled and diseased animals (Mal. 1:8) and were therefore showing "contempt" for God's name (Mal. 1:6). God was so displeased with what they were doing that he told the people, "Oh, that one of you would shut the temple doors, so that you would not light useless fires on my altar! I am not pleased with you and I will accept no offering from your hands" (Mal. 1:10).

God was not only disgusted with their religious offerings; he was also deeply offended by their moral practices. He lamented that "Judah has broken faith" and he exclaimed that "a detestable thing has been committed in Israel and in Jerusalem" (Mal. 2:11). God condemned His people because they were breaking faith with the wife of their marriage covenant (Mal. 2:14) and they were "marrying the daughter of a foreign god" (Mal. 2:11). The LORD made His feelings about that behavior abundantly clear with this three word declaration, "I hate divorce" and then He went on to issue this warning, "guard yourself in your spirit, and do not break faith" (Mal. 2:16).

What was behind this terrible decline in moral conduct and religious practices? God laid the blame for all these abuses at the feet of His priests. He leveled a charge against them that is both shocking and direct. First, God reminded them of their priestly responsibilities, "For the lips of a priest ought to preserve knowledge, and from his mouth men should seek instruction – because he is the messenger of the LORD Almighty" (Mal. 2:7). Then the Lord makes the following accusation, "But you have turned from the way and by your teaching have caused many to stumble; you have violated the covenant with Levi" (Mal. 2:8).

God's people were living in a state of complete moral and religious disarray. Even the priests had violated God's covenant and instead of teaching the people how to live they had actually caused them to stumble and fall, but what could be done to change their religious corruption and moral indifference? Malachi outlines three important steps that, if followed, could bring about an important reformation in both faith and lifestyle.

Step #1: Respect God! As God began to speak through His prophet Malachi, He confronted his people for their obvious lack of honor and respect. God reminded them that "a son honors his father, and a servant his master" and then the Lord asked "If I am a father, where is the honor due me? If I am a master, where is the respect due me?" (Mal. 1:6). In his classic book, The Knowledge of the Holy, noted author and teacher, A. W. Tozer, claimed that "It is impossible to keep our moral practices sound and our inward attitudes right while our idea of God is erroneous or inadequate. If we would bring back spiritual power to our lives, we must begin to think of God more nearly as He is" (viii). In other words, people never rise above their concept of God; therefore, Malachi calls for a renewal of respect!

Step #2: Remember the law! As Stuart Briscoe insightfully explained, "We have a remarkable propensity to forget – a striking capacity to overlook – a built-in ability to ignore the things that God has already shown us" (162). That explains why God made this heartfelt appeal, "Remember the law of my servant Moses, the decrees and laws I gave him at Horeb for all Israel" (Mal. 4:4). The only way to improve the way people live and worship is by going back to God's original plan. There can be no meaningful reformation without authentic restoration.

Step #3: Return to God! "Ever since the time of your forefathers you have turned away from my decrees and have not kept them. Return to me, and I will return to you" (Mal. 3:7). Doesn't that sound remarkably like our Lord's invitation, "Come to me, all you who are weary and burdened, and I will give you rest" (Mat. 11:28). The command to return and the invitation to come both imply that God's people had drifted away from Him, but they also indicate not only that a return was possible, but also that it was desirable. God has always sought to restore and reconcile with those who have been separated from Him. He sought it then and He continues to seek the same thing today.

Now let us turn our attention from the goals and tasks assigned to these men and shift our focus to the role they play in God's overall plan of salvation and the events about which we read in the New Testament with the coming of Christ. As we make that transition, please consider the challenge set forth by G. Campbell Morgan in his book, Malachi's Message for Today. According to Morgan:

You cannot say, "I take the New and not the Old." If you accept the New, the Old is interwoven into every book that the New contains. In this connection I would suggest a profoundly interesting experiment to Bible students. Take your New Testament, and for once read it through from a literary standpoint, with the object of finding out how many chapters there are in which there is no quotation from and no allusion to, the Old, and see how much you have left…In other words, when the Holy Spirit of God moved men of old to write, He not only moved them to write with a view to the interests of the times in which they lived, but with a view to all who should come after (Morgan 13-14).

With that thought in mind, let's consider some of the contributions that Haggai, Zechariah and Malachi make to the story of the New Testament. Beginning with Malachi, I'd like to point out his rather obvious reference to the preparatory work of John the Baptist. First of all, in Malachi 3:1, "See, I will send my messenger, who will prepare the way before me" and then in Malachi 4:5-6, "See, I will send you the prophet Elijah before that great and dreadful day of the LORD comes. He will turn the hearts of the fathers to their children, and the hearts of the children to their fathers; or else I will come and strike the land with a curse".

This prophecy, as was already pointed out, had its fulfillment in the life and work of John the Baptist. The angel who announced his birth explained that John would "go on before the Lord, in the spirit and power of Elijah, to turn the hearts of the fathers to their children and the disobedient to the wisdom of the righteous--to make ready a people prepared for the Lord" (Luke 1:17). Jesus later confirmed that John the Baptist was indeed the Elijah who was to come. "Jesus replied, 'To be sure, Elijah comes and will restore all things. But I tell you, Elijah has already come, and they did not recognize him, but have done to him everything they wished. In the same way the Son of Man is going to suffer at their hands.' Then the disciples understood that he was talking to them about John the Baptist" (Mat. 17:11-13).

There is nothing of note in the book of Haggai that I want to include in this particular discussion, but David Pharr points out that, "With the exception of Isaiah, there are more Messianic prophecies in Zechariah than in any other prophet" (40). In fact, Messianic prophecies seem to fly off Zechariah's inspired pen in rapid fire succession. Starting in chapter 9 and running through chapter 13 Zechariah employs the following language to describe future events that will be fulfilled in the life and ministry of Jesus Christ:

Rejoice greatly, O Daughter of Zion! Shout, Daughter of Jerusalem! See, your king comes to you, righteous and having salvation, gentle and riding on a donkey, on a colt, the foal of a donkey (Zech. 9:9). I told them, "If you think it best, give me my pay; but if not, keep it." So they paid me thirty pieces of silver. (Zech. 11:12). And the LORD said to me, "Throw it to the potter"--the handsome price at which they priced me! So I took the thirty pieces of silver and threw them into the house of the LORD to the potter (Zech. 11:13). They will look on me, the one they have pierced, and they will mourn for him as one mourns for an only child, and grieve bitterly for him as one grieves for a firstborn son (Zech. 12:10). Strike the shepherd, and the sheep will be scattered, and I will turn my hand against the little ones (Zech. 13:7).

In these verses we have the triumphal entry of Jesus into the city of Jerusalem (Mat. 21:5), we have the desertion of Christ (Mat. 26:31), the price paid to His betrayer (Mat. 26:15), a clear description of what would ultimately be done with that blood money (Mat. 27:5-8) and also a vivid description of the Lord's death (John 19:34).

In addition to all these wonderful predictions we have one more to add to the list. As David Pharr explained, "Though not quoted in the New Testament, Zechariah 13:1 is among the most beautiful and meaningful of all prophecies. Messiah would be pierced, his blood would be shed and 'In that day there shall be a fountain opened to the house of David and to the inhabitants of Jerusalem for sin and uncleanness'" (42). As Burton Coffman is quick to point out, "This is the fountain of the blood of Christ, the only fountain in all history that ever afforded cleansing from sin and uncleanness" (193). In the words of William Cowper's beloved hymn, "There's a fountain filled with blood drawn from Emmanuel's veins; And sinners plunged beneath that flood lose all their guilty stains."

While the writings of the post-exilic prophets might seem obscure to some people, they offer a rich contribution to the story of the New Testament; they announce prophetically the coming of John the Baptist and put the people of God on notice that a savior is coming. He will be betrayed, sold at a price and deserted. He will be pierced, blood will flow and sins will be forgiven. "In him we have redemption through his blood, the forgiveness of sins, in accordance with the riches of God's grace" (Eph. 1:7).

Our study of these marvelous books would be incomplete if we did not make some effort to consider the great lessons that can be gleaned from these writers and this crucial period of time in sacred history. As the apostle Paul so eloquently explained, "For whatever things were written before were written for our learning, that we through the patience and comfort of the Scriptures might have hope" (Rom. 15:4 NKJV). If these things were written for our learning, then what are some of the practical lessons God wants us to understand?

From the book of Haggai we learn that "difficult duties should be faced courageously and without delay" (Yates 204) and that "discouragement however profound is not an adequate reason for neglecting duties [we learn that] 'Be strong and work' is a glorious motto for human life" (Hailey 301). From the book of Zechariah we learn that "it is important for God's followers to maintain a hopeful, optimistic outlook – knowing that He cannot fail" (Yates 212) and His plans will always come to pass. From Malachi we learn that "insincerity in worship is an insult to God" and that "divorce is an abomination in his sight" (Yates 218). Also in Malachi God professes His great love (Mal. 1:2) and His unchanging nature, "I the LORD do not change" (Mal. 3:6). When you put those two verses together you discover that "The unchanging God is unchanging in his love toward His people" (Briscoe 177).

Finally, these three books teach us that "what has been will be again, what has been done will be done again; there is nothing new under the sun" (Ecc. 1:9). Since that is the case, these books also teach that the word of God is always relevant and always effective because the word that goes out from God's mouth does not return empty – it will always "achieve the purpose" for which God sent it (Isa. 55:11). Therefore, the best way to impact our own generation is to faithfully follow Paul's instruction to Timothy. "Preach the Word; be prepared in season and out of season; correct, rebuke and encourage – with great patience and careful instruction" (2 Ti. 4:2).

WORKS CITED

Briscoe, D. Stuart. *Taking God Seriously: Major Lessons from the Minor Prophets.* Waco, Texas: Word Books Publisher, 1986.

Coffman, James Burton. *Commentary on the Minor Prophets Volume 4 Zechariah and Malachi.* Austin, Texas: The Firm Foundation Publishing House, 1983.

Hailey, Homer. A Commentary On The Minor Prophets. The United States of America: Religious Supply, Inc., 1993.

Lanier, Jr., Roy H. "Give Your Best." *The Spiritual Sword* 26.4 (1995): 43-46. Print.

Lewis, Jack P. "Post-Exilic Minor Prophets: Historical Background and Archeological Insights." *Today Hear His Voice: The Minor Prophets Speak.* Searcy, Arkansas: Gospel Light Publishing Company, 1993.

Morgan, G. Campbell. *Malachi's Message for Today.* Eugene, Oregon: Wipf and Stock Publishers, 1998.

Pharr, David. "Repent and Build - Zechariah." *The Spiritual Sword 26.4* (1995): 40-43. Print.

Robinson, George L. *The 12 Minor Prophets.* Grand Rapids, Michigan: Baker Book House, 1926.

Tozer, A. W. *The Knowledge Of The Holy.* New York, New York. Haper Collins Publishers, 1961.

Yates, Kyle M. *Preaching from the Prophets.* Nashville, Tennessee. Broadman Press, 1942.

CHAPTER 3

The Significance of the Minor Prophets To The New Testament

Kristy Woodall

> A study of the prophets will enrich the life of anyone who applies himself to learn their teachings; conversely, it will only add to the confusion of those who would use their writings as a basis on which to speculate about the future. An understanding of the prophets" teaching concerning Israel and Judah, the heathen nations of the day, and the Messiah who was to come will strengthen the faith of the one who sees the fulfillment of those predictions in history and in the New Covenant. An understanding of how the prophets dealt with the religious, political, social, and moral corruptions in their day will give courage to the Lord"s faithful today (Hailey 11).

Those wise words from Homer Hailey have been smothered under the cries of "More heart, less history," "More spiritualism, less Scripture," and "More joy, less judgment." These are cries of those who desire a faith not based on Biblical knowledge, but rather based on a subjective feeling. There is no concern for Scriptural truths. Their Bibles may be prominently displayed, but they are perpetually discounted. A few hand picked verses may be quoted, but the Old Testament, even more so, the Minor Prophets, are flicked aside as bothersome lint on a fine garment, cast away without thought. Righteousness is proudly represented by a cross that hangs from the wall as a beautiful symbol of God"s love with no thought given to the cost of it. The true meaning of the cross is lost as some seek to solace the soul rather than solicit the holy script.

Frowned upon or ignored, the Minor Prophets are the annoying siblings of the religious brotherhood. Are they even acknowledged in the New Testament? Are they relevant today? Can we not ignore them like we do the tiresome list of genealogies?

God forbid! The Minor Prophets "pack a concentrated punch of teachings, warnings, calls to repentance, and promises of vengeance and blessing..." (Ritenbaugh).

To start, we will consider just three areas of specific references of the Minor Prophets in the New Testament and then we will conclude with some overlying themes of the Minor Prophets.

SPECIFIC MENTIONS OF THE MINOR PROPHETS IN THE NEW TESTAMENT

The Confirmation of the Incredible

In order to bring about an understanding of our God which has no limitations (Rom.11:33), let us consider the story of Jonah. It is perhaps the most ridiculed Biblical account which provides fodder for the skeptics. Even many who believe the Bible as the word of God have trouble swallowing a tale about a man living in the belly of a fish for three days! Atheists mock it as a fairytale and many religions label it as didactic fiction rather than a true historical record. Could it be real or is it just a great story with a moral message? Consider this: if it is indeed fiction, why is Jonah named in 2 Kings 14:25, even so far as to say who his father is? Also none can doubt the existence of Nineveh, which was specifically mentioned. Can you believe Jonah was swallowed by a great fish? Our Lord did (Mat.12:39-41). That should certainly be enough to authenticate this Scripture. Yet, is it just too incredible to believe? "Oh ye of little faith." Our God is an awesome God! Surely, He who spoke this great world into existence can manage what we can"t wrap our feeble minds around. A fish was prepared (Jon. 1:17). This was not your typical large whale—it was special, touched by the hand of God. He created life from nothing. Without any effort He can certainly accommodate Jonah. This brief mention in the New Testament may seem incidental but it speaks volumes as it confirms the incredible!

The Coming of Christ

There are a multitude of references in the Minor Prophets concerning the great coming of Christ!

- Micah 5:2 with Matthew 2:3-6, Out of Bethlehem a ruler will come who will shepherd my people.
- Haggai 2:6 with Hebrews 12:25-29, I will shake heaven and earth, the sea and dry land;

- Zechariah 11:12,13 with Matthew 27:5-10, They took the 30 pieces of silver, the value of him who was priced.
- Zechariah 12:10 with John 19:37 and Revelation 1:7, They shall look on him who they pierced.
- Malachi 3:1 with Matthew 11:7-10, Mark 1:1-4, and Luke 7:26-28, I send my messenger before your face, who will prepare your way before you.

When a young family shares the news of their imminent newborn arrival we want all the details! When is the baby due? Male or female? Is the name picked out? Don"t hold out—tell us! Many of us, particularly females, even want to know the decor of the nursery. We smile as the story is shared of when the parents found out they are expecting. These are not tedious details; rather they fill our hearts with joy!

What about the prophecies of the coming Christ? They are certainly worthy of attention and rejoicing! The prophecies tell of Christ, the Messiah to come. Not just a sweet baby, but the Son of God who will take away the sin of the world and reconcile us back to the Father! That is something to be excited about! Do you seek to know every detail? Do you care to know the story? Does it make your heart glad, or do you sigh when the preacher calls out a passage from the Minor Prophets?

"Prophetic books cover over one quarter of the Bible, yet no section is more neglected"(Padfield 2). We easily turn to some of our more beloved verses, yet when called upon to find a passage in a Minor Prophet, it requires a little more searching. The pages there are not as worn. Granted, they are smaller books (hence the label "minor"), but even their location does not come as quickly to mind. However, within these pages we can read of the coming of Christ and so much more! As if the intriguing messianic prophecies are not enough, you can also find beautiful poetic language there:

- "Though you build high like the eagle, Though you set your nest among the stars, From there I will bring you down," declares the Lord" (Oba. 1:4).
- "But let justice roll down like waters and righteousness like an ever-flowing stream" (Amos 5:24).
- "He has told you, O man, what is good; and what does the Lord require of you but to do justice, to love kindness, and to walk humbly with your God" (Mic. 6:8).

Give the Minor Prophets another look. Each book is relatively short but found within those concise words are a wealth of knowledge and a glimpse of the coming Messiah!

The Circumspection of the Congregation

Presently, let us notice some warnings to the Lord"s people, and make personal application.

Love Him Most
- "For son treats father contemptuously, daughter rises up against her mother, daughter-in-law against her mother-in-law; A man"s enemies are the men of his own household" (Mic. 7:6).
- "Do not think that I came to bring peace on the earth; I did not come to bring peace, but a sword. For I came to set a man against his father, and a daughter against her mother, and a daughter-in-law against her mother-in-law; and a man"s enemies will be the members of his household" (Mat. 10:34-36). Verse 37 continues, "He who loves father or mother more than me is not worthy of Me; and he who loves son or daughter more than me is not worthy of me."

This is a reminder to the Lord"s people then, and to us today, that we are to love Him above everything and everyone else. Because of that we will stand in opposition to many, even family. This may include both distant relatives and acquaintances as well as those who are closest and dearest to us. Jesus comes with a sword because we are fighting a spiritual war. A battle does not consist of holding hands with all people and religions and singing "Kumbaya." Lines are drawn. Loyalties are tested. What is your priority? Peace with all men or peace with the Father? We must love Him most!

Consider the heart
- "For I desire mercy and not sacrifice, and the knowledge of God more than burnt offerings" (Hos. 6:6).
- "And when the Pharisees saw it, they said to His disciples, "Why does your Teacher eat with tax collectors and sinners?" When Jesus heard that, He said to them, "Those who are well have no need of a physician, but those who are sick. But go and learn what this means: "I desire mercy and not sacrifice" For I did not come to call the righteous, but sinners, to repentance"" (Mat. 9:11-13; see also Mat.12:7).

The nation of Israel was being rebuked because they were going through the motions to offer a sacrifice. They appeared righteous outwardly, but inwardly lacked goodness and sincerity. This does not dismiss the need for sacrifice according to the specific law of God, but instead speaks to the matter of the heart. Some today would use this as a basis for sentimentalism, claiming importance is only placed on the heart and that works and actions are of no account. To believe this, however, you would have to rationalize or ignore all the other passages that speak of our works (see Mat. 5:16, Tit. 3:8, Heb. 6:10, Jas. 3:13 and Rev. 22:14) as well as God"s desire for our obedience (see John 15:14, 2 Jn.1:6, Luke 11:28, and Rom.2:6-8). Are we as the Pharisees? Do we question the deeds and motives of others because we care about righteousness? Is it our motivation to appear more holy to others? We indeed need a heart of mercy. Sacrifices are worthless without a broken and contrite spirit. "The sacrifices of God are a broken spirit; a broken and a contrite heart, O God, you will despise" (Psa.51:17). Is our service to God, our sacrifice, offered with a contrite heart or are we simply going through the motions? We need the appropriate service combined with the appropriate attitude. John 4:24 covers both bases teaching, "God is a spirit, and those who worship Him must worship in spirit and truth." Our actions are vain if we neglect to consider the heart.

Steadfastness in Him

- "Behold the proud, his soul is not upright in him; but the just shall live by his faith" (Hab. 2:4).
- "For in it the righteousness of God is revealed from faith to faith; as it is written, "The just shall live by faith" (Rom. 1:17).
- See also Galatians 3:11 and Hebrews 10:35-38.

This is another lesson on the attitude of man. We are to live a life of humility and firm steadfastness in Him. We are to be grounded in our faith, acquired by prayer and study of Scripture. Our faith cannot be grounded in the faith of our spouse or parents; such faith is without proper foundation and will not survive life"s struggles. Proverbs10:25 teaches us, "When the whirlwind passes, the wicked is no more; but the righteous has an everlasting foundation." When trials blow your way and you are beaten down, do you feel distraught and hopeless? Do you feel abandoned? Have you put your faith in yourself just to find out that you are actually wretched and weak? Whatever comes, reliance on God will carry you through. Your journey is a testimony to His righteousness. Remain steadfast in Him.

Speak in Truth

- "Speak each man the truth to his neighbor"(Zec. 8:16).
- "Putting away lying, "Let each one of you speak truth with his neighbor"" (Eph. 4:25).

Lying is mentioned abundantly throughout the Bible and is even named among the things the Lords hates, listed beside murder (Pro.16:16,17). Yet it is treated so casually in our culture. Rather than being offensive, lying is simply overlooked. You don"t have to follow politics to know that we don"t call a lie a lie anymore. Rather, it is an exaggeration, half truth, misinformation, fabrication, misreport, fib, or mistake. This allows us to more easily shrug our shoulders, give a sheepish grin and brush it under the rug. John 8:44 reminds us of the origin of lies, "You are of your father the devil, and you want to do the desires of your father. He was a murderer from the beginning, and does not stand in the truth because there is no truth in him. Whenever he speaks a lie, he speaks from his own nature, for he is a liar and the father of lies." Your speech determines your father. Speak in truth!

Those are just a few examples; I challenge you to find more in your own study! You will find *A Commentary On The Minor Prophets* by Homer Hailey to be a valuable resource.

In conclusion, let us simply consider the common theme we find within the pages of the Minor Prophets.

OVERLYING THEMES OF THE MINOR PROPHETS

Judgment Against The Sinful Nation

The sinful nation was condemned for idolatry, violence, perversion of justice, oppression of the poor, lewdness, indifference, corruption, pride and complaining...just to name a few. Is this relevant today? Certainly! These are no less common today, and are no less condemned. We can make a check list and mark off each one. Though our knees may not be dirty from bowing to an idol, the guilt remains as the dollar is glorified over God. Could there be anything more violent than abortion? Watch the news to witness the perversion of justice and oppression of the poor. Even commercials and popular songs demonstrate lewdness. Indifference? No one cares about it. Corruption? Check. Pride and complaining—a daily occurrence in every home. Our nation is guilty of it all and as we have learned from the Minor Prophets, God will bring us into judgment.

The Call For Repentance

The word for repent is from a Hebrew word meaning, *"to turn, to return.* Refers to turning toward or away from something, often used with the sense of turning away from God (apostasy) or turning back toward God (repentance)" (Jones n.p.). This Hebrew word is found 82 times in the Minor Prophets. Repentance is of no small concern. God is perfectly just. He is always righteous. He doesn"t reject sinful man just because He can. The holy nature of God prevents Him from being in the presence of sin. His love provided a way to absolve that sin and bridge the gap to redeem us to Him. The cost was great: "And He himself is the propitiation for our sins, and not for ours only but also for the whole world" (1 Jn. 2:2). "In this is love, not that we loved God, but that He loved us and sent His son to be the propitiation for our sins" (1 Jn. 4:10). Love motivates God"s call to repentance. 2 Peter.3:9 tells us that God is "not willing that any should perish but that all should come to repentance." While many focus on the judgments of God, they neglect to see His call for repentance!

A Promise For Future Deliverance

As we saw earlier, the Minor Prophets are filled with promises and allusions to the coming of Christ! We have the same promise today. Christ will come again (Heb.9:28).

He will judge the World (2 Co. 5:10). The wicked will be punished (2 Th.1:8, 9). The righteous will be rewarded (Jas.1:12). Our nation romanticizes sin and ridicules the saint. Don"t lose heart. God"s promises *never* fail. We have a guarantee of deliverance through Jesus Christ.

The Minor Prophets are of great significance to the New Testament and to Christians today. They are inspired, instructional and relevant forever. "The prophets, properly interpreted, speak to issues as though they were among us today, presenting their thoughts in unforgettable figures of speech... Their message will never be out of date" (Lewis 8).

WORKS CITED

Hailey, Homer. *A Commentary on the Minor Prophets*. Religious Supply, Inc., 1993. Print.

Jones, M.R. Apostasy. D. Mangum, D.R. Brown, R. Klippenstein, & R. Hurst (Eds.), *Lexham Theological Wordbook*. Bellingham, WA: Lexham Press.

Lewis, Jack Pearl. *The Minor Prophets*. Grand Rapids: Baker Book House, 1966. Print.

Padfield, David. "Survey of the Minor Prophets." The Church of Christ in Zion, Illinois. David Padfield. Web. 14 Apr. 2015.

Ritenbaugh, Richard. "Further Reading." Meet the Minor Prophets (Part One). Church of the Great God. Web. 14 Apr. 2015. http://www.cgg.org/index.cfm/fuseaction/Library.sr/CT/pw/k/1552/

CHAPTER 4

In That Day
A Study of Zechariah 12–14

Denny Petrillo

A few years ago I had the good fortune of traveling to Israel. Those of you who have had the blessing of going to the "Holy Lands" know the thrill of treading where Jesus walked.

However, if you had a tour guide like we had, you were inundated with Old Testament passages which he and many others believe are soon to be fulfilled. The book of Zechariah was one of the main books our tour guide frequently referred to (he was a former Jew, converted to "Christianity.")

"This book tells us," the tour guide explained, "that Jesus is going to return and from the Mount of Olives provide life giving water for His people. He will stand on the Mount of Olives and it will be split down the middle (Zec. 14:4)." "As a matter of fact," he explained, "geologists tell us that there is a water fault under the Mount and that it can easily split into two and a river will flow down to Jerusalem, thus fulfilling this passage."

"You believe this is going to *literally* happen?" I asked. "Well of course" he replied. "What else could it refer to?" This is a common belief among the Jews (and premillennial "Christians"). Note:

> The Jews, have a notion, that, at the general resurrection of the dead, the mount of Olives will cleave asunder, and those of their nation, who have been buried in other countries, will be rolled through the caverns of the earth, and come out from under that mountain. This is what they call "*gilgul hammetim*", the rolling of the dead; and "*gilgul hammechiloth*", the rolling through the caverns. So they say in the Targum of (Song of Solomon 8:5) ``when the dead shall live, the mount of Olives shall be cleaved asunder, and all the dead of Israel shall come out from under it; yea, even the righteous, which die in captivity, shall pass through subterraneous caverns, and come from under the mount of Olives" (Gill).

Therein lies our problem. What is this great section of Scripture talking about? It is tragic that this passage, and others, is not properly applied.

Far too often, men have looked at various Old Testament texts and used them to "leapfrog" right over the single most important event in the history of mankind: Calvary. In addition, they have ignored how *inspired* writers applied these passages. The New Testament saw the death of Jesus as a fulfilling of numerous Old Testament prophecies. The events at Calvary were part of what was written.

> Now He said to them, 'These are My words which I spoke to you while I was still with you, that all things which are written about Me in the Law of Moses and the Prophets and the Psalms must be fulfilled.' Then He opened their minds to understand the Scriptures, and he said to them, 'Thus it is written, that the Christ should suffer and rise again from the dead the third day...' (Luke 24:44-46 NASB).

Jesus had earlier quoted from Isaiah 53, and noted "for that which refers to Me has its fulfillment" (Luke 22:37).

Paul explained that "I delivered to you as of first importance what I also received, that Christ died for our sins according to the Scriptures" (1 Co. 15:3). He frequently used the Sabbath day to reason with the Jews regarding the Scriptures, "explaining and giving evidence that the Christ had to suffer and rise again from the dead..." (Acts 17:2-3). He stated to King Agrippa:

> And so, having obtained help from God, I stand to this day testifying both to small and great, stating nothing but what the Prophets and Moses said was going to take place; that the Christ was to suffer, and that by reason of His resurrection from the dead He should be the first to proclaim light both to the Jewish people and to the Gentiles (Acts 26:22-24).

Peter, on the day of Pentecost, demonstrated that the death of Jesus was a part of the predetermined plan of God and was the fulfilling of Scripture (Acts 2:22-28). Peter and John reasoned with those at the portico of Solomon, saying "But the things which God announced beforehand by the mouth of all the prophets, that His Christ should suffer, He has thus fulfilled" (Acts 3:18).

> This strong emphasis upon the death of Jesus as fulfillment of the Old Testament is significant since there was little if any preparation or expectation

for a suffering Messiah. It is easy to see why the disciples at first resisted the notion of the death of Jesus (Mk. 8:32-33). To the Jew a crucified Christ was a "stumbling block" a *skandalon* (1 Cor. 1:21). The cross was a curse which cried out for explanation (Deut. 21:22-23; Gal. 2:13-14). It is easy to see why the disciples were "foolish men, and slow of heart to believe all that the prophets have spoken (Lk. 24:25-26) (Williams 6).

While there are many passages that could be considered for this study, we will devote our attention to this amazing text in Zechariah 12-14.

ZECHARIAH 12-14

These remarkable three chapters have received considerable attention through the centuries, especially by those of the premillennial persuasion. However, the careful student will notice a trend that links chapters 12, 13, and 14 together: the phrase "in that day." Note the occurrences of this phrase:

Chapter 12 – verses 3, 4, 6, 8 (twice), 9, 11
Chapter 13 – verses 1, 2, 4
Chapter 14 – verses 1, 4, 6, 8, 9, 13, 20, 21

It is clear that this section is dealing with one great event, one magnificent day, one special time when God accomplishes all of these wonderful things.

Is Zechariah speaking of days yet to be fulfilled? The answer lies in how New Testament writers applied this section. The simple question is, "what *day* is being referred to?

In chapter 12, Zechariah makes the following prophecy:

And it will come about *in that day* that I will set about to destroy all the nations that come against Jerusalem. And I will pour out on the house of David on the inhabitants of Jerusalem the Spirit of grace and of supplication, so that they will look on Me whom they have pierced; and they will mourn for Him, as one mourns for an only son, and they will weep bitterly over Him, like the bitter weeping over a first born-born. *In that day* there will be great mourning in Jerusalem, like the mourning of Hadadrimmon in the plain of Megiddo (verses 9-11, italics mine).

While men may speculate as to when this "day" might be, it is crucial to note that the inspired writer John quotes from this section in John 19:35-37:

> And he who has seen has borne witness, and his witness is true; and he knows, that he is telling the truth, so that you also may believe. For these things came to pass, that the Scripture might be fulfilled, 'Not a bone of Him shall be broken.' And again another Scripture says, 'They shall look on Him whom they pierced.'

This significant day is the day that they looked "on Him whom they pierced." As we consider this prophecy, a number of specifics are worthy of note. Here are some of the events that will take place "in that day."

1. God will destroy all the nations that come against Jerusalem. John applies this to Calvary. Therefore, Zechariah is obviously not speaking of literal Jerusalem. What Christ did on the cross was to provide spiritual protection for all of the true people of God (Jerusalem). To those who have accepted Christ through obedience to His gospel God promises "I will never desert you, nor will I ever forsake you" (Heb. 13:5). In the Revelation, those who gain the victory do so because of the "blood of the Lamb" (Rev. 12:11). Paul says we are "more than conquerors through Him who loved us" (Rom. 8:35-37).

2. On that day God will pour out "the Spirit of grace and supplication." When Jesus went to the cross, His shed blood provided forgiveness of sins through grace (cf. Rom. 6:1-10; Eph. 2:1-10). This prophecy notes that "on that day" – the day Jesus died on the cross – God offered grace to the world. Only through the blood of the cross can one have access to the Father, and have the right to become children of God (John 1:12).

3. There will be great mourning and weeping over Him. The gospel accounts certainly confirm this truth. The events at Calvary were, at first glance, horrifically tragic. God's "only Son" (cf. John 1:18), the "first-born" was put to death (cf. Col. 1:18 – the "first-born of all creation," meaning Jesus had pre-eminence over all that had been created).

As Zechariah continues his discussion of "that day" he notes:

> 'Awake, O sword, against My Shepherd,
> And against the man, My Associate,'
> declares the Lord of hosts,
> 'Strike the Shepherd that the sheep may be scattered;
> And I will turn My hand against the little ones.' (13:7)

This passage is quoted in Matthew 26:31 and Mark 14:27, where Jesus is explaining to the apostles that the events of Calvary will scatter them. Again, the New Testament writers place a time frame where the events of "that day" in Zechariah are to take place. As with the earlier reference, this prophecy has a number of interesting features:

1. Jesus is referred to as God's Shepherd. Jesus called Himself the "Good Shepherd" (John 10:11, 14). Jesus had declared that the good shepherd lays down his life for the sheep. At Calvary, Jesus proved His qualification to be God's Shepherd.
2. Jesus is referred to as God's Associate. The events of Calvary enhanced the position of Jesus as the Son of God. When Zechariah prophesies regarding Jesus being God's "Associate," he is describing the Shepherd as being of the same nature as God (cf. Phi. 2:5-11; John 10:30).
3. God will turn His hand against the little ones. The word translated "against" is better translated "upon" (as in KJV), indicating love, care and protection. While the events of Calvary scattered the disciples (cf. Mark 14:50), God will gather them together again. The cross proved to be the unifying act that this passage predicted it would be (cf. Eph. 2:13-16).
4. In 13:9 God says: "They will call on My name, and I will answer them; I will say, 'They are My people,' and they will say 'The Lord is my God.'" This text is strikingly similar to Jeremiah 31:31-34, which announced the coming of the New Covenant. This text was quoted twice in the book of Hebrews (8:8-12; 10:16-17). The idea of 'calling on the name of the Lord' is a key concept in the book of Acts (Acts 2:21; 4:12; 7:59; 9:14-15; 22:16). This passage is also reminiscent of Hosea 2:23, which is quoted in Romans 9:25.

As we continue to study the text of Zechariah 14, a number of allusions to the work and character of Christ are noted:

1. "In that day there will be no light; the luminaries will dwindle" (14:7). Jesus came as the "light of the world" (John 9:4). In the prologue John stated, "In Him was life; and the life was the light of men. And the light shines in the darkness; and the darkness did not comprehend it.... There was a true light which, coming into the world, enlightens every man" (John 1:3-5, 9).
2. "In that day living waters will flow out of Jerusalem" (14:8). Jesus told the Samaritan woman that he could give her "living water" (John

4:10). On the last day of the Feast of Tabernacles Jesus said, "If any man is thirsty, let him come to Me and drink. He who believes in Me, as the Scripture said, 'From his innermost being shall flow rivers of living water'" (John 7:37). Zechariah also notes that this water will flow east and west, all year long. The life giving water of Jesus flows to all men, all the time. The gospel is for all (Col. 1:23; cf. Mat. 28:18-20).

3. "And the Lord will be king over all the earth; in that day the Lord will be the only one, and His name the only one" (14:9). The events of Calvary established the kingdom of Christ. That event made Him the "ruler of the kings of the earth" and "made us to be a kingdom" (Revelation 1:5-6). The Lamb overcomes all enemies "because He is the Lord of lords and King of kings" (Rev. 17:14).

Properly understood, the great events described in Zechariah 12-14 are centered around the events of Calvary and the first century. The New Testament writers clearly established this truth through their quotations from these chapters. Feinberg notes:

> God promises that in that day of holiness no unclean shall defile the house of the Lord. In short, what is stated positively in the first part of verse 21 is repeated negatively in the latter part of the verse. God's great object in Israel is holiness; His great aim in the Church is holiness; His great longing for your life and mine is holiness, and only holiness. Our chapter which began in darkness (as did, indeed, the entire prophecy of Zechariah) ends in the radiant and transparent light of holiness. And throughout the prophecy there is presented to us on every page the spotless, blemishless Holy One of Israel, the Lord Jesus Christ, the Messiah and King of Israel (Feinberg 103:161-5).

THE SIGNIFICANCE OF ZECHARIAH 13:2

Perhaps one of the most intriguing statements made in these remarkable three chapters is what the Lord says in 13:2:

> "It will come about in that day," declares the LORD of hosts, "that I will cut off the names of the idols from the land, and they will no longer be remembered; and I will also remove the prophets and the unclean spirit from the land."

Several observations need to be made from this section:

1) God is Declaring What Will Happen "In That Day."

It has already been established above that the "day" (time) to which God is referring is the time of Jesus and the New Testament era (first century). In 13:1 Zechariah predicted a time when a "fountain will be opened" that will be "for sin and impurity." That occurred when Jesus was "pierced" (12:10), shedding His blood for all of mankind. Plus, in verse six (immediately after this section in 13:1-5) there will be a clear prophecy regarding Jesus. Both Matthew (26:31) and Mark (14:27) will quote this text and apply it to Jesus and His disciples.

Need we be reminded that God is omniscient, and thus certainly knows what is to come? To announce the demise of prophecy and unclean spirits is certainly within the predictive powers of God Almighty. In addition, of what value or purpose might there be for God to announce such, when it was not going to happen? Or, that it was going to happen at the end of time? What would be the value of that information? Any logically thinking person would know that such would disappear at the end of time. Rather, God is giving His people a glimpse into the time of the Messiah.

2) In The New Testament Era, God Will "Cut Off The Names Of The Idols From The Land, and They Will No Longer Be Remembered."

The Old Testament texts are full of the idolatrous ways of the Jews. From their days in Egypt to the centuries in the Promised Land, they were guilty of idolatry. Jeremiah said that is was so bad that they practiced idolatry "on every high hill and under every green tree" (Jer. 2:20). He said later that "according to the number of your cities are your gods, O Judah" (Jer. 2:28). Yet, it has been well established that the Jews "learned their lesson" regarding idolatry after 70 years in Babylonian captivity. There is no record of their practicing idolatry once they returned from captivity. So what would be the purpose of making such a statement here? In the Messianic age Satan will make a determined push to get the people of God to return to idolatrous practices (cf. 2 Th. 2:4; Rev. 9:20; 13:1ff). This is why John warned them, "Guard yourselves from idols" (1 Jn. 5:21).

3) In the New Testament Era, God Will "Remove The Prophets...From The Land."

It is true that a vast majority of commentators consider the reference to prophets here to be false prophets. Their reasons for this view, however, are lacking. They are mostly attempting to defend the existence of true prophets in modern times. However, I believe that the evidence supports the argument that true prophets are in view here. When we continue on through this text (vv. 3-6), we see the reaction of God's people toward those claiming to be prophets. Their reaction is based upon the fact that God "removed the prophets...from the land." Since true prophets are removed, all that is left are false prophets, and the people of God know it. That is why even parents will turn against false-prophet sons (3), as will their own friends (6). In addition, these men will themselves be ashamed of their deception (4). Why? Because they know they are lying!

In addition, there has never been a time throughout history that there have been no false prophets. The New Testament makes it clear that there are many (Mat. 24:4-5, 11, 23-24; 2 Th. 2:2-4; Rev. 13:4-15), and there will always be many (cf. 1 Ti. 4:1-2; 2 Pe. 2:1-3; 2 Co. 11:13-15; 1 Jn 4:1-3).

Does the New Testament give any indication of a time when there will be no more true prophets of God? Indeed it does. Notice the words of the Apostle Paul:

> Love never fails; but if there are gifts of prophecy, they will be done away; if there are tongues, they will cease; if there is knowledge, it will be done away. For we know in part and we prophesy in part; but when the perfect comes, the partial will be done away (1 Co. 13:8-10).

Here we note that Paul specifically mentions "prophecy," and says that it will be "done away." The word for "done away" is καταργέω (*katargeo*). This word means "to cause something to lose its power or effectiveness, invalidate, make powerless" (BDAG 525). God says in this text that the prophets will be "removed." The similar terminology is striking.

When did this take place? Paul says that it would occur "when the perfect comes." The "perfect" is in the same category as the "partial" (prophecy, knowledge and tongues). The only logical explanation is that Paul is referring to the completed revelation of God's will. Numerous New Testament texts point to the completed revelation of God's word (2 Ti. 3:16-17; Jude 3; 2 Pet. 1:3; Rev. 22:18-19). The manifested gifts of the Holy Spirit served a limited purpose (Heb. 2:1-4). In addition, one could only receive the gift of prophecy through the laying on of an apostles' hands (Acts 8:18; 2 Ti. 1:6). Once the last apostle died, the ability to pass on this gift died as well. Therefore, naturally, the gift of prophecy was "done away." There are even some early church fathers who indicate that the gift of prophecy had ceased (Justin, *Dialogue With Trypho* 51; Chrysostom, *Homilies on Thessalonians* 4).

In his excellent study on prophecy, F. David Farnell, made the following concluding statement:

> From the nature of the discussion in this series, the evidence demands the view that the New Testament prophetic gift ceased its operation very early in the history of the church. Furthermore, although no one single argument alone demonstrates this, the aggregate weight of the total evidence decisively points to this conclusion. When claims to prophetic activity today (and indeed throughout church history) are compared to the biblical record, woeful inaccuracy and inadequacy of such practices are evidenced (201-2).

4) In the New Testament era, God will "remove the unclean spirit from the land."

The phrase "unclean spirit" is found 22 times in the New Testament (Mat. 10:1; 12:43; Mark 1:23, 26, 27; 3:11, 30; 5:2, 8, 13; 6:7; 7:25; 9:25; Luke 4:36; 6:18; 8:29; 9:42; 11:24; Acts 5:16; 8:7; Rev. 16:13; 18:2). It has a direct connection with Satan and his activity with men. In the gospels and Acts, these "unclean spirits" are cast out (showing an obvious link to what we call "demon possession"). In Matthew 10:1, Jesus gave the apostles the power to cast out these unclean spirits. When the apostles returned from this "limited commission," they were excited that "even the demons are subject to us in Your name" (Luke 10:17).

If the power to cast out demons perished with the apostles (and those who were given this gift through the laying on of their hands), then it is logical to assume that God no longer allowed Satan to send his "unclean spirits" to inhabit human bodies.

> With the termination of the supernatural era of the early church, demon possession, and the corresponding gift of expulsion ceased. Satan's supernatural power was bound (Matthew 12:29). Certainly, the devil exerts great influence today. However, just as God no longer works miraculously, but influences men through His Word and providence, so also, Satan wields his power indirectly and non-miraculously through various media. Modern cases of supposed demon possession are doubtless the results of psychosomatic problems, hysteria, self-induced hypnosis, delusion, and such like. They have natural, though perhaps not always well-understood,

causes. When the Bible discusses demon possession, it is always from a specific, historical vantage point. As such, it does not endorse myth or superstition (Jackson).

CONCLUSION

Through the writings of the prophet, Zechariah, God has provided a number of significant prophesies related to the time of Jesus and the first century. The section in chapters 12-14 do not look beyond the time of Jesus (as many claim), but certainly point to the first century. By following the flow of the repeated "in that day" phrases, much can be learned about the flurry of first century activity.

WORKS CITED

Baldwin, Joyce G. *Haggai, Zechariah and Malachi: An Introduction and Commentary.* Vol. 28. Downers Grove, IL: InterVarsity Press, 1972. Print. Tyndale Old Testament Commentaries.

Bauer, Walter, William Arndt, Frederick W. Danker. *A Greek-English Lexicon of the New Testament and Other Early Christian Literature.* Chicago: University of Chicago Press, 2000. Abbreviated as BDAG in the text.

Biblia Hebraica Stuttgartensia: With Westminster Hebrew Morphology. Electronic ed. Stuttgart; Glenside PA: German Bible Society; Westminster Seminary, 1996. Print.

Brown, Francis, Samuel Rolles Driver, and Charles Augustus Briggs. *Enhanced Brown-Driver-Briggs Hebrew and English Lexicon* 2000. Print.

Carson, D. A., R. T. France, et al., eds. *New Bible Commentary: 21st Century Edition.* 4th ed. Leicester, England; Downers Grove, IL: Inter-Varsity Press, 1994. Print.

Clark, David J., and Howard A. Hatton. *A Handbook on Zechariah.* New York: United Bible Societies, 2002. Print. UBS Handbook Series.

Farnell, F. David. "When Will the Gift of Prophecy Cease?" Bibliotheca Sacra 150:598 (April 1993): 170-202.

Feinberg, Charles Lee. "Exegetical Studies in Zechariah." *Bibliotheca Sacra* 102 (Oct 1945):417

---. "Exegetical Studies in Zechariah." *Bibliotheca Sacra* 103 (Apr 19445):161-

175.

Gaebelein, Frank E., Gleason L. Archer Jr, et al. *The Expositor's Bible Commentary: Daniel and the Minor Prophets*. Vol. 7. Grand Rapids, MI: Zondervan Publishing House, 1986. Print.

Gill, John. *John Gill's Exposition of the Bible*. Zechariah 14:4. http://www. biblestudytools.com/commentaries/gills-exposition-of-the-bible/

Harris, R. Laird, Gleason L. Archer Jr., and Bruce K. Waltke, eds. *Theological Wordbook of the Old Testament* 1999 : n. pag. Print.

Hughes, Robert B., and J. Carl Laney. *Tyndale Concise Bible Commentary*. Wheaton, IL: Tyndale House Publishers, 2001. Print. The Tyndale Reference Library.

Jackson, Wayne. "Demon Possession, the Bible, and Superstition." *Reason and Revelation* (1983). http://www.apologeticspress.org

Jamieson, Robert, A. R. Fausset, and David Brown. *Commentary Critical and Explanatory on the Whole Bible*. Oak Harbor, WA: Logos Research Systems, Inc., 1997. Print.

Keil, Carl Friedrich, and Franz Delitzsch. *Commentary on the Old Testament*. Peabody, MA: Hendrickson, 1996. Print.

Klein, George L. *Zechariah*. Vol. 21B. Nashville, TN: B & H Publishing Group, 2008. Print. The New American Commentary.

Lange, John Peter, Philip Schaff, and Talbot W. Chambers. *A Commentary on the Holy Scriptures: Zechariah*. Bellingham, WA: Logos Bible Software, 2008. Print.

Pusey, E. B. *Notes on the Old Testament: The Minor Prophets: Micah to Malachi*. Vol. 2. New York: Funk and Wagnalls, 1885. Print.

Smith, James E. *The Minor Prophets*. Joplin, MO: College Press, 1994. Print. Old Testament Survey Series.

Smith, Ralph L. *Micah–Malachi*. Vol. 32. Dallas: Word, Incorporated, 1998. Print. Word Biblical Commentary.

Williams, Steve. "The Cross as the Crux of Christianity." *Firm Foundation* (December 21, 1982):6.

Zodhiates, Spiros, and Warren Baker. *The Complete Word Study Bible: King James Version*. electronic ed. Chattanooga: AMG Publishers, 2000. Print.

SECTION  2

The Text

CHAPTER 5

Nahum:
"God's Vengeance On Nineveh"

Mike Vestal

O nly two of the Minor Prophets end their book with a question. In the book of Jonah, an important question is posed to the calloused and reluctant prophet, "Should I not have compassion on Nineveh, the great city?" asks God (Jon. 4:11). In the book of Nahum, the king of Assyria (Nineveh being the capital) hears these words, "There is no relief for your breakdown, your wound is incurable. All who hear about you will clap their hands over you, for on whom has not your evil passed continually?" (Nah. 3:19, NASB). The NIV translates the last part of the verse as "your endless cruelty" while the ESV renders it "your unceasing evil." A sure formula for God's anger and judgment is the "endless cruelty" and "continual, unceasing evil" of individuals and nations! Nahum can thus be summarized in three short words: Nineveh will fall.

By concluding the book of Nahum with a question, it is almost as if the prophet wishes to draw his readers' minds back to the book of Jonah and events that transpired some one hundred and fifty years earlier. The two books "share far more" or "have in common" than simply ending with a question; they also share an exclusive focus on God and his dealings with Nineveh. The two books together form a lens which allows us to see even more clearly the rich and perfect character of God, especially His grace and mercy (Jonah) along with His wrath and judgment (Nahum). Interestingly enough, three of the Minor Prophets deal in considerable length with prophecies against nations that had long been notoriously cruel enemies of God's people: Edom (Obadiah), Assyria (Nahum) and Babylon (Habakkuk).

In three short chapters and 47 verses in our English translations, and against the backdrop of the Assyrian empire's constant and century-long cruelty, a magnificently comprehensive portrait of God shines forth. Indeed, Nahum vividly brings to mind a couple of foundational passages of Scripture regarding the nature of God to which people of every generation should cling: (1) "Behold then the goodness and severity of God" (Rom. 11:22); and, (2) "The Lord, the Lord God, compassionate and gracious, slow to anger and abounding in loving kindness and truth; who keeps loving kindness for thousands, who forgives iniquity, transgression and sin; yet he will by no means leave the guilty unpunished" (Exo. 34:6-7). This study will serve as an overview of Nahum by giving consideration to four important matters.

CONSIDER THE AUTHOR, DATE AND STYLE OF NAHUM

The name Nahum means "comfort" or "consolation." It appears that God chose a spokesman whose very name perfectly suited the essence of his message - comfort for Judah who had endured the cruelty of Assyria for years, and the righteous indignation of God against Nineveh. For Nineveh, no comfort would be found (Cf. 3:7)! Less is known about the prophet Nahum than almost any other prophet. We know Nahum was an "Elkoshite" (1:1), but the precise "location of Elkosh is another matter" and "there is really slight evidence for any of the identifications" commonly given as possibilities (Lewis 53).

We can date the book of Nahum with considerable precision due to his allusions to two dateable events. Nahum mentions the fall of the Egyptian city of Thebes or No-Amon (NASB) in 3:8, an event that occurred in 663 B.C. The prophet also speaks at length of Nineveh's eventual fall, which took place in 612 B.C., as something yet future. "Consequently, we may date Nahum's prophetic ministry between 663 B.C. and 612 B.C." (Arnold and Beyer 456). Given these parameters, Nahum would have prophesied during the reign of either Manasseh (697-642 B.C.) or Josiah (640-609 B.C.). Richard Patterson, after a somewhat thorough discussion of the external history of the time, the internal evidence within the book itself (cf. 1:13, 15; 2:1, 3) and a consideration of the nature of predictive prophecy, states: "All things considered, a date between 660 and 654 B.C. would appear to be most likely for the setting of the book" (4).

Nahum may rightly be called, "the poet laureate among the Minor Prophets" due to his "consummate craftsmanship" (Patterson 4-5). Nahum characterizes his message as both an "oracle" (NASB) or "burden" (KJV, ASV) and a "vision" - "something he felt and something he saw" (Wiersbe 406). The first expression is regularly used of statements of a threatening nature as part of a prophetic announcement of judgment (cf. Isa. 13:1; 15:1; Mal. 1:11), while the second indicates that the message is a revelation from God Himself and not merely out of spite on Nahum's part (Austel). This double heading (1:1), as well as the occurrence of "book" in the verse, "is unique to this book" (Lewis 56).

The book of Nahum beautifully blends the comfort God's people can have in His goodness and patience with the threat of His anger and certain judgment against those who repeatedly mistreat both God's people and the Lord Himself. Of the personality and style of Nahum, Walter Maier makes this observation:

> His reverence for the almighty, trust in divine justice and goodness, condemnation of national iniquity, positive conviction that God will keep his word - these are qualities of true greatness. Add to that Nahum's mighty intellect, his patriotism and courage, his rare, almost unequaled gift of vivid presentation, and he indeed looms as one of those outstanding figures of human history who have appeared only at rare intervals (20).

Nahum further displays depth of insight and ability regarding nature (1:4-8), history (3:4-8), the city of Nineveh, Assyrian culture itself and is a master of metaphor and a wide variety of literary techniques. A number of scholars have detected a chiastic (parallel) structure to the book:

A   Assyrian king taunted / Judah to celebrate (1:2-15)
  B   Dramatic call to alarm (2:1-10)
    C   Taunt (2:11-12)
      D   Announcement of judgment (2:13)
        E   Woe oracle (3:1-4)
      D   Announcement of judgment (3:5-7)
    C   Taunt (3:8-13)
  B   Dramatic call to alarm (3:14-17)
A   Assyrian king taunted / All celebrate (3:18-19) (Chisolm, p. 428).

Nahum contains a number of verbal and stylistic parallels with the books of Exodus and Isaiah (cf. Nah. 1:15 with Isa. 52:7). A good case also can be made for parallels with the Song of Deborah in Judges 5. None of these should be shocking due to the character and content of the material under discussion. Like the book of Obadiah, Nahum offers no real rebuke of the sins of Judah, but primarily chooses to deal with the sins of a violent and cruel oppressor. Richard Patterson offers a respectful conclusion regarding the style of Nahum (which may, in truth, be applied to the whole of Scripture):

> Even more important for exegetes of the book is the realization that Nahum's literary skill is not merely a display of his craftsmanship for his readers or a means of enlivening an otherwise colorless statement. Rather, his literary figures not only assist and enrich the understanding of the

meaning of the text but are the very form and content in which its meaning is to be apprehended. Further, they demand that the reader respond to their message in the totality of his being. One will not appreciate so fine a piece of literature as Nahum's prophecy unless he approaches it with his whole person - intellectually, emotionally and volitionally (6).

CONSIDER THE THEME AND KEY WORDS OF NAHUM

The theme is only too plain: Nineveh will fall. Nahum told the story in prophecy through the use of vivid prose, but what he predicted is now history. Nahum lived in a time when powerful Assyria was threatening Judah's very existence; it had placed Judah under a "yoke" and in "shackles" (1:13). The prophet declared in great detail that God would destroy the proud capital of the Assyrian Empire: Nineveh. So thorough was Nineveh's destruction that for centuries travelers passed over its ruins without knowing that this mighty and terrible city lay buried beneath their feet. "Only in fairly modern times (1842, to be exact) have archaeologists laid bare its ruins. Such was the literal and complete fulfillment of Nahum's prophecy" (Constable 4).

The basic theme of Nahum can be stated in this sentence: *God is good and is a great comfort to those who trust Him, but His anger and wrath are like a consuming flood and a fire against His wicked and cruel adversaries.* This sentence utilizes six key words / concepts of Nahum. The first key word / concept to keep in mind is "God." The book of Nahum is remarkably theocentric; it is about God. In chapter one alone, God is referred to specifically by name no less than eleven times, and personal pronouns are used of Him at least twenty-one times! Although historically Nineveh fell to the Babylonians, Medes and Scythians in 612 B.C., it ultimately fell to God. God's goodness and comfort to those who trust Him is another key concept to appreciate (cf. 1:7, 12-13). The book was not merely written to state that Nineveh would fall, but to comfort those who trusted God that Nineveh would fall. Third, the concept of God's anger, wrath and vengeance is accentuated. They are referred to at least ten times just in the first eight verses of the book!

A fourth key word / concept is the word "consuming" (cf. 1:10; 3:13, 15), reminding us that "It is a fearful thing to fall into the hands of the living God" (Heb. 10:31) and "our God is a consuming fire" (Heb. 12:29). Yet again, God's anger and wrath are likened to a "flood" (cf. 1:8) or a "fire" (cf. 1:6). The place of flooding and fire in the defeat of Nineveh has been well chronicled historically;

in fact, most scholars feel very certain that Nahum quite accurately describes the available historical information (Kohlenberger 80-81). Nahum simply does it years before it actually occurred. A fifth key term or concept is "against" (2:13; 3:5). Assyria was the great power in that region of the world in the eighth and most of the seventh century B.C. Its capital city of Nineveh was one of the grandest and most powerful cities on earth. Its size, power and wealth inspired fables (Dever 816). Tiny Judah could not have had less control of their dire circumstances than they did (cf. 2 Ki. 18:13-17; 2 Ch. 32:9; Isa. 36:1-2), but the message of Nahum would bring them comfort in the knowledge that God was "against" Nineveh. A time of reckoning would indeed come for all of Assyria's cruelties and atrocities. If God is against us, it really does not matter how great and mighty we are. Neither does it matter who else may stand with us or who may be for us.

The final key word / concept found in the theme sentence given earlier for Nahum is the idea of being God's "adversary" or "enemy." Such terminology bookends Nahum in 1:2, 8 and 3:11, 13. A consistent pattern of wickedness and oppression on the part of Nineveh led a merciful and longsuffering God to regard it as an adversary (cf. Acts 5:39). Years before Nineveh had repented at the preaching of Jonah (Jon. 3:8-10); now a pattern of sin had been so pursued by later generations in Nineveh that it indicated they had "repented" of a prior generation's repentance!

CONSIDER THE MESSAGE AND STRUCTURE OF NAHUM

From thematic, exegetical and structural considerations, Nahum may be outlined as follows:

Introduction (1:1)
  I. *The Doom of Nineveh Declared (1:2-15)*
      A. Theme: God is a Just King Who will Punish the Wicked and Avenge His Own (1:2)
      B. Development: Hymn to the Sovereign God (1:2-10)
      C. Application: God's Justice for Nineveh and Judah (1:11-15)

  II. *The Doom of Nineveh Described and Deserved (2:1-3:19)*
      A. Theme: God is a Just King Who will Punish Wicked Nineveh and Restore His Own (2:1-2)
      B. Development: The First Description of Nineveh's Destruction (2:3-10)

    C.   Application: The Devastation and Desolation of Nineveh (2:11-13)

    D.   Development: The Second Description of Nineveh's Destruction (3:1- 7)

    E.   Application: The Results of Nineveh's Destruction (3:8-19)

       1.   Nineveh is like Thebes or No-Amon (3:8-13)

       2.   Nineveh is utterly destroyed to the delight of those she had oppressed (3:14-19).

While such an outline is exegetically sound, it might be wise due to the wealth of material being dealt with for the preacher and teacher to deal with Nahum and its three chapters in the following manner: (1) God's Judgment Declared; (2) God's Judgment Described; and, (3) God's Judgment Deserved. A slight but helpful variation on this idea would be a "courtroom approach" to the book where in chapter one we see "The Judge." The one who judges Nineveh is beyond eminently qualified. He comforts the oppressed and promises judgment to the wicked. In chapter two we see "The Penalty." A vivid portrait of siege warfare is depicted, with short, staccato statements utilized to present events with "all possible force" (Lewis 57). The chapter concludes in verses 11-13 with a mocking taunt and announcement of judgment. Where are the mighty Assyrian "lions" now that God has come in judgment? Finally in chapter three we see "The Crimes." The Assyrians were cruel, bloodthirsty and "full of lies" (3:1). They were so oppressive and ruthless that Nazi Germany is said to have looked at them as a pattern for the Third Reich. The Assyrians were also guilty of idolatry and harlotry (3:4). They were guilty of sorcery (3:4). They took great pride in their military might, their alliances, their fortifications and abilities to defend themselves - they believed they were impervious to being overtaken (vv. 8-19). How wrong they were!

James Bruckner is among a number of scholars who contend that Nahum consists of seven literary parts (134-135). One can see the homiletic value of this approach as it incorporates vivid terminology reflecting each rhetorical section in the example that follows:

1. The Lord Our Just Avenger (1:2-11)
2. The Wicked Will Be Cut Off and Pass Away (1:12-15)
3. The Plunderer Will be Stripped and Laid Bare (2:1-10)
4. The Lion of Assyria Will be Routed (2:11-13)
5. The Harlot Will be Exposed (3:1-7)
6. The Invincible Will be Destroyed (3:8-13)
7. The Mortal Blow Will Spell Relief (3:8-14)

One can learn a great deal about the book of Nahum and about life in general by considering the rhetorical questions of the book. There are at least five such questions. The first one concerns God. "Who can stand before his indignation? Who can endure the heat of his anger?" (1:6). The second concerns Assyria as a great "lion" politically and militarily. "Where is the lion's den, the feeding place of the young lions, where the lion and lioness went, where his cubs were, with none to disturb?" (2:11). Another is found in Nahum 3:7, "Wasted is Nineveh; who will grieve for her? Where shall I seek comforters for you?" Then again, another such question follows immediately, "Are you better than Thebes that sat by the Nile with water about her, her rampart a sea, and water her wall?" (3:8). Finally, note the last verse of Nahum, "For upon whom has not come your unceasing evil" (3:19). Each of these questions can be answered with one of the following: (1) No one. (2) Nowhere to be found. (3) No.

CONSIDER THE MESSAGE OF NAHUM FOR TODAY

While a number of these may have been touched on earlier in this study, here are twelve truths to think about in our time from the book of Nahum.

1. God still rules in the kingdoms of men (Dan. 4:34-37; 5:21). The Lord God is still on the throne. He has not abdicated. He still comforts the oppressed and brings into judgment the wicked.

2. We must better stress the priority of a more biblically rigorous, richly comprehensive view of God (cf. 1:2-8). This will keep us from sinful behavior on the one hand and from biblically uninformed, extremist beliefs on the other. The theocentric view of God displayed by Nahum needs to be taken in deeply by elders, preachers, teachers and other children of God today (Pro. 1:7; 9:10; John 17:3).

3. The wrath of God is a biblical topic; God is as perfect in His anger as He is in any of His other attributes (Rom. 1:18; Eph. 5:5). His anger is never mindless, out-of-proportion or inappropriate. If sin is man's contradiction of God and His expressed will, if it is tantamount to idolatry and rebellion, God simply cannot be complacent about sin and still be God.

4. In Scripture, we have received a complete and all-sufficient revelation from God (2 Ti. 3:16-17; 1Th. 2:13). This God-given message is to be proclaimed so that others may know the Lord and His will. The message of God rebukes sin in all its forms and gives people hope because of what the Father has done in Christ Jesus. It is the good news of salvation in Jesus Christ that truly brings peace (Nah. 1:15; Eph. 2:14-17).

5. It is not wrong for Christians to have a biblically appropriate sense of comfort and relief when oppression and cruelty are dealt with (cf. Rev. 6:10). While properly balancing Matthew 5:44-48 and Romans 12:17-21 may be difficult, it is not impossible.

6. It is possible for generations to come to "repent" of the biblical repentance manifested by prior generations. Nineveh did. Oh, the necessity of training faithful men to teach generations to come (2 Ti. 2:2)! There must not be a "generation gap" as it concerns the relationship of people to God! We must leave a legacy of loving faithfulness to future generations.

7. We must more greatly appreciate the power and accuracy of predictive prophecy in Scripture. Have you ever thought about using the book of Nahum in order to evangelize an unbeliever? Its portrait of God, emphasis upon justice, comfort for the oppressed, etc., make it a book that might be worth considering in this regard. Further, the study of such a book would build up the faith of every Christian!

8. There is a genuine place and need for a "sanctified imagination" on the part of Christians, especially those who preach and teach. Divine truth can be taught imaginatively! Preaching and teaching that honors God must be true; it cannot be anything less. But it also must be more - it must be passionately and imaginatively conveyed. To think otherwise is to ignore not only the book of Nahum, but the teaching of our Lord himself!

9. The Lord is a "stronghold in the day of trouble" and a "refuge" (Nah. 1:7). How we need to remember and apply this truth at all times. Often when times are hard and things get tough, we tend to lose sight of this glorious truth.

10. Those who "live by the sword will perish by the sword" (Mat. 26:52). Violence, oppression and abuse do not go unnoticed by God.

11. If God says, "I am against you" (2:13; 3:5), all the "success," allies and power in the world mean nothing. Because of Jesus, we can know God is for us (Rom. 8:31-32).

12. To spurn God's mercy and goodness is the greatest of all tragedies. If ever anyone in the Old Testament positively experienced a "Romans 2:4 Moment," it was the people of Nineveh in Jonah's day. Yet the generations that came afterward turned from God to sin and forgot how blessed they were. Neglecting salvation often leads to rejecting it altogether (Heb. 2:4)! Nineveh had once been the object of God's mercy through its humble repentance; later it became the object of His wrath through its continued wickedness.

Although Nahum is a seldom studied book listed among a group of prophets known as the Minor Prophets, its message is powerful and desperately needed by the world today. May more of the spirit and character of Nahum be seen in God's people today!

WORKS CITED

Arnold, Bill T. and Beyer, Bryan E., *Encountering the Old Testament*, Baker, 2008, Second Ed.

Austel, Hermann J., *"Nahum,"* in The Baker Illustrated Bible Commentary, Baker, 2012.

Bruckner, James K., *"Jonah, Nahum, Habakkuk and Zephaniah,"* in NIV Application Commentary, Zondervan, 2004.

Constable, Thomas L., *Notes on Nahum*, www.soniclight.com

Dever, Mark, *The Message of the Old Testament*, Crossway, 2006.

Herrick, Greg, *The Book of Nahum*, www.bible.org

Kohlenberger, John R., *Jonah and Nahum* in Everyman's Bible Commentary, Moody Press, 1984.

Lewis, Jack P., *The Minor Prophets*, Baker, 1982, Eighth Printing.

Maier, Walter, *Nahum*: Concordia Classic Commentary Series, Concordia, 1987.

Patterson, Richard A., *Nahum* - published in its entirety online at www.bible.org

Wiersbe, Warren W., *The Old Testament Prophets in The Bible Exposition Commentary*, 6 Volumes, 2002.

CHAPTER 6

Habakkuk:
"Seeking The Divine Through The Difficult"

Donnie Bates

"I don't know why I even bother to pray!" Sitting here together on a beautiful morning, made beautiful by the occasion and not the weather, it may be hard to imagine uttering such a statement or entertaining such a thought. However, it is entirely possible, even likely, that someone reading this has at least been tempted to think a thought like this one, due to frustrations that often arise in our lives. It may even be the case that someone reading this, at this moment, is feeling this level of frustration, anxiety, or stress. If that be the case, then the short book of Habakkuk has something to say to you about being able to see God's love, power and ability to care for His people through the most difficult of times in our lives.

Very often we hold up King David as a man after God's own heart (1 Sa. 13:14) and David did say, "The Lord is my light and my salvation; whom shall I fear? The Lord is the defense of my life; whom shall I dread? When evildoers came upon me to devour my flesh, my adversaries and my enemies, they stumbled and fell. Though a host encamp against me, my heart will not fear; though war arise against me, in *spite of* this I shall be confident." (Psa. 27:1-3). David was able to utter such a strong statement of faith and trust in God even though he faced many trials and afflictions in his life; however, many of the afflictions David faced were of his own making; consequences of his own actions. And that is where most of us live, is it not?

The "oracle" (burden) of Habakkuk is not so much one of his own making, but it gives us a great lesson in how to face whatever may come in this life from whatever direction; whether it be as a result (consequence) of our own actions, or from the efforts of our enemy, the devil. It is a short book comprised of only three chapters with a total of 56 verses. While different commentators offer outlines with slight variations of the book, the structure seems to be fairly straightforward. The first two chapters contain an exchange between the prophet and Jehovah, with the final chapter being entirely composed of the powerful and emotional resignation of Habakkuk to the truth that God is in control, even though what is coming is terrifying.

It seems appropriate to lay some groundwork at this point of our study, before delving into the text itself. Not much is known about the man Habakkuk, other than that he was a prophet and, apparently, a known prophet. Even the meaning of his name is uncertain, although some have opined that it comes from a Hebrew word meaning "to embrace" (McComiskey par. 1). "Very little can be ascertained concerning the identification or provenience of this prophet. Historical allusions and linguistic characteristics of his prophecy suggest that he ministered in Judah *ca. 600 B.C.*" (Myers par. 2). Harper's Bible Dictionary offers: "The reference to the coming of the Chaldeans in 1:6 makes it likely that Habakkuk was active in the last quarter of the seventh century b.c. [sic]" (Achtemeier par. 2).

If we are correct in understanding that the time frame coincides with the coming of the Chaldeans as part of the judgment of God on Judah, near the end of the seventh century B.C. and the beginning of the sixth, then we can understand somewhat better the "burden" (oracle) under which the prophet was operating. Almost 100 years had passed since the invasion of Israel and Judah by the Assyrians, which resulted in the end of Israel and the near-defeat of Judah, which was only averted by the faithful and humble submission of good King Hezekiah to Jehovah. Since that time, however, Judah had moved further and further from a right relationship with God.

Judah had just experienced the exhilaration of the glorious days of Josiah, marked by freedom, prosperity, and a great religious revival. The Assyrians, once the scourge of the Middle East, were only a shadow of their former selves. In their place, however, stood the Babylonians. In the book of Habakkuk, they are called the Chaldeans, so named for the region from which their rulers came. The Babylonian armies were led by the energetic Nebuchadnezzar, who was soon to succeed his father Nabopolassar as king. Nineveh, Assyria's capital, fell in 612 b.c.[sic] The powerful poetry of Nahum celebrates its fall. In 609 b.c. [sic] disaster struck. King Josiah, attempting to block the Egyptians as they moved north along the Palestinian coast to aid Assyria, was killed at Megiddo in northern Palestine. In his place the Egyptians set up Josiah's son, Jehoiakim. Unlike his father, Jehoiakim was a petty tyrant. Over the next 10 or 11 years, Jehoiakim tried to pit the Babylonians against the Egyptians until he finally exhausted the patience of Nebuchadnezzar. In 598 he laid siege to Jerusalem. That same year Jehoiakim died, leaving his son, Jehoiachin, to become Nebuchadnezzar's prisoner when Jerusalem fell in 597 b.c. [sic] (Holman par. 1, 2).

This time of shallow spirituality would have been of great concern to a man of faith. "The Book of Habakkuk reveals a man of great sensitivity. His deep concern about injustice and his prayer (Hb 3) show that Habakkuk was characterized by profound religious conviction and social awareness." (McComiskey par. 4).

This "deep concern" of Habakkuk for his people is seen at the beginning of the book. Habakkuk does not begin by questioning the wisdom of bringing in the Chaldeans as a punishment of the evil Judeans. He is not aware of God's plan at this point, but he is concerned about the great sin and injustice that exists among his people. It is only when God explains His plan to him, that Habakkuk's real struggle begins.

Whether or not we understand all the reasons for and implications of what we endure in this life, God is in control and man's responsibility is to trust Him to get us through, even if that costs us our physical lives.

FIRST EXCHANGE (1:1-11)

Habakkuk's First Question (1:1-4)

Habakkuk is upset. There is injustice in Judah and he has prayed for justice and deliverance and as far as he can tell, there has been no answer from God. In fact, Habakkuk's problem seems to be with Jehovah Himself, at this point. It is as though he could have put it in the words with which we began this lesson: "I don't know why I even bother to pray!"

Life has its frustrations, certainly, but if we are not careful we can let those frustrations take over and we become easy prey to the thought that God is no longer listening, or worse, is no longer in control. The prophet does not appear to have fallen this far into his depression or frustration. God is going to answer him with a shocking solution to the problem, shocking, at least, to Habakkuk's way of thinking.

Jehovah's First Response (1:5-11)

God begins His answer to Habakkuk by saying, "Open your eyes!" God *is* doing something and what He is doing is something the prophet would scarcely believe!! The answer to the problem of injustice and unrighteousness in the land of Judah is to raise up the Chaldeans who would invade Judah and punish (or judge) them on God's behalf.

The Chaldeans (Babylonians) were a fierce, warrior people. Militarily, they were the super power of the day and no army could resist them. Egypt would try, but fail. The Chaldeans had only recently destroyed the once all-powerful Assyrian empire. Jehovah's answer ends with a warning that the Chaldeans would bring about their own end through their arrogance.

Let us make some application here. How many times have you felt your were suffering unjustly and wondered if God was ever going to answer your prayers? How many times have you cried out, at least in your mind, "How long, O, Lord?" Perhaps we should open our eyes and observe. It might just be that Jehovah God is working His own purpose through our suffering!

SECOND EXCHANGE (1:12 - 2:20)

Habakkuk's Second Question (1:12 - 2:1)

God's answer to the prophet did not satisfy Habakkuk. In fact, Jehovah's plan seemed even more outrageous than the initial problem. I want us to think through this. Habakkuk complains that God is not addressing a problem. God responds by telling Habakkuk, "I *am* addressing the problem; I have a plan that is so great you wouldn't believe it if I told you, but I'm going to tell you anyway." And then He tells him, and the prophet's response is, "I can't believe it!" Read 1:13 again: "Your eyes are too pure to approve evil, and You can not look on wickedness with favor. Why do You look with favor on those who deal treacherously? Why are You silent when the wicked swallow up those more righteous than they?" Apparently, Habakkuk felt it was better to suffer injustice and suffering in the family than to bring in a bunch of outsiders.

I would like us to pause here for a moment and consider the kind of relationship that Habakkuk had with his heavenly Father. He does not have any difficulty in bringing his concerns to God in prayer. We see a confidence here that many do not possess. Some might even call it brash or arrogant. We should note that at the end of this particular exchange (2:1), the prophet seems to acknowledge that he might have gone too far in chastising Jehovah God Himself and expects to be reproved. We should also note that God never reproves Habakkuk for a lack of respect or for his impatience. This suggests that it is not necessarily wrong to bring our concerns to God in such a (seemingly) forceful way as long as our basic attitude is one of humility and righteousness, which is what we see in Habakkuk's oracle (burden) when taken as a whole. Now that the prophet has had his say about God's plan, God answers again.

Jehovah's Second Response (2:2-20)

Jeff Jenkins, made this point about this portion of our text. Verse two is about as close to a reproof of Habakkuk as God seems to come. If we were to put this into our own vernacular, the Lord says, "Habakkuk, your job is not to understand My plan! Your job is to write down what I tell you and write it clearly enough so that the faithful can read and know what to do to survive what is coming."

This seems to be a great place for some more application. Does this not apply to us today every bit as much as it did for Habakkuk? Of course it does! It is not our job to understand fully all the ways of God or every nuance of every command. Our job is to preach (or write) the truth of God's Word and to preach it (or write it) clearly enough so that those who hear (or read) can understand what is necessary to survive the judgment that is coming. When we start questioning God because we don't understand how He could mean what He appears to mean (to the point of studying more and digging deeper into God's word), that's one thing, but when we take the next step of changing what He says to make it more understandable in our own minds, or more appealing to the ears of others, we have gone too far; we have gone far beyond what the prophet Habakkuk did.

Jehovah makes it perfectly clear that judgment is coming! Rather than worrying over the fairness or justness of the plan, Habakkuk has a job to do, and time is running out. If a person is going to be prideful and insist that the plan is not fair, why, there is something wrong with that man's soul! The contrast to that proud man is the righteous man, who will survive judgment because of his faith. Neither in Habakkuk 2:4 nor when the apostle Paul quotes this verse in Romans 1:17, is this meant to be a commentary on daily Christian living. "The righteous shall live by his faith" simply means that the righteous will survive judgment because he is a man of faith.

Continuing His response, Jehovah makes it clear that while He is quite willing to use the Chaldeans for His purpose of judging Judah, He is not willing to overlook their sin in the process. Babylon will not escape their own judgment. In bringing Jehovah's justice to the Jews, the Chaldeans will exhibit their own injustice (nakedness, verse 16) and will be brought down in their turn for it.

Historically speaking, the Chaldeans that destroyed Jerusalem and took away the captives were not as evil as Habakkuk feared they would be. They were led by Nebuchadnezzar, who recognized that he was a servant of Jehovah. A very interesting historical side note is that this Nebuchadnezzar who destroyed Jerusalem in 586 B.C., who was as pagan as they come (he built the giant statue in Susa and ordered all of Babylon to worship it or be thrown into the fire (Dan. 3), had, by 586 B.C., been exposed to four godly young men named Daniel,

Hananiah, Mishael and Azariah (Shadrach, Meshach and Abed Nego) for several decades. Wow! It's almost as though God had a plan, isn't it? It was not until Nebuchadnezzar's descendants were ruling over Babylon that their arrogance led to their destruction, but that destruction will come as the wages of sin always do.

The response of Jehovah concludes with a commentary on idolatry (verse 18-20). I do not know if you have ever seen verse 20 posted in a church auditorium with the intent of encouraging a quiet and reverent attitude when we assemble together. I think my first memory of this verse came with the "encouragement" (although "threat" might be a more applicable term) to remember that I was in "God's house" and so I had better be quiet! Such is a gross misapplication of this passage. The verse does not mean to keep quiet in the assembly, but that we worship a living God. In idolatry, the worshippers do all the talking because there's nobody home on the other end. In our worship, however, our God is alive, and we would do well to listen to Him, rather than tell Him what we think He needs to know! Even though audibly (in a physical sense) we hear men speaking, or all of us speaking in psalms, hymns and spiritual songs, it is God speaking to us through those who faithfully lead us in worship (1 Pe. 4:11).

We may be tempted to ask God why the unrighteous seem to "get away" with their unrighteousness. It is true that there are things in this life that do not seem to be fair. God says here, in His second response to Habakkuk, that the unrighteous do not "get away" with anything. Righteousness will prevail and unrighteousness will be punished (Rom. 1:18). The lesson for us is that we may trust our God. Now, go back to 2:1 where the prophet says he will see how he will reply to whatever Jehovah says next. Chapter three is that reply.

HABAKKUK'S PRAYER OF PRAISE (3:1-19)

Habakkuk was deeply moved by Jehovah's response. I have found many explanations for the meaning of Shigionoth, but none seem any more clear or easy to explain than the footnote in my Bible: "a highly emotional poetic form." Yes, Habakkuk has questioned God; some might even say he chastised God. However, it clear by this prayer that Habakkuk was always disposed to humble himself before God. He seems willing to accept whatever God has in store for the Jews.

In verses 3-15 we find what might be termed a theophany (an appearance of God to man), but it is not any kind of physical appearance. God appears in a figurative manner in judgment of Judah. These verses describe the very elements of creation and their reaction to the judgment of God. Verses 12 and 13 gives us a sense of the purpose of God's judgment:" In indignation You marched through the earth; in anger You trampled the nations. You went forth for the salvation of Your people, for the salvation of Your anointed. You struck the head of the house of the evil to lay him open from thigh to neck." God was not sending judgment on His people because He no longer loved them, but precisely because He *did* love them and wanted to save them. That is where the job of Habakkuk and his colleagues (the prophets) comes in; they were charged with the responsibility of getting that message out. And that is precisely the same charge we have today. Judgment is coming, but this time it will not be to convince the unrighteous to come back to God. This time, judgment is final! The unrighteous must come back to God *before* judgment, or it will be too late. As Christians, we simply *must* understand the urgency of that fact.

I find verses 16-19 to be among the most powerful in all of Scripture. They indicate a level of faith on the part of Habakkuk that may be hard for some to comprehend, but which also serves as an example of what our faith must be. Habakkuk is terrified of the judgment he now understands cannot be avoided. It is an acknowledgement akin to Jesus' statement, "Not My will, but Thine be done!" (Lk 22:42). However, even in his fear the prophet is ready to accept whatever comes because he knows that God is in control. It does not matter how bad things get. He will trust Jehovah. If the invader destroys the economy so that there is no food, Habakkuk says, "I will rejoice in the God of my salvation."

Do you have that kind of faith? What if those who have stated publicly that they want to destroy our nation succeed in doing so? What if they destroy our economy so that there is no food, as happened to Jerusalem? What if God, in judging this nation, causes us to be ruled by another? Will the Lord be your strength, or will you give in to despair, lose your faith and turn your back on God because He must be too weak to stop it? My prayer is that all of us will have the faith of Habakkuk. Remember, faith does not mean laughing at physical danger. We may hear and our inward parts may tremble, but our verse 16 must lead to a verse 18.

CONCLUSION

Habakkuk had a reason to hope. He knew that even though the future was so scary that it terrified him, Jehovah was still in control. He could still say at the end that he trusted in God to be his strength. And we can take hold of that same hope.

Habakkuk is truly an example of faith. When things get desperate in your life, remember this short prophecy. When faith is hard to come by, look to Habakkuk, and see the Divine through the difficult.

WORKS CITED

Achtemeier, Paul J., Harper & Row and Society of Biblical Literature. *Harper's Bible Dictionary* 1985 : n. pag. Print.

Brand, Chad, Charles Draper, et al., eds. "Habakkuk." *Holman Illustrated Bible Dictionary* 2003 : n. pag. Print.

Elwell, Walter A., and Barry J. Beitzel. *Baker Encyclopedia of the Bible* 1988 : n. pag. Print.

Myers, Allen C. *The Eerdmans Bible Dictionary* 1987 : n. pag. Print.

CHAPTER 7

Zephaniah:
"The Day of Jehovah"

Bart Warren

There's a great day coming, a great day coming;
There's a great day coming by and by,
When the saints and the sinners shall be parted right and left,
Are you ready for that day to come?

So wrote brother Will L. Thompson back in 1887. The lines of this beloved traditional hymn convey eternal truth. All of Scripture testify to the fact that a day is coming when the faithful and obedient will be separated from the rebellious and wicked (cf. Mat. 25:31-46). This eschatological event will be a day of joy and celebration for some and a day of terror and anguish for others. The key, as in the lyrics of the song, is to be ready for that day to come.

The prophet Zephaniah, though often overlooked by modern audiences, has much to say on this particular subject and remains perpetually relevant. In fact, one quarter of the prophet's 53 verses makes specific reference to the "day" of the LORD. Zephaniah boldly proclaimed to his audiences that "a great day" was coming. This monumental event would bring judgment in the form of unbearable wrath and punishment. But the day would not be limited to suffering and retribution. The day of the LORD is also a harbinger of restoration and hope. We expect such to be the case knowing what we know about the awesome God we serve. "He is by nature the God of holy wrath and the God of holy hope – inseparable components of his deity" (Motyer 897). The book of Zephaniah contains a loving and compassionate call to be humble before, and submit heart and soul to, Almighty God – while also making the reader completely aware of the terrible consequences and harrowing destiny that awaits those that know not God.

HISTORICAL SETTING

The ministry of Zephaniah took place during the reign of King Josiah (Zep. 1:1). This information gives us a good deal of contextual insight. Josiah, known as one of the reformer kings who sought to bring the hearts of the people back to God, came to the throne of Judah following the wicked and disastrous reigns of Manasseh and Amon (2 Ki. 21; 2 Ch. 33). Manasseh left quite a legacy after his 55 years in power. He was said to have done what was evil and despicable in the eyes of the LORD. He rebuilt the pagan altars that his father, Hezekiah, had torn down. He worshipped the stars and other heavenly bodies. He built pagan altars in the Temple. He burned and sacrificed his own sons. He attempted to utilize information received from mediums and necromancers. In short, Manasseh led Israel astray (2 Ki. 21:9). It was in this setting of deep-seated wickedness that Josiah sought to rule and Zephaniah labored to preach. Though there is no justification for being dogmatic, it seems within reason to conclude that Zephaniah's message from God could have played a role in the reforms of the young king.

THE DAY OF THE LORD

It was during this time that Zephaniah would preach, "the day of the LORD is near" (Zep. 1:7). How are we to understand this message? What did the prophet's audience think of this phrase? The term "day of the LORD" occurs throughout the Bible referring both to impending historical judgments from God and to His final judgment at the end of time. At the heart of the term is divine action. The "day of the LORD" is indicative of those times when God would break into time and act in human history. Israel viewed this day as a time when God would come to the aid of those who are His. It was thought to be a time when all enemies would be put down and Israel and her God would be exalted. It was seen as a day in history in which a nation would receive its doom.

For Zephaniah and his contemporaries, the harsh reality was this day would be tragically horrible for both Judah and the surrounding nations. They would come to know the wrath of God. However, this same day would be glorious and happy for a remnant of God's people. The day would find fulfillment in the sixth century BC when Judah was destroyed by Babylon and taken captive (Zep. 1:7). Beyond even this, the day would find fulfillment in the first century with the coming of Jesus and the Roman destruction of Jerusalem (Luke 11:20; Mat. 24:3-35). And finally, the day will find ultimate fulfillment in the second coming of Jesus and Judgment Day (2 Pe. 3:10-12, 18; Acts 17:31; 1 Th. 5:2; 2 Ti. 4:8; et. al.).

Zephaniah's audience would have expected the LORD to work on their behalf. They assumed that God would exalt them and destroy their enemies. To their great shock and dismay, the prophet would inform them that, in addition to the wicked nations around them, they too would fall victim to the mighty wrath of God. The only way to avoid such a painful demise would be to turn their hearts and minds over to the God of heaven. Humble submission to Him and seeking His will was required. The prophet describes a coming time when God will crash into human history and, according to His plan, bring about salvation and blessing for His people who trust Him, as well as terrible wrath on those who have rejected Him.

SUMMARY OF THE TEXT

With some obvious exceptions, the book can be generally outlined accordingly: Chapter One = Judgment of Divine Wrath against Judah; Chapter Two = Judgment of Divine Wrath against the Nations; Chapter Three = Declaration of Hope and Restoration. Zephaniah taught a straightforward message: Judgment is coming and it is unavoidable. However, the judgment may well be positive if one will humbly submit to God.

Chapter one opens with a terrifying prediction. Everything, man and beast included, will be destroyed. The prophet seems to make a historical reference to the days of Noah in verses two and three (cf. Gen. 6:17; 7:4, 21-23). There was a time in the past when God destroyed mankind because of their great wickedness. It stands to reason that He could and would do such again. The prophet of God does not make an idle threat.

After the wide-ranging announcement of destruction, God gives a specific list of who will be punished. The priests who led people astray and encouraged false worship head the record (Zep. 1:4). Although all men are free and must make up their own minds about the truth (1 Th. 5:21; Acts 17:11), teachers are held to a higher standard – one that is indeed daunting and challenging (Jas. 3:1; Jer. 2:8; 5:31; 2 Pe. 2:3, 9-10). Almighty God is very serious and careful about what His flock of sheep is being fed. We must be, as well. Next on the list are those involved in pagan worship and those caught up in syncretism (Zep. 1:5). Some thought they could worship both God and various pagan gods at the same time. They were actually worshipping multiple gods so that they could cover all of their bases. Today our issue is more often the hearts of men that are given to the world, to pleasure, to leisure, to being entertained, etc., and then they want to "go to church" on Sunday morning to express their "devotion" to God. The LORD will sweep away those with divided attention (Jas. 1:8; 4:8). The God of Heaven must hold our hearts and captivate our minds without competition (Mat. 22:37). Next on the list are those who have left the LORD altogether. They may have loved Him at one time, but now He never even enters their minds. Note: not even the Old Testament knows anything about the false doctrine of once-saved-always-saved. One can be part of kingdom and leave (Heb. 6:4-6). One can be part of the fold and escape (2 Pe. 2:20-23). These people no longer cry out to God or seek His wisdom. They will be swept away. Next on the list are the materialistic (Zep. 1:11, 13, 18). When money is the source of our security…our satisfaction…our significance…instead of God, we are lost (1 Ti. 6:9-11)! Finally, the prophet calls out the complacent (Zep. 1:12). These are the people who claim to believe in God, yet they live as though He does not exist. They live without any fear of retribution whatsoever. This is dangerous. When we live without proper fear and do not appreciate the significance of God's wrath, we are doomed. We must live in light of the fact that God's wrath is eternal (Mark 9:43-48), terrible (Mat. 13:41-42), and deserved (Rom. 2:5; 3:23; 6:23), albeit escapable (2 Th. 1:7-9; 2 Pe. 2:9).

The remainder of chapter one emphasizes just how terrifying and horrible the day will be (Zep. 1:14-18). The day is near and getting closer all the time (cf. Rom. 13:11). The day will have all of the sights and sounds that would shock and frighten even the mightiest of battle-tested warriors. Nothing and no one will be able to stand against it. Nothing and no one will be able to prevent the day from coming. All we can do is be ready for that day to come.

Chapter two focuses on the nations around Judah. The prophet depicted God's judgment falling on various nations representing the four points of the compass (all inclusive). To the west, major Philistine cities would be given to Judah (Zep. 2:5-7). To the east, the Moabites and Ammonites would be annihilated (Zep. 2:8-11). To the south, the Cushites would be cut down by the sword (Zep. 2:12). To the north, arrogant Nineveh would be reduced to a pile of rubble (Zep. 2:13-15) (Chisholm 448). Our pride will destroy us, but our dependence upon Him will sustain us (Pro. 16:18; 1 Co. 10:12; Mat. 5:3, 5; Gal. 2:20).

Chapter three changes everything. After all of the doom and gloom…after all of the language designed to stir up the emotion of fear…here we find some of the most uplifting and thrilling lines in all of Holy Scripture (Zep. 3:7-20). The prophet closes his book with a stirring message of hope. The LORD will cure His people and purify their unclean lips (Zep. 3:9; cf. Isa. 6:5-7). God has set a time when He will sweep away the proud, the indifferent, and the corrupt. Those who seek the LORD diligently with humility, longing for the day of redemption, will be sheltered on that day (Dockery 491). Most amazing of all, Zephaniah affirms that it is God who will be rejoicing over His people (Zep. 3:17)! God delights in His children (Deu. 30:9-10; Isa. 62:4). This was illustrated famously in the parables recorded in Luke 15. Whether it was a coin, a sheep, or a boy, the people rejoiced when that which was lost was found. Moreover, heaven itself rejoices (Luke 15:7, 10). The Father Himself demands that there be a celebration of the dead finding life (Luke 15:24, 32). Oh, to live a life of trust and humble submission that would make God sing!

CONCLUSION

The grace of God is available in abundance to those of a humble and contrite heart. He will exult over us with loud singing! Yet He has told us what we must do to enjoy and experience such a phenomenon. First, we must be silent (Zep. 1:7). We must be prepared to listen and be prepared to move/act when instruction is given. Second, we must seek Him (2:3). Knowing and living by His commands are vital and indispensable components to life as a child of God. Third, we must wait for Him (3:8). Let us long for His return and place our confident trust in Him as we wait for and watch His plan unfold. If we will live this way, we can join with Paul and say that we long for and love His appearing (2 Ti. 4:8)! J. I. Packer once wrote, "Run from Him now, and you will meet Him as Judge then – and without hope. Seek Him now, and you will find Him (for "he that seeketh findeth"), and you will then discover that you are looking forward to that future meeting with joy, knowing that there is now 'no condemnation for those who are in Christ Jesus' (Rom. 8:1)" (147).

> *There's a bright day coming, a bright day coming;*
> *There's a bright day coming by and by.*
> *But its brightness shall only come to them that love the Lord.*
> *Are you ready for that day to come?*

WORKS CITED

Chisholm, Robert B., Jr. *Handbook on the Prophets: Isaiah, Jeremiah, Lamentations, Ezekiel, Daniel, Minor Prophets*. Grand Rapids, MI: Baker Academic, 2002.

Dockery, David S. et al. *Holman Bible Handbook*. Nashville, TN: Holman Bible Publishers, 1992.

Motyer, J. Alec. "Zephaniah." *The Minor Prophets: An Exegetical and Expository Commentary*. Ed. Thomas Edward McComiskey. Grand Rapids, MI: Baker Academic, 2009.

Packer, J. I. *Knowing God*. Downers Grove, IL: IVP, 1973.

CHAPTER 8

Haggai 1:
"From Indifference To Industry"

Wade Webster

Have you ever tried to push a stalled car? If you have, then you know how hard it is to move a stationary object. Now, imagine trying to push a car that has been sitting in the same spot for years; a car that has four flat tires and grass growing up through it. No doubt, it would be nearly impossible to move. Haggai faced a very similar task in Jerusalem. The work of the Lord had stalled. In fact, it had not moved in sixteen years. The people had settled comfortably into their daily lives and routines. Haggai was sent by God to get them up and moving again.

INDIFFERENCE – "YE SAY, THE TIME IS NOT YET COME"

When Haggai arrived on the scene in Jerusalem, he came face to face with indifference. God's house was in ruins, and the people were living in "ceiled houses" (Hag. 1:4). "Ceiled" houses were houses that were wainscoted or paneled. They were more than shelters to protect the residents from the elements. They were ornately finished houses. They were finished with fragrant and beautiful cedar. They were the kinds of houses that kings built for themselves (1 Ki. 7:3, 7; Jer. 22:14). Where had they found the wood to decorate their houses? Had it come from the king's grant? Had it come from the wood that was originally to be used on the temple? Although we cannot know for sure, it seems likely that they had procured the wood for the Lord's house and used it on their own houses. When they finally did get around to building the temple, they would have to go to the mountain to get wood to finish it (Hag. 1:8). Each day the people must have thoughtlessly passed by the ruins of God's house as they ran to their own ceiled houses (Hag. 1:9). The condition of God's house was nothing to them (Hag. 1:12). They were more concerned with their own gain, than they were with God's glory. They were more concerned with ceiling their own houses than they were in completing God's house.

The 50,000 Jews that returned with Ezra in 536 BC came into the land with great enthusiasm and zeal. They quickly rebuilt the altar and started offering sacrifices again. Then, they laid the foundation to the temple in 535 BC. God's house was on its way to being rebuilt. However, opposition arose, and the work soon slowed and stopped. Although opposition stopped them from building God's house, it did not prevent them from building their own houses. I am reminded today of people who let almost anything and everything prevent them from doing God's work, but not from doing the things that they want to do. I know people who will get up well before daylight on Black Friday and fight large crowds to save a few dollars on a gift, but can't make it to Bible class on Sunday morning because it starts too early. I know people who will go into an opposing team's stadium to cheer on their football team, but won't knock on a door because they might face a person from another religion.

God's people were arguing that the time had not yet come to build God's house (Hag. 1:2). Yet, they had found the time to build their own houses. There was no way around it. They had put the building of their own houses before the building of God's house. I am reminded of church members today who say that they don't have time to visit, but they do have time to do other things. They find time to attend sporting events, to play golf, to go fishing, and to do a host of other things. For sure, there is nothing inherently wrong with these things. In fact, I believe that a strong case can be made for doing them; especially, going fishing. I really like fishing. However, there is something wrong when worldly things come before spiritual things. God and His kingdom are supposed to come first (Mat. 6:33). Our affections are supposed to be on things above and not on things on the earth (Col. 3:2).

No doubt, the people of Haggai's day had good intentions. They were planning to build God's house one day. They were simply waiting for a convenient time (Acts 24:25). Likely, they never would have gotten around to it, had it not been for the prophet Haggai. After all, those who observe the wind do not sow, and those who regard the clouds do not reap (Ecc. 11:4).

In their indifference, Haggai's people did not realize that their priorities were out of order until the prophet came and called their attention to it. Like those at Laodicea, they did not know their true condition. Dwelling in their custom houses they must have thought that they were rich and in need of nothing. However, they were poor, wretched, miserable, blind, naked, and in need of everything. They were neither hot nor cold, but lukewarm. The prophet Haggai was sent to chasten them in love. He was sent to call upon them to repent and to be zealous again (Rev. 3:19).

Today, indifference continues to plague God's people. God's work in many places is in ruins as men run to their own houses. Like Haggai's people, people today live in great luxury. They have about every comfort that can be imagined. Sadly, at the same time, missionaries struggle to raise funds to be able to carry the gospel to those who are lost and dying in sin. I am convinced that God continues to want his ministers to call His people to repentance and revival (2 Ti. 4:2).

INVENTORY – "CONSIDER YOUR WAYS"

Haggai encouraged the people to "consider," or take inventory, of their ways (Hag. 1:5, 7). He wanted them to examine their ways and to prove themselves (2 Co. 13:5). If their priorities were right, then they had nothing to fear from such an examination. If their checkbooks were in order, then the register of where they were spending their money would prove it (Mal. 1).

I think that it is interesting that Haggai encouraged them to "consider" their ways. He could have easily commanded them to change their ways. For sure, that is what they needed to do. No doubt, it would have been acceptable for him to have done so. However, he chose a softer approach. I believe that he was hoping to make them sorry so that he did not have to come with a rod (1 Co. 4:21). He was speaking the truth in love (Eph. 4:15). As God's servant, he was being very gentle, meek, and patient with them (2 Ti 2:24-26). He knew that they were opposing themselves by their actions. They were earning wages, only to turn around and put them into a bag with holes. They were sowing much, but reaping little. Haggai hoped that as they took inventory of their ways that they would realize it.

The absence of dew, the poor harvests, and other things should have been a clear indicator to them that their actions were not pleasing to God. Years earlier, Moses had spelled out exactly what would happen to them if they forsook God. We read,

> But it shall come to pass, if thou wilt not hearken unto the voice of the Lord thy God to observe to do all His commandments and his statutes which I command thee this day; that all these curse shall come upon thee, and overtake thee. Cursed shalt thou be in the city, and cursed shalt thou be in the field. Cursed shall be thy basket and thy store. Cursed shall be the fruit of thy body, and the fruit of thy land, the increase of thy kine, and the flocks of thy sheep… And thy heaven that is over thy head shall be brass, and the earth that is under thee shall be iron. The Lord shall make the rain of thy land powder and dust from heaven shall it come down upon thee, until thou be destroyed…Thou shalt carry much seed out into the field, and shalt gather but little in; for the locust shall consume it (Deu. 28:15-18, 23-24, 38).

These very things were happening to them. Consider Haggai's record:

> Ye have sown much, and bring in little; ye eat, but ye have not enough; ye drink, but ye are not filled with drink; ye cloth you, but there is none warm; and he that earneth wages to put it into a bag with holes…Ye looked for much, and, lo, it came to little; and when ye brought it home, I did blow upon it. Why? saith the Lord of hosts. Because of mine house that is waste, and ye run every man unto his own house. Therefore the heaven over you is stayed from dew, and the earth is stayed from her fruit. And I called for a drought upon the land, and upon the mountains, and upon the corn, and upon the new wine, and upon the oil, and upon that which the ground bringeth forth, and upon men, and upon cattle, and upon all the labour of the hands (Hag. 1:6, 9-11).

Clearly, the people were suffering the consequences of their own actions; or, in this case, the consequences of their own inaction. However, it did not have to be this way. If they would put God first again, curses would turn into blessings.

On a weekly basis today, God challenges us to consider our ways. Of course, this is done as we examine ourselves in preparation for partaking of the Lord's Supper (1 Co. 11:28). Indifference for us should never go for sixteen years. It should never go more than six days. It should be checked and corrected on the first day of every week.

INDUSTRY – THEY CAME AND DID THE WORK IN THE HOUSE OF THE LORD

Haggai delivered God's message for the people to go up to the mountain, to bring wood, and to build His house (Hag. 1:8). The people heard this message, took inventory of their lives, abandoned their indifference, and began to build again (Hag. 1:12, 15). They changed their mindset from thinking that it was not time to build God's house (Hag. 1:2) to realizing that it was past time to do so (Heb. 5:12; Rom. 13:11). Many years ago in preacher training classes, we were given a wonderful definition of repentance. We learned that repentance is "a change of the mind that is brought about by godly sorrow and which results in a reformation of life." We see this lived out among Haggai's people. Haggai's message pricked their hearts. Godly sorrow changed their minds, and they began to build God's house again. I am reminded of the son who at first refused to go into the vineyard at his father's command, but afterward, repented and went (Mat. 21:28-29).

Amazingly, after 16 years of inaction, Haggai had the people up and working within 24 days. He started speaking on the first day of the sixth month (Hag. 1:1) and they started working on the 24 day of the sixth month (Hag. 1:15). That is a pretty quick turnaround. Likely, during these 24 days careful planning was done to ensure that when the work started, it continued unto completion. The work itself would take four years, six months, and two days to finish (Hag. 1:1; Ezra 6:15). Four godly men, Zerubbabel, the governor, Joshua, the high priest, Haggai, the prophet, and Zechariah, the prophet (Ezra 5:1; 6:14), brought the work to completion. In like manner, godly men must work together to complete the work of God today (1 Co. 3:9). Just as God promised to be with them, He will be with us (Hag. 1:13; Heb. 13:5). We can be assured that if we will abound in the work of the Lor, that our labor will not be in vain (1 Co. 15:58).

The prophet Haggai moved the people from indifference to industry by calling on them to take inventory of their lives. What he was able to accomplish in such a short time is truly amazing. The effectiveness that Jonah had with the pagan people of Nineveh, Haggai had with the passive people of Jerusalem. Through the inspired record, God is trying to do the same with His people today (Rom. 15:4).

CHAPTER 9

Haggai 2:1-9:
"The Latter Glory of The Lord's House"

Eli Schnell

I n Haggai, the people have returned from Babylonian captivity which Jeremiah prophesied would last only 70 years (Jer. 29:10). Those who have returned are only a small piece of the original population, a remnant (Hag. 1:12). As they returned, the people built homes for themselves and made their own lives comfortable, but they left the house of the Lord, the temple, as rubble. By the end of Haggai one the people have begun rebuilding the Lord's house at His command. However, in a month's time they have become disappointed in the house of the Lord which they are building. As they become worn down, the Lord sends encouragement through Haggai.

In Haggai 2:1-9, God encourages the remnant to renew their enthusiasm for the work He had given them, and as we study we, too will gain new enthusiasm and courage for the work God has given to us. As the remnant looked on the temple being built, they fretted over its lackluster appearance. So, God encouraged them.

- **God encouraged them to acknowledge their feelings about the past (Hag. 2:1-3)**
  God's people accomplish nothing when they are consumed with and discouraged by nostalgic, backward looks at "the good old days."
- **God Encouraged Them to Work Now, because He was with them, blessing their work (Hag. 2:4-5)**
  God expects us to work enthusiastically in the present because He is with us even today.
- **And God Encouraged Them to Look to the Future, to hope for what would be rather than being discouraged by what is or what was (Hag. 2:6-9)**
  Hope for the future is what drives us forward in the present. If the church is to grow and thrive today, we must know what we hope for and be confident that we will receive it from the Lord.

ACKNOWLEDGE YOUR FEELINGS ABOUT THE PAST (HAG. 2:1-3)

On the twenty-first of the seventh month, the word of the Lord came by Haggai the prophet saying, "Speak now to Zerubbabel the son of Shealtiel, governor of Judah, and to Joshua the son of Jehozadak, the high priest, and to the remnant of the people saying, 'Who is left among you who saw this temple in its former glory? And how do you see it now? Does it not seem to you like nothing in comparison?

God is not afraid to acknowledge our feelings. When they saw the work they were doing and the temple they were building, they were disappointed. It did not have so much gold, it did not have so much physical beauty as Solomon's temple had, and the old men who saw the foundation laid wept because it did not compare with the former glory (Ezra 3:12).

Sometimes we fall into this trap by allowing Bible passages to discourage us concerning our present work. Take Acts 2:36-46 for example. After reading this section of Scripture a number of depressing things might be exclaimed:

- "Too bad there aren't soft hearts today" (v.37)
- "Nobody really wants to hear the gospel today" (v.41)
- "People never want to attend church anymore" (v.42)
- "Everyone's so selfish today!" (v.45)
- "We'll never have unity like that" (v.46)

We must never, ever speak such discouraging and untruthful statements in the church today. By accepting statements like these some churches have decided to simply wait for the lost to come to them! That is not God's pattern for us. Jesus gave a clear command to us to preach, not to wait (Mark 16:15). As you are going along, as you see people, as their ears are present, preach the gospel! Don't wait for them to ask you! Waiting does not accomplish "preach the gospel" (Mark 16:15).

Instead of becoming discouraged by the accounts of success in the New Testament, be encouraged because they prove that the gospel truly is the power of God and that there are people who want you to share it with them.

Our older and younger generations perceive success very differently because of their experiences, especially in the church. One from the younger generation may see or do something good, perhaps they have been studying with a friend and they are making slow progress, and they are thrilled! They could not be happier, save for the moment when that friend decides to put Christ on in baptism and continue their studies.

The older generation, however, remembers tent meetings and grand outreach opportunities that were had in the 1950s, where hundreds were being saved each day, and everyone wanted to know what God's Word said. They look on the one or two who are willing to listen with disappointment, discouraged that the one or two isn't 50 or 60. Where the younger generation is often thrilled with progress of some kind, the older generation is easily discouraged by their memory of the good old days of the church.

So what is the cure? How can we get past our "good old days" depression? Isn't it by the same message God gave to the remnant in Haggai 2:1-9? First, we have to acknowledge that we have lived beyond the "good old days" and realize that we live in the present. If you are discouraged by what has been and what you see now, then admit that to yourself. But do not wallow in despair. Instead, realize that the "good old days" were good because people were doing what God commanded with enthusiasm, and there's time to do that today.

WORK NOW (HAG. 2:4-5)

'But now take courage, Zerubbabel,' declares the Lord, 'take courage also, Joshua son of Jehozadak, the high priest, and all you people of the land take courage,' declares the Lord, 'and work; for I am with you,' declares the Lord of hosts. 'As for the promise which I made you when you came out of Egypt, My Spirit is abiding in your midst; do not fear!'

God provides comfort and encouragement for His people by reminding them, "I am with you, and My Spirit is abiding in your midst." They should work because God had commissioned them and because their work was blessed by the Lord, and that is something which had not been the case for most of Israel's recent history.

When you look back fondly on the good old days, be encouraged by them, but then remember to return to the present and work. Why? Because the Lord is with you, that's why. When we set out to spread His gospel, the Lord is with us and we need to gain courage from that. God is with us today and is blessing our efforts to spread His gospel. Instead of becoming discouraged because the Bible shows such great successes, we need to work today with enthusiasm!

Let me share something with you. When my wife Katherine and I arrived in Citrus Heights where I currently preach, the congregation was practicing vain worship in many of their devotional gatherings and at Bible camp especially. The congregation was not large, about 130-140 people. Rather than become discouraged by their mistakes, I met with our elders and studied with them and any of the men in our congregation who were willing, and we began pulling the reigns back so that we would praise God both in spirit and truth (John. 4:24).

We lost several people because we returned to God's way. We lost almost all our young people. Our congregation was taunted and insulted by many of the surrounding churches, and for a while we had to help our members remember that they serve God in good times and bad, and that no matter what is said, we stand for the truth. No matter what, we work today at what God has given us.

We are only four years removed from those decisions, and already families who are moving to the area from across the nation and beyond are choosing to worship with us and work with us because they see and hear the truth being proclaimed and practiced by us. Stand for the truth and work today. Preach and teach the truth today. Correct your course when it strays. Share encouraging words with others both near and far. People will see that and recognize that you are serving the Lord.

We need to gain courage and enthusiasm in the Lord's work today. It seems to me that some churches are becoming afraid that nobody truly wants to follow God's way, and because of that some turn away from God's truth to attract people. That is the coward's way, and it does not accomplish salvation even for those you reach. Instead, stand courageously and enthusiastically for the truth. God is with us today and He blesses our efforts to spread His gospel.

In the same way that God blessed the Israelites as they began the work of rebuilding the temple, He blesses us today when we continue to help Him build up the church. Even though we focus enthusiastically on the work at hand, the present is not our goal. We seek something more than what we see with our eyes, and touch with our hands. God reminds His people in Haggai 2:6-9 that He has plans for more than today. He has plans that are greater than the good old days, if His people work today.

HOPE IN GOD'S FUTURE BLESSINGS (HAG. 2:6-9)

"For thus says the Lord of hosts, 'Once more in a little while, I am going to shake the heavens and the earth, the sea also and the dry land. 'I will shake all the nations; and they will come with the wealth of all nations, and I will fill this house with glory,' says the Lord of hosts. 'The silver is Mine and the gold is Mine,' declares the Lord of hosts. 'The latter glory of this house will be greater than the former,' says the Lord of hosts, 'and in this place I will give peace,' declares the Lord of hosts."

God promises, "I will fill this house with glory; I will shake all the nations." A grand event is approaching, and this temple will be involved. Don't fret about the silver and the gold. Those physical things belong to the Lord already, and they will arrive to bring physical glory to this house when He calls for them. God has no shortage of possessions (Psalm 50:10–12).

God's people should never worry or fret over physical decoration or physical possessions. All the world is God's and all it contains. If He needs it, He will call for it, and it will be provided (Genesis 22:7-8, 13).

Sometimes we wonder whether there will be enough resources for us to complete God's work. The people in Haggai two were worrying about how much gold they would have to place on the walls or what sort of decoration or treasure they might place in the house of the Lord. It's good to want to glorify God in every way, and we will bring Him glory if we follow the all-important principle found in Psalm 50:12: "The world is Mine, and all it contains." In Acts 2:45, why did Christians sell their property and possessions and share? Because they understood what we so often forget-- Everything I own belongs first to the Lord. Let your life be guided by that truth. Everything you own belongs first to the Lord. If He has need of it, then He already has it from me. There is no reason I should withhold God's possessions from Him when He calls me to use them.

God makes another promise to the people in Haggai two, that the latter glory of the house would be greater than the former. This house would have some glory when they had finished building it, since by God's own words it would be filled with gold and silver at His command. But the true latter glory of that house would come not with gold and silver, but with Jesus. He would come and through His sacrifice He would make peace between God and man.

Those who are building the temple in Haggai two could bring some glory to it by their work, but the true, surpassing glory would come from Christ. When Jesus came to this world, He displayed glory the likes of which had never before been known (John 1:14). He was presented in that temple (Luke 2:29ff). He drove out the moneychangers from that temple (John 2:15). He taught in that temple (Luke 21:37), and He established peace between man and God by His sacrifice (Eph. 2:14-16) (Roper, 435). Jesus is the peace which God would provide for all. It is by His sacrifice that we are given peace and reunited with God. Because of Christ's sacrifice, we have a home prepared beyond the boundaries of this life.

Our hope, our goal, what keeps us going today, is the home which Christ has gone to prepare for us (John 14:1-3). That home with God is what keeps us working today. We want to be with God, and if we work until He comes, He has promised that we will be.

CONCLUSION

The Israelites in Haggai two were growing discouraged in their work. They had seen some glorious things with their own eyes, and all they saw in that day was rubble. And so God encouraged them by reminding them that He is with them, that He owns everything in the earth, and that "the silver is Mine and the gold is Mine, declares the Lord of hosts" (Hag. 2:8). Not only are the silver and gold the Lord's, but He has glory planned which they cannot remember because they have never seen its equal. And so they worked because the latter glory of the Lord's house was greater than the former.

So what about the tent meetings of the '50s that brought in hundreds? What about the 3,000 in Acts two? The glory which is remembered, which some of you have experienced, even that pales in comparison to the glory of our promised heavenly home. And so we work today because the latter glory of the Lord's house is greater than the former.

WORKS CITED

New American Standard Bible: 1995 Update. LaHabra, CA: The Lockman Foundation, 1995. Print.

Roper, Coy D. *The Minor Prophets, 2.* Ed. Eddie Cloer. Searcy: Resource Publications, 2013. Print. Truth for Today Commentary.

CHAPTER **10**

Haggai 2:10-23:
"Renewed Blessings and Renewed Promise"

Neil Richey

"Restoration" is the weary soul's greatest need. "Renewal" is the wandering soul's greatest discovery. The passage under consideration for this study underscores two primary thoughts—restoration and renewal.

God's people have been blessed tremendously. Delivered from Egyptian bondage,\ and directed to the promised land of Israel, they were God's conquering heroes as they took one heathen town after another, and established Jehovah's presence on both the west side and east side of the Jordan. Jerusalem was occupied and established as God's city. This city would become the religious hub of God's people for the next 1,100 years (ca. 1050 B.C. - A.D. 70).

Though the benefits were innumerable, the blight of Israel was their desire to be like the nations around them. They wanted to live like them, be led like them, and worship like them. Many of the children of Israel intermarried. In short order, they left the counsel of the judges and sought to be led by a monarchy. Eventually they established the high places and left sacrificing at the altar of God for sacrificing to the deaf and dumb idols of the heathens.

The consequences of their conformity would be decades, yea centuries, of domination by the world powers of the day—Assyria and Babylon to be specific. Israel's Northern Kingdom failed to listen to God's warning to give up their idolatry and was taken captive by the Assyrians in 722 B.C. Despite the tragic example of disobedience and consequences of their brethren to the north, Israel's Southern Kingdom of Judah would likewise be conquered. In three stages, beginning in 606 B.C., the new dominant power of the Babylonians would take Judah into captivity where they remained for the next 70 years.

Lesson learned? One would think so. After decades of captivity, a remnant would return to Jerusalem under the authority of the new world power—the Medo-Persians. The books of Ezra and Nehemiah tell us about the returning remnant. This remnant, along with some of the Jews who had been left behind, would gradually restore the city of God. The altar of God was, rebuilt establishing the worship of the people of God. The foundation of the Temple was likewise laid. The Temple would of course represent the presence of God Himself. Sixteen years after the Temple's foundation was laid, it would finally be completed. Later, under the oversight of Nehemiah, the walls of the city which had been destroyed by Nebuchadnezzar would be rebuilt in just 52 days.

It is that 16 - year - period of "nothingness" that serves as the timestamp for this particular study. Thanks to the bully pulpit of Judah's adversaries and the weak-kneed Israelites, there was a lull in the building of God's Holy Temple (Ezra 4). So, God raised up prophets to stir up the hearts of the people. These men were Haggai and Zechariah. This study will only deal with one of those prophets— Haggai.

The book of Haggai can be summarized in four distinct sermons. In the first sermon Haggai calls his brethren to the mat for using their time, talents, and treasure to build their own houses but not God's house (Hag. 1:1-15). In the second sermon the prophet challenges the thinking of his contemporaries to not compare the temple yet to be finished with the temple that Solomon was charged to build (Hag. 2:1-9). In the third sermon Haggai challenges Israel for their rebellion to God and reminds them of God's goodness toward them (Hag. 2:10-19). Finally, the fourth sermon of Haggai describes the prospect of Judah's restoration and God's renewed promise ultimately to be fulfilled in the Christ (Hag. 2:20-23). The third and fourth sermons will serve as the context for this study, as the thought is considered: the rebellious children of God must heed His reminders and be restored if they are to be the recipients of God's promises.

JUDAH'S REBELLION AND JEHOVAH'S REMINDERS (2:10-19)

It was a serious grievance for one to touch a dead body. The Bible says, "He that toucheth the dead body of any man shall be unclean seven days…And whatsoever the unclean *person* toucheth shall be unclean; and the soul that toucheth *it* shall be unclean until even" (Num. 19:11, 22). Sandwiched between these bookends is God's reason for this particular law.

But the man that shall be unclean, and shall not purify himself, that soul shall be cut off from among the congregation, because he hath defiled the sanctuary of the LORD: the water of separation hath not been sprinkled upon him; he *is* unclean (Num. 19:20).

To defile oneself by touching that which was unclean was to defile the sanctuary. To defile the sanctuary was to offend God. So, unholiness was and is an offense to God.

The priests were to be asked this question by the prophet Haggai: "If one bear holy flesh in the skirt of his garment, and with his skirt do touch bread, or pottage, or wine, or oil, or any mean, shall it be holy?..." (Hag. 2:12). To which the priests replied with "no." Further, Haggai asks "...If one that is unclean by a dead body touch any of these, shall it be unclean?" (Hag. 2:13). The priests once again respond, affirming that this one would indeed be unclean.

God's people, the returners from exile, had reestablished their worship to God per their sacrifices upon the altar. Yet, their lax attitude toward God and their indifference defiled that offering. Speaking for the Lord once more, Haggai says, "...So is this people, and so is this nation before me, saith the LORD; and so is every work of their hands; and that which they offer there is unclean" (Hag. 2:14).

The expression "you can take the boy out of the country, but you can't take the country out of the boy" applies here. God's people had been removed from Jerusalem following their idolatry and disobedience. However, they did not learn their lesson fully and upon their return to Jerusalem years later they were back to some of their old ways. A change in life does not always keep one from having to sort through the consequences of their failures. It becomes necessary then for God to give His people a few reminders.

The Jews are reminded that God,

> ...smote you with blasting and with mildew and with hail..." (Hag. 2:17). Long ago Moses had spoken of this chastisement when he said, The LORD shall smite thee with a consumption, and with a fever, and with an inflammation, and with an extreme burning, and with the sword, and with blasting, and with mildew; and they shall pursue thee until thou perish (Deu. 28:22).

Moses' word picture is that of immediate and enduring ruin. When God's people fail to abide by His commandments, there is nothing that the rebellious sinner can do to escape the wrath of God. So, there is the reminder of God's punishment to the disobedient.

There is likewise the reminder of God's praise for the penitent. Haggai says, "Is the seed yet in the barn? yea, as yet the vine, and the fig tree, and the pomegranate, and the olive tree, hath not brought forth: from this day will I bless you" (Hag. 2:19). The foundation of God's house was complete and it was time to finish construction. With their repentance, demonstrated by getting back to work, came a blessing. God says before you even complete the construction I'm going to bless you. Before you've harvested your crops, I'm going to bless you. Before you take your baskets to pick your grapes, figs, pomegranate, and olives, I'm going to bless you.

Great things can happen to the people of God when they leave the selfishness of building for themselves and begin building for God. Just as Haggai told his brethren not to build their own houses to the neglect of God's house, Jesus reminds the New Testament reader,

> Lay not up for yourselves treasures upon earth, where moth and rust doth corrupt, and where thieves break through and steal: But lay up for yourselves treasures in heaven, where neither moth nor rust doth corrupt, and where thieves do not break through nor steal: For where your treasure is, there will your heart be also (Mat. 6:19-21).

Lest we rebel like Judah, Jesus reminds us to focus our hearts on the eternal and not the temporal. The denominational preacher Johnathan Edwards once said, "Oh, God, stamp eternity on my eyeballs!" Of course, that sentiment deserves a hearty amen! A life that lives in view of eternity every day and in every way will be revolutionized. It will change the way one interacts with people. Every person will be viewed as a soul, not just a warm body. It will change the way one works. Employees will recognize that the job they are doing is "unto the Lord." It will change the way one thinks about worship. Instead of seeing it as something to be done once a week, every heart will rejoice for just one more opportunity to be in His presence.

God is ever present in our world. He sees the good and the bad and rewards both accordingly. Every man would do well to remember that the ground he stands on every day is holy, because it is God's soil that is in the treads of our shoes. When man learns from his mistakes, repents, and follows God's will then he shall be blessed now and in eternity.

JUDAH'S RESTORATION AND JEHOVAH'S RENEWED PROMISE (2:20-23)

The final message from God to the prophet Haggai was a message that was to be placed on the heart of Zerubbabel. God says, "Speak to Zerubbabel, governor of Judah..." (Hag. 2:21). What was to be said to the governor? It was a message of restoration and God's renewed promises.

Zerubbabel, along with Joshua led the first group of Jews home from exile. They rebuilt the altar and built the foundation of the temple, straightway. God began the process of restoring His people to Himself. Zerubbabel would be His special servant, and as a descendant of the family of David, the Christ would come through him (Mat. 1:12; Luke 3:27) .

The restoration of God's people and the renewed promise with them would not be without conflict. Haggai says,

> I will shake the heavens and the earth; And I will overthrow the throne of kingdoms, and I will destroy the strength of the kingdoms of the heathen; and I will overthrow the chariots, and those that ride in them; and the horses and their riders shall come down, every one by the sword of his brother (Hag. 2:21-22).

Heathen nations would rise and fall. God's people would often be in the midst of conflict, but His people would endure/will endure forever (Dan. 2:44). Further, Zerubbabel's position and his status as the one through whom Christ would come was going to remain secure.

The fourth and final message of the prophet was more than a sermon of hope for the remnant who were rebuilding the physical temple of God. It was a message of the fulfillment of a spiritual hope in Christ. Listen to the conclusion of the prophet's final sermon: In that day, saith the LORD of hosts, will I take thee, O Zerubbabel, my servant, the son of Shealtiel, saith the LORD, and will make thee as a signet: for I have chosen thee, saith the LORD of hosts (Hag. 2:23).

Zerubbabel was of great value to God; a point made clear by the fact that he was called God's "signet ring." The owner of a ring like this would have worn it around his neck on a chain or on his finger. It was always with him. It bore the seal of the royals and would be used to show the proof of origination of important documents. God says, "Zerubbabel, you are my special seal of approval. I wear you around my neck and you will not be lost."

Valuable, powerful, and authoritative was this chosen one, but equal to these is the fact that he was God's servant. For the text says that God called him "my servant." He was God's bond-servant or table server. Service is a quality to be had by every leader. The King of kings was a servant. "Even as the Son of man came not to be ministered unto, but to minister, and to give his life a ransom for many" (Mat. 20:28). Likewise, service is to be a quality of every Christian. "Let this mind be in you, which was also in Christ Jesus: Who, being in the form of God, thought it not robbery to be equal with God: But made himself of no reputation, and took upon him the form of a servant, and was made in the likeness of men" (Phi. 2:5-7).

Zerubbabel had been bestowed with the honor of a special place in God's divine scheme of redemption, and was called to be God's servant. However, the spiritual promises for all of God's people were not to be fulfilled in him, but in Christ.

CONCLUSION

Rebellious to God, which led to their ruin and captivity, Judah would be reminded of God's expectation for complete and total holiness and purity. Further, it was demanded by God that Judah set their heart on God and His work. They realized that life was like a bag full of holes when they built great personal dwelling places but neglected the house of God—the Temple. Likewise, when Christians focus on personal plans and interests to the neglect of God's, their lives will be empty and will lack purpose.

Great things happened to the children of God when they were restored to their home, and enjoyed God's presence in His holy city. It is with that thought in mind that today's Christians are the recipients of great and precious promises when they are restored to their home the church, and dwell in God's presence. One can enjoy the forgiveness of his sins (Acts 2:38). There is the benefit of peace (Rom. 5:1). The Christian can come boldly before God's throne (Heb. 4:14-16). The child of God can rest assured of his eternal home (1 Jn. 5:13). These benefits and many more belong to the faithful child of God because of the renewed promise to the Jews through Zerubbabel which was fulfilled in Jesus.

CHAPTER 11

Zechariah 1:
"The Horsemen and The Horns"

John Baker

520 B.C. was an especially eventful year in the history of God's revelation to man. In that year God sent two powerful preachers, Haggai and Zechariah, to stir the indolent citizens of Jerusalem to zealous obedience (Ezra 6:14). Specifically, God wanted His people to finish rebuilding the temple,which had been destroyed in 586. Reconstruction work halted almost as quickly as it had begun in 536 because of enemy threats, and so the temple lay unfinished until the second year of King Darius: 520 B.C. (Ezra 4:5; Hag. 1:15). In the sixth month of that year God began to speak to His people and by the end of the eleventh month the entire book of Haggai and the first six chapters of Zechariah had been composed. As a result of God's word the temple was completed in just four years (Ezra 6:15). Meaningful restoration always begins with faithful preaching.

Zechariah describes himself as the son of Berechiah, the son of Iddo the prophet (Zec. 1:1). "Zechariah," which means, "The LORD Has Remembered," is a common name in Scripture, belonging to at least twenty-nine distinct individuals. This particular Zechariah was a Levite of priestly descent according to Nehemiah 12:16. He was a student of history and had a tremendous respect for the work of the "former prophets" of God (Zec. 1:4; 7:7, 12). As a Levite who had never seen a fully constructed temple, Zechariah longed to see God's house restored. He passionately pleaded with his Jewish brethren to complete the work they had begun. The message of chapters 1 through 8 is summed up in Zechariah 8:9:

"Let your hands be strong, you who have been hearing in these days these words by the mouth of the prophets, who spoke in the day the foundation was laid for the house of the LORD of hosts, that the temple might be built" (Zec. 8:9).

A reading of the first eight chapters of Zechariah raises an intriguing question: what is needed to build a temple? Notice that God ordained everything relating to temple construction. He ordained the time, the place, the pattern, the needed supplies and even the workers. God withholds no needed blessing when He desires to build a temple. What God provided through Haggai and Zechariah was the needed enlightenment and encouragement.

Significantly, the New Testament describes the church as the temple of God (1 Co. 3:16-17; Eph. 2:21-22). Every Christian has a responsibility to be involved in the restoration and building up of God's spiritual temple today (Eph. 4:16). Zechariah chapter one contains three vital truths for those who are yet interested in the restoration of New Testament Christianity.

THOSE WHO BUILD TEMPLES MUST LISTEN CAREFULLY TO GOD'S WORD (1:1-6)

Zechariah's first message was preached approximately two months after temple reconstruction had resumed (Zec. 1:1-6; Hag. 1:14-15). The sermon can be summed up in the word: "Listen!" Zechariah's message reveals four reasons why God's people must listen carefully to God's word.

God's Word Reveals His Will and Disposition.

No one can know God's mind unless He reveals His thoughts in the form of words (1 Co. 2:11-12). Thus Zechariah begins with a statement about God's disposition that, "The LORD has been very angry with your fathers" (Zec. 1:2). Upon that basis, God issues a challenge: "Return to Me, and I will return to you" (Zec.1:3). Far from a tender invitation, this command is a stern warning to the Jews to come home quickly, much as an irate parent might do with wayward, misbehaving children. It is noteworthy that Zechariah's first sermon begins and ends with the wrath of God (Zec. 1:2, 6). Their fathers had stubbornly refused to hear and heed the will of God as revealed by the former prophets, and the consequences of that refusal were disastrous (Zec. 1:4-6). Unless we continually heed what God has spoken we will live in error, for men are incapable of correctly discerning God's mind and will apart from the light of revelation (Jer. 10:23; Rom. 10:17).

God's Word Is Authoritative When Transmitted Through Faithful Servants.

Some today would prefer only to listen to the "red letters" of Scripture (those words they believe to have been directly spoken by Jesus Himself), but authority resides in all that God transmits through His faithful prophets. Zechariah himself delivers exactly what he has heard from God-- "Thus says the Lord of hosts" (1:3). The former prophets had done precisely the same thing (Zec. 1:4). The night visions are said to be, "The word of the Lord," although God uses angels as agents to reveal their meanings to Zechariah (Zec. 1:7-9). At one point God speaks to an angel, who then speaks to Zechariah, who is then told to repeat the message he hears directly to the people (Zec. 1:13-14). To reject the message of one of these recognized servants or prophets was to reject God Himself Zechariah records, "'They did not hear nor heed Me,' says the Lord" (Zec. 1:4). Those who are interested in building temples must heed the inspired words that have been faithfully transmitted from God through all His faithful servants. The church must always be "built on the foundation of the apostles and prophets, Jesus Christ Himself being the cornerstone" (Eph. 2:20). Restoration of New Testament Christianity still depends on our heeding the doctrine of the apostles as revealed in scripture (Acts 2:42).

God's Word Is Aimed At The Hearts of Men.

Zechariah reminds us that all true restoration must begin and continue in the heart. Our message must be His message, our motivation must be His motivation, our will must be His will, and our hope must be His hope. The fathers of Zechariah's countrymen built a temple and offered worship to God, but their well-documented wickedness displayed hearts that were far from Him (Isa. 1:10-17; 29:13). Zechariah later says of those pre-exilic Israelites, "They made their hearts like flint, refusing to hear the law and the words which the Lord of hosts had sent by His Spirit through the former prophets. Thus great wrath came from the Lord of hosts" (Zec. 7:12). The people had obeyed the words of Haggai and begun to build, but God still warned, "Return to Me" (Zec. 1:3). The word of God is intended to win the hearts of men; we miss the mark in New Testament Christianity when we fail to encourage the kind of faith that works through love (Gal. 5:6; 1 Co. 13:1-3). The word of God is intended to produce pure, wholehearted, unreserved love for God (Mat. 22:37).

God's Word Is Enduring and Immutable.

Zechariah 1:5-6 illustrates the enduring nature of God's word. That word had outlasted the former prophets who delivered it and had overtaken the fathers who ignored it. God and His former prophets had been vindicated later by the very people who suffered in captivity due to God's wrath. The captives confessed, "Just as the Lord of hosts determined to do to us… so He has dealt with us" (Zec. 1:6). The eternal, immutable word of God has always been a solid foundation upon which to build. Those who build upon anything else are constructing upon a foundation of sand (Mat. 7:24-27). Thus, we must give careful attention to every word that proceeds from the mouth of God (Mat. 4:4).

THOSE WHO BUILD TEMPLES MUST TRUST IMPLICITLY IN GOD'S GRACE (1:7-17)

When we acknowledge our weakness and recognize our need for God, God can begin to work mightily in us. So it was with the small, frail remnant that had returned to Jerusalem. As work progressed they must have remained acutely aware of their own inadequacies, and so three months after his first sermon and five months after temple reconstruction had resumed, God gave Zechariah eight encouraging visions in one night (Zec. 1:7-6:8). The visions affirm God's gracious involvement in reconstruction and they point out that rebuilding and restoration would not be the result of man's strength and ingenuity. "'It was not by might nor by power, but by My Spirit,' says the Lord of hosts" (Zec. 4:6). These visions especially emphasize God's sovereignty, power, jealousy and wrath on behalf of His people. Vivid and colorful, they are clearly meant to be both surprising and reassuring to those who were building the temple.

The vision of the horsemen was meant to demonstrate God's awareness of world affairs and His intentions regarding Jerusalem and her enemies. To those who needed to trust God's grace, four assurances were given.

To The Powerless, God Is The Lord of Hosts.

God is called "The Lord of hosts" 46 times in the 211 verses of Zechariah, with nine of those occurrences in Zechariah 1. The expression could also be translated, "Lord of armies," and as such it depicts God in military terminology. This designation for God appears to have been used especially when His people were powerless and needed Him to fight a battle they could not win on their own. For example, when Hannah was yet barren she addressed Him as "the Lord of hosts" (1 Sam. 1:11). David used the expression when confronting mighty Goliath (1 Sa. 17:45). Psalm 46 twice repeats the refrain, "The Lord of hosts is with us, the God of Jacob is our refuge" (7, 11). In Isaiah God referred to the Red Sea deliverance and called Himself "The Lord of hosts" (Isa. 51:15). In the New Testament, James

5:4 promises rich oppressors that the cries of their suffering laborers have reached the "Lord of Sabaoth" or "Lord of hosts" (ESV).

How significant, then, that God is called "The LORD of hosts" 82 times in the writings of the post-exilic prophets (Haggai, Zechariah and Malachi). This small remnant of Jews scratching out a living among the ruins of Jerusalem would not have inspired much optimism about their long-term prospects for success. However, Zechariah 1:3 calls God, "The LORD of hosts" three times in one verse. People knew what that meant. God is mighty and sovereign. He fights battles for those who are weak and powerless, and He desires to return to be with His people. Three months later God again spoke as "the LORD of hosts" in Zechariah 1:14-15, saying, "I am zealous for Jerusalem and for Zion with great zeal. I am exceedingly angry with the nations at ease; for I was a little angry and they helped – but with evil intent." Those who build temples must acknowledge their own weakness and place their trust in the LORD of hosts. The battle always belongs to Him.

To The Friendless, Heavenly Beings Are Actively Serving God.

Perhaps it should not be surprising that prophets such as Zechariah and Daniel had much to say about angels. Both men prophesied at times when the people of God stood especially alone and friendless in a hostile world. One is reminded of the words of Elisha: "Do not fear, for those who are with us are more than those who are with them" (2 Ki. 6:16). Angels appear in every one of the eight night visions of Zechariah, either as participants in the visions themselves, or in order to reveal the meaning of the visions. God is so powerful that He does not need to use angels to accomplish His purposes, yet Scripture reveals that He chooses to do so at times. What would have been especially meaningful about these visions to the small, ragged band of Jews building the temple was that these angelic beings were actively serving God on their behalf. These angelic beings were friends of the friendless, "Ministering spirits sent forth to minister for those who will inherit salvation" (Heb. 1:14).

The first vision Zechariah saw was of four angelic horsemen standing in a hollow among myrtle trees (Zec. 1:7-17). Each horse was a different color, although Scripture does not explain how this might be significant. What is significant is that these horsemen had been traveling to and fro throughout the earth, watching the disposition of the nations. They had gathered to bring their report that, "All the earth is resting quietly" (Zec. 1:11). The people rebuilding the temple had been working for five months, and during that time God had promised several times through Haggai to "shake" the nations on behalf of Jerusalem (Hag. 2:6-9, 21-23). This report, which was received much faster than human news could have traveled from distant lands at that time, does not seem to have been good news, for God later expressed anger with the "nations at ease" (Zec. 1:15). Given the promises of Haggai's preaching and the report of the angelic horsemen, the people would have immediately raised this question: "How long until God does what He has promised by shaking the nations and blessing Jerusalem?"

For The Helpless, The Angel of The LORD Is Interceding.

Before the question of God's timing could be asked or answered, an especially important character appears in Zechariah's vision -- the Angel of the LORD. This angel, while somewhat mysterious, seems to arrive on the Old Testament scene at times when people are especially weak and helpless. He comforts Hagar in the wilderness (Gen. 16:7-9). He stops Abraham from slaying Isaac and reaffirms God's promise in Genesis 22. He appears to Moses in the burning bush and commissions him to deliver Israel from captivity (Exo. 3:2). He commissions and instructs Gideon to deliver Israel from the Midianites (Jud. 6:11-22). He strengthens and encourages Elijah in the midst of his discouragement (1 Ki. 19:7). Psalm 34:7 promises, "the Angel of the LORD encamps all around those who fear Him, and delivers them."

It had been almost exactly 200 years since inspired prophets last mentioned the Angel of the LORD. According to Isaiah 37:36, this angel was responsible for slaying 185,000 Assyrian soldiers outside the walls of Jerusalem just after the fall of the Northern Kingdom in 722 B.C. Nobody had seen or heard from the Angel of the LORD since that time, and thus it is especially noteworthy that the book of Zechariah mentions this Angel six times (Zec. 1:11, 12; 3:1, 5, 6; 12:8). How encouraged the people of Jerusalem must have been to have heard Zechariah describe seeing the Angel of the LORD interceding for Jerusalem in 520 B.C! His appearance was a sure sign of God's favor and blessing.

The Angel of the LORD asks a question on behalf of the helpless Jews, "O LORD of hosts, how long will You not have mercy on Jerusalem and on the cities of Judah, against which You were angry these seventy years?" God answers the Angel, "With good and comforting words" (Zec. 1:13). The Angel of the LORD is here presented as an intercessor for the helpless people of God. How like the ministry of Christ on behalf of His church, for Scripture teaches that, "He ever lives to make intercession for them" (Heb. 7:25; Rom. 8:34). Those who are busy about the work of restoration need a heavenly intercessor, advocate and guardian.

To The Hopeless, Powerful Promises Are Graciously Given.

In response to the Angel's question, God began to promise to do a number of things that His people could never do for themselves. As a basis for all He was about to promise He first expressed great zeal, which itself is a measure of love for Jerusalem and Zion, and He expressed great anger with the nations who had exceeded His will in oppressing the Israelites (Zec. 1:14-15).

Verse 16 gives three promises to the people. First, God promised His mercy saying, "I am returning to Jerusalem with mercy." Zechariah's earlier call to return to God had evidently been heeded (Zec. 1:2). Now, God was going to bless Jerusalem with mercy; He is a God who treats men better than they deserve. Second, God promised that, "My house shall be built in [Jerusalem]," and He again called Himself, "The LORD of hosts." Sixteen years earlier temple construction had been halted by force of arms (Ezra 4:23). Though enemies were still present in the second year of Darius, the LORD of hosts was promising to see this project through to the end. It is entirely possible that these promises were made while the Jews still awaited the answer of Darius concerning the rebuilding of the temple (Ezra 5:3-6:13). Third, God promised to stretch a measuring line over Jerusalem. This was a promise to rebuild the city according to the dimensions that He ordained. When God pronounces the size and shape of a city or nation, no power in heaven or on earth can countermand Him.

Verse 17 uses the word "again" four times, signifying that the mission of the Jewish remnant was not novel construction, but re-construction. Three more promises were given. First, God promised that His cities would again overflow with prosperity. While rebuilding the temple, the remnant must have thought frequently about the former prosperity of Israel in the time of Solomon. God promised that He would again bless Israel in a similar manner. Second, God promised to "comfort" Zion. Two centuries earlier Isaiah had explained some of the wonderful details of this promise: "The LORD will comfort Zion, He will comfort all her waste places; He will make her wilderness like Eden, and her desert like the garden of the LORD; joy and gladness will be found in it, thanksgiving and the voice of melody" (Isa. 51:3). Third, God promised to again "choose" Jerusalem. Jerusalem was the city that God had previously chosen to represent Himself before the world (1 Ki. 8:16, 44, 48). However, God later cast off the city due to her impenitent wickedness and idolatry (2 Ki. 23:27). Now after seventy years of captivity, God affirms His re-choosing of Jerusalem three times in the night visions of Zechariah (1:17; 2:16; 3:2).

Scripture teaches that God makes amazing and specific promises to those who are without hope (Eph. 2:1-12). Those who are about the work of building temples and restoring relationships must feed on a steady diet of God's gracious promises.

THOSE WHO BUILD TEMPLES MUST WAIT PATIENTLY ON GOD'S TIMING (1:18-21)

The prophets consistently affirmed that "the Most High rules in the kingdoms of men" (Dan. 4:17). God intervenes in the affairs of nations and He uses their rulers to accomplish His own purposes in history. Although men are not always privy to the specific details of God's interventions, they may rest assured that He is both concerned and involved. Such is the point of the second night vision (Zec. 1:18-21).

Following the wonderful promises of the horsemen vision, God next shows Zechariah four horns (Zec. 1:18). In prophetic literature, horns often represent a political power or ruler (Dan. 7:7-8; Rev. 13:1). Such is clearly the case in Zechariah's vision, for he is told, "These are the horns that have scattered Judah, Israel and Jerusalem" (Zec. 1:19). The vision of the horns serves to explain that God remained angry with a group of nations and powers that had "scattered" His people, although the vision does not name which specific nations and powers God had in mind. Not only was God angry, but Zechariah next witnessed four heavenly "craftsmen" or "blacksmiths" that served God. Zechariah was told that the craftsmen were coming to "terrify" and "cast out" the horns that had scattered Judah (Zec. 1:21). The message for God's people was that they need not be concerned about further saber-rattling, rumors or threats from the foreign powers that had scattered them. God's craftsmen were going to deal with those powers in God's time.

The God who rules in the kingdoms of men knows the times and seasons of history. He chose the time for captivity, and He chose the time for restoration and rebuilding. He chose the time for the birth of His Son, and He chose the time for the establishment of His church (Gal. 4:4; Acts 2). He chose the time for the early church to be scattered by persecution (Acts 8:1-4). He chose the time for the first Gentile to hear and obey the Gospel (Acts 10-11). He chose the time for the Gospel to first travel to the European continent, and He did so while forbidding Paul to preach elsewhere in Asia (Acts 16:6-10). Even today, God rules among the nations for the ultimate good of His Kingdom, and those who are interested in restoring New Testament Christianity must continually look to Him for wisdom concerning the times and seasons of history. Those who would labor as God's fellow workers must sometimes wait patiently on His timing while serving faithfully in their present circumstances (1 Cor. 3:9; 15:58). May He ever grant His people wisdom to understand the times in which they live, so that they might wisely labor to build up His Kingdom (1 Ch. 12:31).

Zechariah chapter one teaches that God's word, God's grace and God's timing are all necessary for restoration. Let us never be guilty of attempting to work in His Kingdom apart from these blessings, and let us never fail to remind all men of God's challenge: "Return to Me."

CHAPTER 12

Zechariah 2–3:
"The Measuring Line and The Filthy Garments"

Chris McCurley

Back when I was young and didn't have good sense, I took sixteen teen-agers to the inner city of Memphis. Our job there was to spend a week fixing up houses for those less fortunate. We scraped, we painted, we did yard work, etc. It was miserable. The heat and humidity were almost unbearable. We started at sunrise and stopped long after sunset. The teens whined and complained the entire time, which made me whine and complain the entire time. It was not the way I would have chosen to spend a week.

However, two of my best friends accompanied me on this endeavor to serve as chaperones. I was looking forward to what little down time we could spend together. One of the area churches was responsible for providing housing. This would be the vacation portion of the trip. I knew, from past experience, that the chaperones always stayed with a very well to do elder that had a house full of amenities. We arrived the first night and awaited our housing assignments. The six boys that came on the trip were placed in a big house that belonged to one of the deacons; that left ten girls who, I assumed, would be split up into various homes. I didn't really care where the ten girls went just as long as my buddies and me got our own space.

But my dreams of relaxing in a hot tub after a long hard day of manual labor were quickly doused when I was informed that one family had signed up to keep all ten girls plus my two friends and me. All thirteen of us, plus the host family, would be in one house with two bathrooms. Suddenly a week seemed like an eternity. After the first full day of work I went upstairs to crash. About that time the homeowner informed me that the air conditioning had gone out and it would be a few days before it could be fixed. This was now officially the worst week of my life. It would have been bearable had my family been with me, but they stayed behind. There I was, tired, hot, miserable, and missing my wife and kids. I remember lying in the bed, drenched in sweat, thinking, "I wish I were home." I missed my family. I missed my air conditioning. I missed my bed. The host family was very sweet. They were really nice people. Their house was beautiful. But I was terribly homesick. I missed the comforts of home. My heart just wasn't in it. I longed to be somewhere else. I couldn't wait to get home.

I'm from Abilene, Texas where there are three universities. And every fall, whether it be at Abilene Christian University, McMurry University or Hardin-Simmons University, there is an epidemic of sickness. It gets students down, they can't study, and they're dissatisfied. They complain about the dorms, the food, and the weather. It sometimes gets so bad they even have to go home. They want to see their folks. They miss their friends. They miss all their familiar places. They are homesick. Have you ever been homesick? Have you ever been stuck far away from home and eagerly anticipated your return? Has your heart ever missed the comfort and security of the place where you call "home?" The place where you feel you most belong?

ISRAEL'S HOMECOMING

The trite old saying is true—"There's no place like home." It was certainly true for God's people. In Zechariah 1 & 2 the Israelites are going home. But God's not just calling them back to Jerusalem. He's calling them back to Him. Let's get up to speed with what has happened up to this point.

The Jews have been in exile in Babylon. God orchestrated their captivity because of their rampant immorality; mainly their turning away from God and turning toward idols. But God is a gracious, merciful and forgiving God. While the people suffered justly for their sins, God promises restoration. A future glory was on the horizon. God would free His children and allow them to go home. However, the excitement of their homecoming would be short-lived.

The story is told of a couple that was away on vacation when they got a call from the police. Apparently, someone had burglarized their home. The couple immediately returned from vacation and found the front door to their house had been busted open. The place had been turned upside-down. The entire place had been ransacked. It was a complete and utter mess. The wife looked at the disaster and stated, "How embarrassing. That's just the way we left it."

Israel would return from captivity to find their home in shambles. Everything was a complete and utter mess. God's temple was lying in ruins and the people had the monumental task of rebuilding it. In fact, the entire state of God's people at this point in history could be defined as "rebuilding." They were rebuilding in a spiritual sense. Their relationship with God was lying in ruins because of their self-destructive behavior. That relationship had to be rebuilt. They needed to repent and restore what had been lost. And, of course, they were rebuilding physically as they sought to reconstruct the city they once called home and the temple that was God's house.

Things went well in the beginning. Israel's rebuilding was moving ahead. Progress was being made. But outside opposition thwarted the people's efforts and construction was halted for sixteen years. It was a dark time in Israel's history. The people were discouraged. Morale was low. The Israelites became apathetic. God sent a prophet by the name of Haggai on the scene that had stirred the people to resume the rebuilding, but after two months enthusiasm waned. Enter Zechariah. God calls this prophet to piggyback on the efforts of Haggai and encourage the people to finish what they started. Finally in 516 B.C. (Ezra 6:15), thanks to the efforts of Haggai and Zechariah, the temple was completed.

That is the *Reader's Digest* condensed, condensed version of Israel's story at this particular point in history. It's against this backdrop that Zechariah's efforts take place. Again, Zechariah is at the heart of God's rebuilding—the rebuilding of the temple, but, more importantly, the rebuilding of His people. The prophet delivers eight divine visions and two oracles for the purpose of turning the people's hearts back to God. The thrust of Zechariah's message is that God's blessings are contingent upon man's loving obedience. Zechariah shows God's people what the future holds—a day and time when the Messiah would reign supreme (cf. Zec. 3:6-8; 9:9). Jesus will provide a *fountain* (Zec. 13:1), which will flow from His *pierced* body (Zec. 12:10) so that all of God's people may have cleansing for their sins (Zec. 13:1). Christ the King will supply these *living waters* (Zec. 14:8) that will flow out of Jerusalem over all the earth.

THE THIRD VISION

This brings us to Chapter two and Zechariah's third vision.

> "Then I lifted up my eyes and looked, and behold, there was a man with a measuring line in his hand. So I said, 'Where are you going?' And he said to me, 'To measure Jerusalem, to see how wide it is and how long it is.' And behold, the angel who was speaking with me was going out, and another angel was coming out to meet him, and said to him, 'Run, speak to that young man, saying, "Jerusalem will be inhabited without walls because of the multitude of men and cattle within it." For I,' declares the Lord, 'will be a wall of fire around her, and I will be the glory in her midst.' 'Ho there! Flee from the land of the north,' declares the Lord, 'for

I have dispersed you as the four winds of the heavens,' declares the Lord. 'Ho, Zion! Escape, you who are living with the daughter of Babylon.' For thus says the Lord of hosts, 'After glory He has sent me against the nations which plunder you, for he who touches you, touches the apple of His eye. For behold, I will wave My hand over them so that they will be plunder for their slaves. Then you will know that the Lord of hosts has sent Me. Sing for joy and be glad, O daughter of Zion; for behold I am coming and I will dwell in your midst,' declares the Lord. 'Many nations will join themselves to the Lord in that day and will become My people. Then I will dwell in your midst, and you will know that the Lord of hosts has sent Me to you. The Lord will possess Judah as His portion in the holy land, and will again choose Jerusalem. 'Be silent, all flesh, before the Lord; for He is aroused from His holy habitation'" (Zec. 2:1-13).

Chapter 2 of the book of Zechariah begins with a vision of a man with a measuring line in his hand. He is measuring the width and length of Jerusalem. The question becomes, "Why measure the city of Jerusalem?" This vision seems to be a picture of mindset of the God's people versus God's eternal purpose. The young man is about to lay out walls for the city, but he is stopped because Jerusalem is to be a city without walls. Walls were built to fortify a city in ancient times. They kept the enemy out. But Jerusalem would not need walls in the future because she had the greatest protector of all—Jehovah. God would provide "a wall of fire around her" (Zec. 2:5). Not only that, He would also be the glory within her (Zec. 2:5).

I live in West Texas, and in West Texas any rancher worth his salt knows that in order to keep your cows or horses from wandering off you must build a fence. Fences are vital to keep livestock in and, hopefully, keep predators out. In Australia, however, ranchers take a different approach. Because ranches are so vast building fences would be an effort in futility. Instead, ranchers dig a well at a certain location on their property. Water is precious in the Outback, but that is not the only purpose of the well. Livestock will stray, but they will never roam too far from the well, lest they die. As long as there is a supply of fresh, clean water the animals will stay close, thus eliminating the need for fences "The Shaping of Things to Come" (Hirsch and Frost, np).

God would be Israel's "well." His divine presence would assure a constant supply of fresh clean water. He would be at the center of the city and their lives. Therefore, walls or fences would be unnecessary. As long as the people stayed close to God and did not stray they would have protection and fulfillment. There would be no need for the inhabitants of Jerusalem to fear because God would be in their midst. He would be their wall. God is telling the captives to flee from Babylon and enter a place without walls. Remember, the Israelites had been held in captivity. All they knew were walls and the restriction of them. They knew that they were in that situation, at least in part, because the enemy had burst through their walls and destroyed what they had built. A city without walls must have been an exciting notion to these people, not just the absence of walls, but also the absence of the need for walls.

Imagine a life without walls. Picture a life without the need for fences. We like walls. We feel comfortable behind our fences. They provide protection. They make us feel secure. They give us privacy. But they can make us too safe. There is no need for risk when you hide behind walls. Walls hold us in. We get used to them, and are uneasy about stepping outside of them. They keep us from enjoying life to the fullest. We construct these walls because we have been torn down by life. We build fences because we are ashamed of our sinful existence. We put up walls because we're afraid of anyone seeing who we really are. Many times, the very walls we build to protect us are the same walls that imprison us. Jesus came to make us free (John 8:32-33). He came to bring us an abundant life (John 10:10). We will never experience such a life, such an existence while choosing to stay locked behind our walls. God was setting His people free. They had a glorious future awaiting them. And so do we. But I'm not just referring to heaven. We can enjoy an abundant life in Christ right here, right now by tearing down the walls and living at the center of God's will.

Like Zechariah's audience we, too, have a glorious future awaiting us. We are going home. John described it figuratively with these words: "Then I saw a new heaven and a new earth; for the first heaven and the first earth passed away, and there is no longer any sea. And I saw the holy city, new Jerusalem, coming down out of heaven from God, made ready as a bride adorned for her husband. And I heard a loud voice from the throne, saying, 'Behold, the tabernacle of God is among men, and He will dwell among them, and they shall be His people, and God Himself will be among them, and He will wipe away every tear from their eyes; and there will no longer be any death; there will no longer be any mourning, or crying, or pain; the first things have passed away'" (Rev. 21:1-4). We are going to a place that John describes as a foursquare city, 1500 miles wide, 1500 miles long and 1500 miles high. In other words, it's 3,375,000,000 cubic miles. It's a city made of precious stones. Walls and gates are constructed out of gems. The streets are of purest gold. Think of the number of dump trucks full of gold dust needed to pave the streets of a city 1500 miles long and 1500 miles wide. Though John's picture includes walls constructed out of gems, the gates in these walls are never shut (Rev. 21:25). In the heavenly city there is no need to keep the enemy out because there are no enemies. There is no need to keep the rebels in because there are no rebels.

How do you describe an igloo to someone living in Africa? How do you describe the Minnesota lakes to an Arab man? It's nearly impossible because such is beyond experience. How do you describe the eternal in terms of the temporal? And how do you describe heaven in a way that man can understand? It's next to impossible. It is beyond the scope of our comprehension. Just as I am sure the Israelites had a hard time picturing a restored Jerusalem and a future glory, we have a hard time picturing heaven. Our finite minds cannot possibly grasp the infinite glory that awaits us, which is why God used these word pictures—to give us some idea of the incredible magnitude of a place we call home.

THE FOURTH VISION

Zechariah's fourth vision begins with Joshua, the high priest, and Satan. It ends with a picture of the Messiah. The high priest stands as a symbol of the redeeming power of Jehovah. Satan had been behind the sins of the priesthood. As the priesthood was defiled so were the people. Satan believes he has won. In this fight of good versus evil, the devil claims victory. He feels as though he has separated the people from their God. Judah no longer has fellowship with Jehovah God. The Israelites, however, were a "brand plucked from the fire" (Zec. 3:2). Satan only thought he had won. Though the people had endured the punishment for their disobedience, God was not finished with them.

Joshua not only represents the priesthood, but all the people of God. His garments are filthy because they are stained with the sins of the people. God says to remove the sin-soaked garments (Zec. 3:4). This was symbolic of God's power to forgive. God would have the final say in whether His people would be restored or live in exile, not Satan. God's grace is on full display as the high priest is clothed with clean garments. This not only symbolizes the loving forgiveness God has toward His people, but it also stands as a new beginning for Israel. Verses six and seven read: "⁶ And the angel of the Lord admonished Joshua, saying, ⁷ 'Thus says the Lord of hosts, "If you will walk in My ways and if you will perform My service, then you will also govern My house and also have charge of My courts, and I will grant you free access among these who are standing here."' The people had been forgiven. Satan, as well as the conquering nations, had been defeated. Now it was up to them to live a lovingly obedient existence, not staining their garments again.

The fourth vision closes with a prophetic picture of the coming Messiah. Verses eight and following read: "Now listen, Joshua the high priest, you and your friends who are sitting in front of you—indeed they are men who are a symbol, for behold, I am going to bring in My servant the Branch. For behold, the stone that I have set before Joshua; on one stone are seven eyes. Behold, I will engrave an inscription on it,' declares the Lord of hosts, 'and I will remove the iniquity of that land in one day. 'In that day,' declares the Lord of hosts, 'every one of you will invite his neighbor to sit under his vine and under his fig tree'" (Zec. 3:8-10). Can you see the cross in these verses? God's dealing with the people of Israel was just a snapshot of the future deliverance that would come through Jesus Christ. The perfect Lamb of God would come to this earth to live, to serve, to die, and to rise from the dead. Sin, death, and Satan would be defeated once and for all. The "Branch" has its root in David. Jesus is a shoot coming from the house of Jesse, David's father. Thus, He fulfills the promise made to David in 2 Samuel 7:12-16. There is some debate as to what the "stone" represents. Some believe it to be a reference to God's people as a whole—the redeemed, the kingdom of God, the church. I think the more logical explanation is that the "stone" is symbolic of Jesus and the "seven eyes" represent that He is all seeing. A stone is strong. It is solid. It is enduring. Peter wrote, "Behold, I lay in Zion a choice stone, a precious corner stone, and he who believes in Him will not be disappointed" (1 Pe. 2:6). The Apostle Paul stated, "Christ Jesus Himself being the corner stone, in whom the whole building, being fitted together, is growing into a holy temple in the Lord, in whom you also are being built together into a dwelling of God in the Spirit" (Eph. 2:20b-22). The corner stone is the building block that forms the base, joins the walls, and governs the lines of a structure. Christ serves as the keystone for the church. He is the linchpin upon which our entire spiritual livelihood is founded. He purchased the church with His own blood. He founded it, member by member, by removing our filthy garments and giving us festal robes.

OUR HOMECOMING

The first thing I did when I got home from my trip to Memphis was hug my wife. I played with my kids. I turned the air conditioner way down. And I climbed into my own bed. The stress, the heartache, and the discomfort were finally over. All the things I had missed and had longed for were no longer out of reach. I was home. All of us are born with an expiration date. Physical death is a fate that awaits every single one of us. But beyond the grave lies something far greater for the Christian. There lies our eternal destination; our final dwelling place; our home.

There are many people living a life of captivity. They are locked in a prison of sin and self-destruction. They are living in exile away from the presence of God. Like the Israelites in Zechariah's day, they need hope. That hope is found in God's Son. It is Jesus who tears down the walls and releases us from the bondage of sin.

When we live at the center of our Father's will, and when we make Him the center of our lives, we don't need walls. It is Christ who removes our filthy garments. It is God's only begotten Son who makes us free. And it is our Lord who takes us home.

WORKS CITED

Hirsch, Alan & Frost, Michael. *The Shaping of Things to Come: Innovation and Mission for the 21ˢᵗ-Century Church*. Baker: Ada. 2013.

CHAPTER 13

Zechariah 4:1–5:5: "The Candlestick, Olive Trees, and Flying Scroll"

Travis Bookout

A dream is what one has while sleeping; a vision is what one has while awake. It appears that Zechariah has not been getting much sleep lately. As this prophetic work begins by detailing eight night visions of Zechariah, there is a tremendous amount that can be learned. These night visions, along with the prophecies of Haggai and the rest of Zechariah, were fundamental to the rebuilding of the temple after its destruction by Nebuchadnezzar (Ezra 5:1-2; 6:14-15). These were not all good times, however. They were not rebuilding their temple at the zenith of prosperity, like under Solomon, but after years of captivity, they were impoverished, without a king, and in need of real encouragement (Hag. 2:1-9). Zechariah's visions seek to provide encouragement, warning, and justification for the work which God has in store for them.

The fifth and the sixth night visions, which we will call "The Candlestick and Olive Trees" (Zec. 4:1-14) and "The Flying Scroll" (Zec. 5:1-4), find a unique place in these visions. Picture these scenes in your mind. You have been awakened by an angel to behold something incredible. You see a golden lampstand holding up seven lamps. Immediately this might bring to your remembrance the lampstands (Menorahs) in Solomon's temple (2 Ch. 4:7). Above the seven lamps you see a big bowl on top with seven spouts connecting to each lamp. Oil from the bowl flows through the spouts in order to keep the lamps lit perpetually. As one commentator puts it, "What the prophet sees is an elaborate lampstand of pure gold that has a bowl on its top as well as seven lights and seven pinched lips to hold the wicks… Archeologists have so far discovered at least two lampstands in Palestine that resemble the features Zechariah describes" (Brown 150). Then to the sides of this lamp, to the right and to the left, there are two olive trees (Zec. 4:2-3). These olive trees connect to the bowl on top of the candle by two golden pipes. The trees produce the "golden" oil that flows through the pipes and is gathered in the bowl (Zec. 4:12), which pours through the spouts into each of the 7 lamps. It supplies a never ending supply of oil to keep the lamps continually lit. What a contraption!

103

Following this vision, you look up again and see a scroll. But not just any scroll, this scroll is enormous and it is flying. "The image of a 'flying scroll' is unparalleled in biblical and nonbiblical sources" (Meyers and Meyers 278). So this is unlike anything you have ever seen or heard of before. Its dimensions were 20 cubits in length and 10 cubits in width (Zec. 5:1-2). These are no ordinary dimensions for a scroll. "The dead sea scroll of Isaiah, by comparison, is more than 24 feet long, but only less than a foot wide. What is unusual about Zechariah's scroll is that it is disproportionatsic half as long as it is wide, not to mention, of course, that it flies" (Brown 153). While these dimensions might not fit those of any normal scroll, they are the exact dimensions of the porch at Solomon's temple (1 Ki. 6:3). The size of the scroll possibly serves, like the lampstand mentioned earlier, as a reminder of Solomon's temple (Coogan 421). The scroll is flying throughout the land, purging those who steal (Exo. 20:15; Lev. 19:11) and swear falsely by the Lord (Exo. 20:7; Lev. 19:12), entering and consuming their houses (Zec. 5:3-4).

These are two vastly different visions. Not only are the images quite different, but the corresponding meanings are polar opposites. The first image is one of perpetual light and blessing while the second image is one of curse and destruction. There appears to be a major shift in focus in between these visions. In interpreting these visions, it is helpful to see how they connect with the other night visions that Zechariah sees.

The Vision of The Golden Lampstand and The Olive Trees

This vision is explained to Zechariah by the angel who woke him. Zechariah did not know how to interpret what he was seeing, so he asked the angel, "What are these, my lord?" (Zec. 4:4). The angel might be somewhat disappointed that Zechariah did not understand the vision (Zec. 4:5), but after Zechariah again admits ignorance the angel reveals the vision as an encouraging word of the Lord to Zerubbabel. "'Not by might nor by power, but by My Spirit,' says the Lord of hosts. 'What are you, O great mountain? Before Zerubbabel you will become like a plain; and he will bring forth the top stone with shouts of "Grace, grace to it!"'" (Zec. 4:6-7). God promises His Spirit will be with Zerubbabel. In a time of discouragement and while facing a massive task, this is exactly what one needs to hear. The Lord continues, "The hands of Zerubbabel have laid the foundation of this house, and his hands will finish it. Then you will know that the Lord of hosts has sent me to you. For who has despised the day of small things?" (Zec. 4:9-10a).

Now, who is Zerubbabel and why would he need this encouragement? He is called by Haggai, "the governor of Judah." He is the political and royal leader of Judah after the return from captivity. He is the grandson of Jehoiachin, (Jeconiah/

Coniah), the former king of Judah. His grandfather was rejected by God when He said, "Even though Coniah the son of Jehoiakim king of Judah were a signet ring on My right hand, yet I would pull you off; and I will give you over into the hand of those who are seeking your life…into the hand of Nebuchadnezzar" (Jer. 22:24-25). So Zerubbabel does not have a great family track record. Add to that his name, Zerubbabel, which literally means "seed of Babylon." And yet he is the one in whom the people have placed their hope to rebuild the temple and their former way of life. Yet, the temple still lay in ruins. He did lead them in laying the foundation of the temple (Ezra 3:10; Zec. 4:9), but it has been left dormant for roughly 16 years and "a spirit of indifference and defeatism predominated" (Lewis 70). Not only do the people have many important tasks ahead of them, like rebuilding their own houses and businesses (Hag. 1:2-11), they do not yet have the means to make the temple anywhere nears as splendid or lavish as it was under Solomon. In fact, the new temple looks like nothing in comparison (Hag. 1:3), and the elderly who remembered the first temple wept when they saw it (Ezra 3:12-13). There is simply no confidence, trust, or motivation. Zerubbabel needs a lot of encouragement if he is going to take on this task.

In an effort to encourage Zerubbabel for this task, Haggai prophesied that the Lord chose him and made him like a signet ring (Hag. 2:23). This is the exact opposite of what happened with Zerubbabel's grandfather (Jer. 22:24-25). In much the same way, Zechariah assures Zerubbabel that God's Spirit will be with him and that he will finish what he started. Even if it looks like "small things," he should not despise it (Zec. 4:10). This message connects perfectly with the night vision immediately before it. The previous night vision dealt with the high priest Joshua. As Zerubbabel was the political leader, Joshua was the spiritual leader. Joshua stood on trial before God as a priest in filthy clothes, with no turban on his head, covered in his, and all the people's sins. He had great reason to be discouraged. Even Satan showed up, as the prosecutor, to point out his every failure and ensure a guilty verdict. Yet, God had another thing in mind. He removed Joshua's filthy clothes and replaced them with festival robes. A clean turban was placed on his head. Zechariah was shown that God is with Joshua and will work through him. This is the same message that Zerubbabel needed and this is the message that he received. God's Spirit is with him and God will accomplish great things through him. The plumb line will be in Zerubbabel's hands, he will be working, and God will be ensuring his success (Zec. 4:10). No matter how difficult things appear, no matter how high the mountain, God's purpose will not be stopped

The end of this night vision combines Joshua and Zerubbabel as those whom God is using and who stand with Him. After Zechariah asks twice what the two olive trees are and again explains his ignorance as to their meaning, the angel gives him a response: "These are the two anointed ones who are standing by the Lord of the whole earth" (Zec. 4:14). The two anointed ones are no doubt Zerubbabel and Joshua the political and religious leaders of the people. God will be with them, helping them, as they fulfill His requirements in leading the people, rebuilding the temple, and restoring temple worship.

The Sixth Night Vision

"The Flying Scroll," is not a vision of blessing but is a vision of a curse. The scroll that flies through the air is called "the curse that is going forth over the face of the whole land" (Zec. 5:3). That is an interesting phrase (Zec. 1:11; 4:14; 6:5; 14:9). In the night vision of the golden lampstand and olive trees, the seven lamps are said to represent "the eyes of the Lord which range to and fro throughout the earth" (Zec. 4:10). This is similar to the occupation of the patrolling horsemen in the first night vision, who "the Lord has sent to patrol the earth" (Zec. 1:10), and the patrolling chariots of the eighth night vision (Zec. 6:5-7). The Lord's horsemen, chariots, eyes, and scroll are all keeping close watch on the earth.

The "scroll" is an important part of Ezekiel's message. As he is first commissioned to prophecy to a rebellious house, God gave him a scroll full of "lamentations, mourning and woe" (Eze. 2:10). Ezekiel had to eat this scroll, "and it was sweet as honey in my mouth" (Ez. 3:3). "Zechariah's scroll, however, is not to be consumed but to consume" (Brown 153).

This scroll would be a curse and purge those who steal and swear and consume their houses. It is possible that upon returning home after captivity, it became a serious temptation to lie about one's property boundaries, and thus, steal someone else's. Whatever the cause of the stealing and false swearing was, the Lord will have none of it. While the Word of God written on a scroll has been one of the greatest blessings mankind has ever received, it surely has the power to be a curse. Deuteronomy presents God's law as either a blessing or a curse depending on how one chooses to respond to it. The thief and liar might run, they might hide in the darkest corner of their houses, but they will be found. God will "spend the night within that house and consume it with its timber and stones" (Zec. 5:4).

This prophecy serves as a great introduction to the night vision that follows. The seventh night vision is about a woman in an ephah. This woman represents wickedness. She is cast into the middle of the ephah and a large lead weight is placed on top. Then she is carried by two women with wings, far away from God's land. She is carried to Shinar (cf. Gen. 11:2) where they build a temple for her. As the flying scroll will purge those who steal and lie, God will remove wickedness from the land.

While these are not messages of hope or blessing, by any means, they are necessary additions to the more pleasing night visions. The night visions about Joshua being made clean and about Zerubbabel being given God's Spirit are powerful messages of hope. They build confidence and inspire trust. They are great to read and learn. But it is equally important to remember that many of God's promises are conditional. They are predicated on the obedience of His people. Do not think that God will bless His people because He owes them or because of their genealogy. If you swear falsely by God's name, He will purge you from His land. If you seek to steal your neighbor's property, God will purge you and consume your property. Equally important to knowing about the great blessings of God is knowing the requirements of God. God has not forgotten His people. He has not abandoned them forever. He "will again choose Jerusalem" (Zec. 1:17; 2:12; 3:2). He will be jealous for Jerusalem (Zec. 1:14). He will protect Jerusalem with a wall of fire (Zec. 2:5). He will bless her leaders (Zec. 3, 4). But He will not tolerate sin in the camp.

He wants Jerusalem to be called "the City of Truth" (Zec. 8:3). He wants "to be their God in truth and righteousness" (Zec. 8:8). He desires them to "speak the truth to one another; judge with truth and judgment for peace in your gates" (Zec. 8:16). Simply, they need to "love truth and peace" (Zec. 8:19). That will not happen while there is theft and false swearing in the land. God will send His scroll to clean house.

There are numerous applications that we can glean from these two night visions. We will point out three of them. These can be a true benefit to us in our personal lives, church work, and relationship with God.

The First Application

Put your trust in God rather than yourself (Zec. 4:6). When the synagogue in Cologne, Germany was destroyed on November 9, 1938, by Nazi forces, hope seemed lost. After being rebuilt in the 1950's, the front of the synagogue was inscribed with Zec. 4:6, "Not by might nor by power, but by My Spirit." This passage has been one of comfort throughout the ages. This is a common idea throughout the Biblical literature (Exo. 14:13-14; Jos. 1:5, 9; Psa. 42:5, 11; 43:5; Rom. 1:16, etc.) While it might be easy or encouraging to read, it is surprisingly difficult to put into practice. It goes against our natural inclinations. To quote Agamemnon from the movie Troy, "The gods protect only the strong!" Or a famous expression that many think is in the Bible, "God helps those who help themselves." We often feel that if only we could be strong enough, talented enough, or good enough, then God will work for us. But God tells Zerubbabel,

"Not by might nor by power, but by My Spirit" (Zec. 4:6). Zerubbabel cannot be strong or mighty enough to accomplish this task, but for God's Spirit it will be no problem.

Paul recognized that no matter how much he planted, or Apollos watered, it was God who would give the increase. This is often a difficult concept for ministers. We need to perfect our speaking ability, be more creative than the competition, outsmart our adversaries, and if we are good enough, just maybe the church will grow. When the numbers dwindle, it must be our fault. If they boom, then we must be the greatest ministers, nay, humans, ever! We often judge our worth in the kingdom based on the decisions of others: baptisms, repentance, attendance, etc.

Sometimes when you preach it is really hit or miss. One Sunday morning I finished my lesson and could not wait to step away from that pulpit. I felt I had studied and prepared properly, but that the lesson just went flat. I did not feel any real connection to by brethren, I thought it seemed difficult to follow, the faces looked bored, and even I was a little bored. I stepped away from the microphone and literally uttered under my breath, "That was terrible." I hate that feeling, like I squandered a Sunday by my ineptitude. What happened next, however, was something of a shock. Not one or two, but five people came forward to request prayers and confess sins during the invitation song. Now, honestly, I have no idea how many decided to do that during my lesson or during the week before. I do not know if my lesson played a role in them growing closer to God. But I did come to acknowledge something that day,: It is not about me. God's purposes will not fail because I am not talented enough. It is not by my might or by my strength.

When we can come to accept this truth, it will change us. It will take away a lot of the stress, anxiety, worry, and frustration of ministry. It should give us confidence that God is involved and active. It is not all on our shoulders. It will hopefully change our motives. I want to be the absolute best preacher that I can be, not to beat out the other preachers for members and not because the church on earth will collapse if I am not talented enough, but because I want to honor God by giving Him the best that I possibly can. Zerubbabel was definitely supposed to do the best he possibly could. This verse was in no way supposed to produce a laissez-faire attitude to rebuilding the temple. In fact it was supposed to produce the exact opposite. He was supposed to get the plumb line in his hand and as his hands laid the foundation of the temple "his hands would finish it" (Zec. 4:9-10), but to do so with confidence. Sometimes we need confidence that God is on our side as we seek to serve Him. Finally, this concept can help us derive greater joy from the "small things" (Zec. 4:10). Sometimes, with God, small things turn into great big things. This temple might have seemed little in comparison to Solomon's, but "the latter glory of the house will be greater than the former" (Hag. 2:9). Take pleasure in the fact that you have helped a child understand something better, that you have encouraged someone with a timely hospital visit, that you provided a meal for someone who was hungry. They might seem like "small things" at first, but you never know what God can produce with just a "small thing."

The Second Application

Remember that God often works through human leaders (Zec. 4:14). There have been a lot of terrible leaders over the years in political, occupational and spiritual realms. Sometimes people get so attached to a human leader that they will follow him all the way to Guyana and drink cyanide Kool-Aid. Social psychologist Leon Festinger wrote a book entitled *When Prophecy Fails* which studied a group of people anxiously awaiting the arrival of a UFO that would remove them from earth the night before its impending destruction. "Cognitive dissonance" is that uneasy feel that we get when two of our beliefs are diametrically opposed to one another. For example, when you are driving with your spouse and you say, "I know the restaurant is right down this road and then, as you drive a little further you see that the restaurant is not down this road. That is not a good feeling. You are left with the realization that you were wrong, or, as I see it, the much more likely solution that someone stole the restaurant! Along with his colleagues, Festinger infiltrated the group and observed as they prepared for the end of the world.

They were basing their beliefs on the prophecies of their leader, a housewife who was given the name Marian Keech. On December 21, 1954, the supposed day that the world would end, Keech and her fellow believers were to be taken away by a UFO at precisely midnight. Shortly after midnight, no UFO had appeared. The group sat in utter silence and dismay. They had quit jobs, dropped out of college, and left spouses to prepare for this moment. And as it turns out, the world was not destroyed and there was no UFO. After hours of sitting in silence, Keech finally, around 4:00 AM, received another prophecy. They had been so faithful and spread so much light in their time together, that God decided to preserve the world from destruction. Not only did the prophecy's failure not destroy the group's faith in Keech, it actually increased as they now had evidence that they saved the whole world!

Some people have been so enamored by human leaders that they have left all reason and logic behind them. In order to make sure that this does not happen to us, many of us have grown to be quite skeptical of all who are in authority. Some I have met have an automatic chip on their shoulder when speaking to an elder or a leader in a local congregation. This is truly a sad thing. Good leadership is rare but it is exceedingly valuable. God accomplishes a tremendous amount through human leaders. Now, in order to make sure that Marian Keech does not end up leading a church, there are qualifications given for one to be an elder in the Lord's church. There is always a plurality of elders who work together within a congregation. And all men, elders included, are subject to the written Word of God, so as to keep any one individual from running things with an iron fist however he sees fit. God has taken precautions against misuse of leadership. But He did not abandon the practice of human leadership altogether. We should never follow blindly those who are leading us away from God, but we must make certain that we never reject God's leaders simply out of fear or distrust. God chose men like Joshua and Zerubbabel to be his "anointed ones who are standing by the Lord" (Zec. 4:14). God chose qualified men like elders and teachers and evangelists, to lead people to accomplish His will and grow closer to Him.

The Third Application

You cannot hide from God's Word (Zec. 5:4). Do not ever think that you can be so sly or secretive that you fool God. I am always amazed at how well some people can lead double lives. Kerri Rawson felt this amazement all too well. When the FBI agent knocked on her door, she did not even know if she should answer. She thought, "Why would someone in the FBI be knocking on my door? Is this person really an agent? Is that badge legitimate?" After she let him in, he nervously talked with her about a man she had heard of before, the notorious BTK killer. BTK serves as an acronym for "Bind, Torture, Kill." While she had heard of the killer, she had no idea why this FBI agent was asking her about it. Little did she know, on that very same day, two other things took place. Her mother's house was stormed by police, and her father, Dennis Rader, was arrested on his way home from work. Kerri had no idea. Her mother had no idea. Kerri had just talked with her dad the night before. She grew up seeing him as a loving father and a very religious man. Yet, he had a secret, second life that he kept all to himself. He was the BTK killer.

He must have been a master at hiding his emotions. He kept major parts of his life a secret for many years. He was able to fool even those closest to him. Sometimes, we feel we can do this very thing. "As long as I am faithful in deleting my user history, then no one will ever know." "If I tell my wife I am just going on a business trip…" "If I never let my church family know what I am like at home…" "If I never let my family at home see what I am like at work…" "If I never let my parents see what I am like at school…" It is so easy to try to hide who we really are, but it is a fruitless endeavor. While we might be able to fool our families, our friends, and our churches, we will never be able to fool God.

His scroll is not only massive, but it is flying. It can move in any direction, and it can see all. It is a curse for those who lead double lives. It is an unwelcome guest in the homes of those who feel they can hide. We cannot escape from God. When it is all said and done, all men, great and small, will stand before the Lord and books will be open (Rev. 20:12). Those books will be compared to our lives and we will be judged accordingly. There will also be another book open. This book will contain all the names of God's faithful people, "And if anyone's name was not found written in the book of life, he was thrown into the lake of fire" (Rev. 20:15). Just like the scroll is a curse for those who steal and swear, so God's Word serves as a curse for all who reject it.

God's Word can either be a great blessing and benefit or a curse to us. As has already been noted, it depends on our response to it. Zerubbabel and Joshua were blessed immensely by God and there were great promises of restoration in the land. But God wanted faithfulness and righteousness among His people. God still wants this today. If we are to have hope in the blessings of God, we need to be diligent to trust and obey.

WORKS CITED:

Brown, William P., *Obadiah through Malachi*. Louisville; Westminster John Knox Press, 1996.

Coogan, Michael D., *The Old Testament: A Historical and Literary Introduction to the Hebrew Scriptures*. New York: Oxford University Press, 2011.

Lewis, Jack P., *The Minor Prophets*. Henderson: Hester Publications, 1966.

Meyers, Carol L., and Eric M. Meyers. *The Anchor Bible: Haggai, Zechariah 1-8*. New York: DoubleDay & Company, Inc., 1987.

CHAPTER 14

Zechariah 5:5–6:8:
"The Woman and The Four Chariots"

Wesley Walker

O ur text for discussion is Zechariah 5:5-6:15. In order to properly understand the text we must place it within its historical and literary context. Since others in this book have the assignment to provide this background in more detail, our time here will be a basic undertaking.

The historical context places Zechariah within the post-exilic period. He is a contemporary to Haggai and their ministries overlap in both time and context. When the exiles first returned from captivity they laid the foundations for the rebuilding of the temple (Ezra 5:16a). The centerpiece of Israelite religion and the place where God dwells among His people needed to take first importance. However, the rebuilding project had become dormant and the people had allowed the temple to stay in a ruined state (Ezra 5:16b). Zechariah rebukes and encourages the returnees.

As to the literary context, the main focus of Zechariah is on God's renewal of His covenant with His people. Zechariah means "Yahweh remembers" and that is what his message entails. God remembers His covenant He made with the forefathers of Israel. This renewal centers on God once again choosing Jerusalem (Zec. 2:12). When the Israelites were exiled God had removed His glory from the city in dramatic fashion (Eze. 10:2-4,18,19; 11:22,23). Now, God is promising once again to renew His relationship with His people and restore the city to its glory. Jerusalem's glory comes from God's presence. The city is important because it is the place where God and His people commune. Its renewal is also a prerequisite to the coming Messianic age.

The book begins with a brief call to repentance. Zechariah tells the people to return to the Lord and leave behind their wicked deeds and wicked ways (1:4). This call to repentance is connected with a promise. If they will return to God, they are assured God will return to them (1:3). The foolishness of continuing in wickedness and the trustworthiness of God's promise to accept those who repent is illustrated with a discussion concerning how God worked among the fathers (1:4-6).

Our text is found at the conclusion of a series of vision, which begin after the call to repentance. The visions start in 1:7 and conclude in 6:8. We should recognize these visions as a single unit. The eight apocalyptic visions take the form of a chiasm. Its structure is as follows:

A   Myrtle Tree/Horses: God patrols the earth
  B   Four Horns: God will punish the wickedness of Israel's enemies
    C   Measuring Man: The Lord will dwell in Jerusalem
      D   High Priest and Satan: Renewal of the Priesthood
      D   Olive Trees: Renewal of Zerubbabel's reign to build the temple
    C   Flying Scroll: Removal of Sin from Israe
  B   Woman in the Ephah: Complete removal of wickedness
A   Four Chariots: God patrols the earth to protect His people

The chiastic structure is a literary device employed to emphasize the center of the structure (A4, B4 in our diagram), namely that God is going to restore the functions of the priesthood and king to Judah. This is made clear by the way the series of visions concludes with a prophetic message that emphasizes the crowning of priest and king (Zec. 6:9-15). The restorations of religious and civil leadership would signal the restoration of Jerusalem's prominence (1:17).

Having established the literary and historical context our task is to examine more closely the final two visions (visions 7 and 8) Zechariah was given by the Lord. Then we must develop the impact of the concluding prophetic message. Thus we will be covering Zechariah 5:5-6:15.

VISION 7

Description

In the 7th vision Zechariah is told to gaze upon an ephah. An ephah was a container used to measure dry goods. It was an essential tool needed in the economy of that day. The sizes varied, but each merchant was responsible for providing an honest measurement of what the container held. This ephah was equipped with a heavy cover. Merchants traveling great distances wanted to ensure that their product was protected. A heavy covering upon an ephah indicated important cargo.

The punchline of the vision is what is found inside the ephah. Instead of dry goods for selling, Zechariah sees a woman when the heavy lid is lifted. The ephah, and the woman inside, is located in Judah. We are told she represents wickedness.

The point is there is wickedness in God's land. Wickedness placed in an ephah with a heavy lid means it is ready to be transferred from the land.

For transporting, two women with stork wings are called upon. These women with unclean wings (storks were unclean) lift the ephah out of the land of Israel and will transport it to Shinar, where a temple is being built. The woman named Wickedness is removed from Judah and brought to her appropriate dwelling place.

Explanation

Other visions within this series are given direct explanation, but no explanation is provided for this vision. We will examine the vision by looking at the key symbols. The first is the ephah. An ephah was used in trade. In the previous vision we are told that God was cursing the land because of stealing. One way people stole, which is condemned throughout the Hebrew Bible, is the use of dishonest weights (Lev. 19:35; Pro. 11:1). The deliberate use of this symbol could indicate a greed dimension to the wickedness in this vision.

The second symbol is the woman. It is not uncommon for a woman to be used to represent wickedness in apocalyptic literature (cf. Rev. 17:1). "Wicked ways and wicked deeds" is the phrase Zechariah uses in chapter 1 to describe the reason the Israelites needed to repent. Repenting means these would be removed from the land. Thus the symbolism of the woman being carried away personifies Israel's repentance. Wickedness and its curses would be removed from the land if they repented. The heavy weight is placed upon the ephah to ensure no wickedness spills out in the travel and falls upon the land. God wants to completely remove all wickedness.

The third symbol to be explained is Shinar. Shinar is significant in the book of Genesis and to these exiles. It is the location of the Tower of Babel (Gen. 11:2). This is the place where the people rebelled against God in order to make a name for themselves. It is symbolic of rebellion against God. Wickedness would be expected in such a place. It is also another name for Babylon. Symbolically, Babylon was representative of the capital of wickedness in other Apocalyptic Literature (Rev. 18:2). Here it could be seen as a literal reference. The exiles had left Babylon, but Babylon had not left them. They needed to allow wickedness to stay in the temple being built at Babylon and remove it from the land where God would reign.

The final symbol is the temple. Mentioning of a temple being built is important to Zechariah's message. This could be a rebuke to the returnees to get to work building God's temple since in Babylon the temple to Wickedness was being built.

Application

Those in the land are asked to return to God by removing wickedness. This vision reiterates the point. The children of God need to clear the land of wickedness so that God's promised renewal and blessing can come upon the land. The removal of wickedness precedes God's restoration of Jerusalem's glory.

VISION 8

Description

This 8th and final vision starts with the formulaic words that Zechariah "lifted up his eyes." The vision he sees is of four chariots. Chariots were instruments of warfare. These chariots were coming forth from two bronze mountains. The chariots are pulled by horses of different colors. The first had red horses. The second had black horses. The third had white horses. The fourth had dappled horses.

The horses then are sent out. The black and white horses head north. The dappled head south. Their job was to patrol the earth. Nothing is said concerning the fourth set of horses. The chariots headed north are said to have appeased God's wrath in the region.

Explanation

Some explanation of this vision is provided directly from the text. The rest we gain from understanding the symbolism. The text tells us that the four chariots represent "the four spirits of heaven going forth, after standing before the Lord of all the earth" (6:5). There is some debate on whether this refers to "spirits" or "winds" since the Hebrew word can be translated either way. Whether it is winds or spirits does not effect the interpretation of the symbol. If it is in reference to winds, it is possible that Zechariah wants us to view them as angelic messengers (cf. Psa. 104:3,4).

What is of more importance to understanding this vision is the symbolism of the number four. Four is used in other texts to refer to the four corners of the earth (Dan. 8:8; 11:4). It has to do with points on a compass. The chariots, which the Lord sends out from the bronze mountains, are sent throughout the entire world (Zec. 6:7). The *four* chariots being sent throughout the earth represent the extent of God's sovereign reign. His chariots are patrolling the totality of the earth.

The chariots specifically go "north" and "south" from the bronze mountains. The mountains seems to symbolize Jerusalem, a city surrounded by mountains (Psa. 125:2). The "north" and the "south" are the directions of Israel's enemies.

The north is the direction from which the Assyrians and Babylonians attacked the land. The south is the domain of the Egyptian superpower. God is saying He is patrolling the whole world, but specifically He comforts Israel by paying special attention to their enemies.

Many readers want to spend time on the meaning of the horses' colors. I believe understanding what the colors represent is not nearly as important to understanding this vision as some suggest. Horses are used in the first vision in Zechariah, but they are not the same colors. In this case the colors seem to be inconsequential background.

Application

The vision shows God has acted on behalf of Israel to calm the earth. In doing so He allows Israel to rebuild the temple and bring renewal to Jerusalem. The superpowers that have tormented Israel (Babylon, Assyria, Egypt) are calmed and God is in control. This should comfort the exiles to put their energy into the work God has left them to do. God will protect His people while they rebuild His temple.

PROPHETIC COMMENTARY

With the visions complete the Israelites should know that God is on their side. Verses 9-15 function as a final prophetic message that provides authoritative commentary to the visions. The emphasis is on the rebuilding of the temple by the renewal of religious and civil leadership.

It is important for us to remember the historical context of this particular passage. Sometimes in passages like this we want to jump quickly to Messianic application. However, that jump is doing an injustice to the context. With this warning in mind, let us look at what Zechariah is saying to the post-exilic Israelites.

The keyword throughout this section is temple. It is repeated in verses 12, 13, 14 and 15. The rebuilding of the temple is what needs to happen if Jerusalem is to be restored. The temple is the place where God dwells and is essential to the Israelite religion. Once the temple is rebuilt the returnees will know that God is with them.

Leadership is needed for the temple to be rebuilt and that is what this prophetic message concerns. Zechariah is involved in the symbolic act of taking gold and fashioning crowns out of it. The first crown is for Joshua the High Priest. The religious leadership of Israel is renewed.

Now there is a second man that is mentioned in this context. Joshua is told to "behold a man." The name of the man is "Branch." This comes from Isaiah 4:2, Jeremiah 23:5, and 33:15. Jeremiah spoke of the descendant of David who would restore Jerusalem's glory after the time of exile. This man is said to be the one who will rebuild the temple. He will lead alongside Joshua to accomplish this task. From both a historical and literary standpoint, the branch is in reference to Zerubbabel. Zechariah 4:9 reads, "the hands of Zerubbabel have laid the foundation of this house, and his hands will finish it." Thus Zechariah has already said the one who will finish the temple is Zerubbabel. Thus Zerubbabel is the man named "Branch."

Joshua and Zerubbabel will work together to rebuild the temple in Jerusalem. God is going to dwell with His people just as He promised. Jerusalem will once again prosper. This promise, though, is conditioned with the last sentence of verse 15. The people must "completely obey the Lord" if they are going to see the temple rebuilt and Jerusalem return to glory.

The question we are left to discuss is whether there is more to this prophetic message than merely the working together of the civil and religious leaders to restore God's temple. It appears there very well might be. Although in its historical context the point of this section is the promise to build the Second Temple in Jerusalem, there seems to be a future fulfillment as well, especially when one considers how the Messianic theme functions in chapters 9-14. This theory is made more certain when we consider the amount of times the Gospel writers reference this prophetic work making application to Jesus. So it is likely the text has a deeper dual fulfillment.

The deeper meaning has to do with the Messiah who will in one person unite the priesthood and royal line. In the case of Joshua and Zerubbabel, they function in unity, but the Messiah will actually be one. The Messiah is the ultimate fulfillment of the Branch prophecy. It is in His day when the final temple will be built that will encompass all the nations (6:15).

Allow me to summarize the textual study portion of this section. Vision seven establishes that wickedness needs to be removed from the land so that God's blessings can return. Vision eight shows that God is the ruler of the nations and will protect the Israelites as they work on rebuilding the temple. The final prophetic message summarizes what the totality of these apocalyptic visions taught, which is the temple will be rebuilt under the leadership of Joshua and Zerubbabel. This rebuilding of the temple reestablishes God's covenant with His people and the glory of Jerusalem. It also allows for, and prefigures, the coming of the Messianic age.

PRACTICAL APPLICATION FOR TODAY

There are many practical applications that can be made from this section of Zechariah. Allow me to share eight:

1. Yahweh is faithful to His covenant. The name Zechariah means "Yahweh remembers" and this book reminds us of God's faithfulness. Yahweh had punished His people through captivity and allowing the city of Jerusalem to be destroyed. By bringing the people back from exile and reestablishing Jerusalem's prominence, and the temple's glory, God displays His faithfulness.

2. Repentance brings blessing. God wants to return to His people, but they must first return to Him. Returning to God requires repentance. Repentance is seen when the people remove the wickedness from the land and obey God completely (6:15). When this happens God will bless the people with a united civil and religious leadership, which will bring glory back to Jerusalem.

3. The renewal of true religion and reign brings about prosperity. Zechariah tells the people that God wants to see prosperity in the city of Jerusalem again (1:17). This prosperity will come whenever the true religion of God is practiced. This is why the priesthood needs to be recognized and the temple needs to be restored.

4. Wickedness is a characteristic of the world, not of God's people. The world is wicked and we should not be surprised by this. In fact, the worlds build temples to wickedness. However, God's people should not be characterized by wickedness. It should be completely removed from our midst. As we see the ethical standards of the world deteriorate, we should not allow that deterioration to influence our way of life.

5. We can trust in God's protection as we do His work. God's sovereign reign over the whole earth means that we know God can protect us as we do His will. We should not be timid in doing the works of God due to fear of persecution or insult. God still patrols the whole world and He is still able to protect His people.

6. Godly leadership brings the people to faithfulness. It is not until the religious and civil leadership is established by God and united in one purpose that the glory of Jerusalem can return. The rebuilding of the temple happens whenever godly leaders unite to accomplish God's

work. What good works could we do if leadership would unite to encourage the people in doing great things for the Lord?

7. God desires to dwell with His people. This could easily be first on this list. Jerusalem, the land, and the temple are repeatedly mentioned in Zechariah. Each of these represent the place where God dwells in the midst of His people. God wants to be with His people. Even today God wants to be with His people as He dwells among us through His Spirit in the spiritual temple of the church.

8. The hope of all nations is the Messianic reign. The last verse of our section (6:15) leaves us not with a word simply for Israel, but that the nations would be a part of the rebuilding of the temple. This seems to find its ultimate fulfillment in the ushering in of the Messianic age, when it is not merely the Israelites who make up God's temple, but rather people from all nations who are the spiritual material that composes the people of God (1 Pe. 2:4,5).

Zechariah 7–8:
"The Question of Fasting"

Dustin Campbell

On the thirteenth day of March in 1863 President Abraham Lincoln proclaimed a national day of prayer and humiliation. This was a day that was to be set aside to remember the power of God and to ask for forgiveness "of the national sins." As Lincoln gave his address he frequently recognize God as the "Almighty Power" and gave God the reverence as Lord. Lincoln wrote:

> It is the duty of nations as well as of men to own their dependence upon the overruling power of God; to confess their sins and transgressions in humble sorrow, yet with assured hope that genuine repentance will lead to mercy and pardon; and to recognize the sublime truth announced in the Holy Scriptures and proven by all history, that those nations only are blessed whose God is the Lord. The awful calamity of civil war which now desolates the land may be but a punishment inflicted upon us for our presumptuous sins, to the needful end of our national reformation as a whole people. "Intoxicated with unbroken success, we have become too self-sufficient to feel the necessity, too proud to pray to the God that made us." It behooves us, then, to humble ourselves before the offended Power, to confess our national sins, and to pray for clemency and forgiveness (Basler 385).

Lincoln continues in this speech to designate April 30, 1863 as a day of fasting and prayer a day that they set aside all other items that flood the brain and give that time to God in focus and repentance. Often times children of God devote time and fast, as a way of devotion to God, but are we doing it right?

THE QUESTION OF FASTING

Fasting is a topic that frequently surfaces in the pages of the Bible. The word occurs 46 times in the Old and New Testaments. Throughout the Old Testament we see times when God's children would devote time away from food or other activities and spend that time in prayer and focus on and to God.

We see mainly three different uses or times that fasting is performed. It was often used as an emergency measure in desperate times. David fasted and wept for his son whom God condemned to die due to the sin David committed with Bathsheba. "He said, 'While the child was still alive, I fasted and wept, for I said, who knows whether the Lord will be gracious to me, that the child might live?'"(2 Sa. 12:22)

The second use that we find is an expression of confession and repentance. In Nehemiah we have an example where the children of Israel find themselves out of favor in the eyes of the Lord, as they so many times did. They realize that the only way for them to entreat favor with the Lord is to repent from their sinful ways. "Now on the twenty-fourth day of this month the people of Israel were assembled with fasting and in sackcloths and with earth on their heads. And the Israelites separated themselves from all foreigners and stood and confessed their sins and the iniquities of their fathers" (Neh. 9:1, 2).

The third use that we find is a means preparation. We mainly see this in the New Testament. In two specific occurrences we see men preparing themselves for an important time in their lives. The first example is taken from Matthew when Christ went up into the wilderness. "Then Jesus was led up by the Spirit into the wilderness to be tempted by the devil. And after fasting for forty days and forty nights, he was hungry" (Mat. 4:2, 3). In this account, Christ is spending time fasting, focusing on God because He is about to be tempted by Satan. The second occurrence for consideration is when Barnabas and Paul are sent out to Cypress to spread the good news of Christ. "While they were worshipping the Lord and fasting the Holy Spirit said, 'Set apart for me Barnabas and Saul for the work to which I have called them.' Then after fasting and praying they laid their hands on them and sent them off" (Acts 13:2, 3) (Erye 34).

In each of these occurrences a common thread maintains unity. That common thread is that each time they are fasting they are doing this to be found right in God's eyes to find favor in Him. Fasting and prayer are performed to set aside earthly desires and give our undivided attention to God. Without the heart of humility and submission to God and what He requires, fasting is only glorified starving.

In Zechariah, we have a case where it was simply glorified starving. In the seventh chapter we have God asking an important question through the prophet Zechariah, "Say to all the people of the land and the priests, when you fasted and mourned in the fifth month and in the seventh, for these seventy years, was it for me you fasted?" (Zec. 7:5). The point of the first rhetorical question is that the fasts commemorating events associated with the fall of Jerusalem "were man-made, not God-ordained" (Smith 287). They were not being observed to please the Lord. Therefore, as far as the Lord was concerned it was a matter of indifference whether these fasts were observed or not. For seventy years people were not fasting out of obedience for God, but out of ritualistic emptiness. They knew this was something they should do but their hearts were far from where they should be. We often times do, things that we think are right, but we are not doing them with the right heart, but simply fulfilling ritual.

A MORE BASIC ISSUE

As we strive to walk through this life we are often ingrained with the idea that we must "dress to impress." Holding the idea that we always have someone to impress and too little, or dare we say "hardly ever" is that someone God. How often do we find ourselves living this life and taking each step to impress God by doing what He wants and how He wants it?

When we look back through biblical accounts of the children of Israel we see the selfishness they often portrayed. As we begin to look at the text of Zechariah we quickly see a selfish people. A people who acted based on what they desired to do. These were a people who did what they did because they thought it was right instead of what the Lord commanded. The fasting they performed was not for God, it was for them. They figured if they did this physical act, or "outward sign," they would find favor in the Lord. The main problem was that it was only physical. Once again we must understand that fasting is to be done with our hearts in focus and meditation to God.

As we evaluate the church today how does this idea apply to us? When we devote time in singing praises, worship, service, giving and others are we doing it in ways we deem acceptable, or are we doing them for God in the ways He desires? When we take the Lord's Supper are we doing it when God deemed appropriate? Are we doing it when it is convenient for us, maybe Saturday night or Tuesday evening? The question of fasting that we are exploring here in Zechariah 7 and 8 is more than just a question of fasting. It is a question of whether we are doing things God's way or our way.

As we do evaluate the fasting we must ask ourselves why. Why fast? As was mentioned above the fasting that they were performing in Zechariah was ritualistically empty. Are the lives we live ritualistically empty? First, we must beware of tradition overcoming doctrine in importance. It is far to easy to use the line "that is the way we always have done it," to answer biblical questions. Rather we should respond with "let me show you in the pages of God's inspired word what He requires." The answers may in the end be the same but the second response holds more validity. Second, we live in a world today that has become a "me" society. The culture today is all about what you can do for you, how you want to do it. Because of this we have become a society that no longer respects authority the way that was intended by God, "Be subject for the Lord's sake to every human institution, whether it be to the emperor as supreme, or to governors sent by him to punish those who do evil and to praise those who do good" (1 Pe. 2:13). In this passage Peter writes to encourage the conduct of the saints (1 Pe. 2:12) in order to ultimately win them to God not so people can praise us but praise God. Our lives should be lived for God and only for God. There is no room for us to serve two masters (Mat. 6:24).

FOCUS ON THE WORD

As we study through this topic the question must arise, "What then does the Lord want?" The word of the Lord comes to Zechariah and He does not fail to tell us what he wants from the people of Bethel. "The word of the Lord" (7:1,4,8; 8:1,18) 5 times and "says the Lord" (7:9; 8:2,3,4,6,7,9,14,19,20,23) 11 times in chapters 7 and 8 shows us that God has made it clear to them and in turn us. As we study through the Bible there are many more times that the Lord called us to action and obey his words. But unfortunately in this "me" society we think we know best. The fasting is what the people thought God required but what did God actually require from His people so they will find favor in His eyes? In chapter 7 we have the answer to the question of what God desires. "Render true judgements, show kindness and mercy to one another, do not oppress the widow, the fatherless, the sojourner, or the poor, and let none of you devise evil against another in your heart"(Zec. 7:8,9). He echoes these in the following chapter and goes one step further stating "these are the things I hate" (Zec. 8:16) It went in one ear and out the other, "they refused to pay attention" (7:10).

The interference of our own minds plays a major part in what we hear. We like to call it selective hearing. Our brains seem to think they know the answer before the question is even asked. The people of Bethel thought they had the answer, they thought that the Lord wanted the fasting, but the Lord wanted much more. The people in Bethel thought they could please the Lord with their fasting. This did not work because their fasting was simply an outward action with the heart disconnected. Their brains interfered with what God desired and ritualistically empty fasting was the result.

Studying through God's holy and inspired word we have a responsibility to watch for what God wants and what He desires. We use excuses from time to time in which we convince ourselves in our heads, "God would want this for me, He wants me to be happy." or "God doesn't understand the circumstances of the 21st century." We are disqualifying God by questioning His authority and His all-knowing power. We are to strive to live our lives for God not for ourselves.

THE POTENTIAL FOR BLESSING

As we venture into chapter 8 of Zechariah we see the benefit of submitting to what God desires from us. We understand the value of reward, a parent rewards a child with a piece of candy or an ice cream if a task is performed at a satisfactory level. Likewise, we have a promise from God that if we as His children walk in a righteous way we will be rewarded with Heaven (Heb. 6:18).

In chapter 8, peace and prosperity (Zec.8:12ff) are promised to a nation who find favor in the Lord. That is what we should be striving for as Christians today is to find favor in His eyes so one great day we can be called up to Heaven to live eternally. Zechariah book-ends chapters 7 and 8 with the phrase "to entreat favor of the Lord" (7:2; 8:21,22). The word "entreat" literally means "to make the face of one sweet or pleasant" (Brown 318). The idea would hold that of appealing to God, causing Him to look down upon us with love, gentleness and forgiving. As they went to "entreat favor from the Lord" in chapter 7 the Lord responds with, when you fasted was it for me? (Zec. 7:5). If we desire to be blessed by God and to one day have a home with Him in Heaven we need to find favor in the Lord. We do this by maintaing His commandments and doing the way he has told us to do them giving those commands all of our heart, mind and soul. Zechariah makes another strong point that parallels our call in Matthew to spread the gospel and make disciples (Mat. 28:19,20). Zechariah encourages the remnant with "People shall come, even the inhabitants of many cities" (Zec. 8:20). He continues to speak how the will desire to "find favor" and "seek" the Lord. When we do the things that God desires for us to do His ways people will see and souls will be converted to Christ. We need to strive to live our lives doing God's things God's ways. Let not our worship and service to God be empty and as Solomon puts it "all is vanity and a striving after the wind" (Ecc.1:14).

Let us put away tradition if they interfere with God's way. Let us put away ideas and opinion if they too interfere with God's way. To the question of fasting, fasting is a godly act if performed a godly way, we see many righteous men fast including

Christ. When these men fasted they gave God what He wanted the way He wanted it. They gave God their hearts, minds, and souls in complete obedient dedication. So when we worship, partake of Lord's supper, pray, fast and other acts let's be sure to devote our hearts, minds and souls to God in complete obedient dedication.

WORKS CITED

Basler, Roy P., Marion Delores Pratt, and Lloyd A. Dunlap, eds. *Collected Works Of Abraham Lincoln, 1809-1865*. Vol. 4. New Brunswick: U, 1953. 385. Print.

Eyre, Stephen D. *Drawing Close To God: The Essentials of a Dynamic Quiet Time*. Downers Grove: InterVarsity, 1995. 34. Print.

Smith, James E. *The Minor Prophets*. Vol. Old Testament Survey Series. Joplin: College, 1994. 34. Print.

Brown, Francis, Samuel Rolles Driver and Charles Augustus Briggs. *Enhanced Brown-Driver-Briggs Hebrew and English Lexicon*. electronic ed. Oak Harbor, WA: Logos Research Systems, 2000. 318.

Chapter 16

Zechariah 9–10:
"Zion Delivered By Her King, The Messiah"

Jason Jackson

T
he praise utterance that concludes Psalm 68 captures the essence of Zechariah 9-10. David said, "Awesome is God from his sanctuary; the God of Israel—he is the one who gives power and strength to his people. Blessed be God!" (Psa. 68:35). Banish any doubt: God is awesome—there is none like him (Jer. 10:6). The Lord powerfully intervenes in time and history for his divine purpose (Dan. 2:21). Hallelujah!

INTRODUCTION

The purpose of this study is to understand the meaning of Zechariah 9-10 and to realize how the Holy Spirit, by the mouth of Zechariah the prophet, magnifies divine power and providence. Truly the Lord God imposes his divine will on the earth, which brings blessings to his people and judgment on his enemies.

This discussion of the text recognizes the sacredness of the prophetic word. We must approach this hallowed ground with reverence, for the meaning of this (and all) scripture is communicated *by the words* of the prophet who was borne along by the Holy Spirit (2 Pe. 1:21). The meaning does not *originate*, therefore, from the reader's musing over the text. The reader is challenged to understand that which God revealed *by the words of scripture*.

The Holy Spirit revealed a single message of abiding significance to multiple generations. Zechariah 9-10 was meaningful to the prophet's contemporaries, to the threatened Jews of the inter-biblical period, to the expectant nation at Christ's first coming, to the first generations of Christians, and to every generation of believers from the coronation of the king until he comes again.

The message is not primarily applicable to one generation over another. Rather, Zechariah 9-10 is equally powerful and relevant to any generation from 500 B.C. to A.D. 2015—in different ways, depending on one's time orientation relative to the events described in the text. Only God Almighty, who calls things that are not as though they were (Rom. 4:17), could produce such a volume.

GOD SHALL ARISE

In Psalm 68:1, David said, "God shall arise, his enemies shall be scattered." All God has to do is "arise" to deal with His enemies. By two figures David described the ease with which God administers judgment on the wicked. "As smoke is driven away ... as wax melts before fire, so the wicked shall perish before God!" (v. 2).

Zechariah 9:1 announced a time when "God shall arise" by declaring "the burden of the word of Jehovah" (ASV). This marked a transition in the book, and the expression was utilized again in 12:1. The ominous word foretold the impending conquest of the infamous neighbors of Judah (Judah at this time was that region, including Jerusalem, populated by many who returned from exile, but was smaller than the pre-exilic territory of Judah)

Zechariah foresaw a seemingly unstoppable force that would leave destruction in its wake and would terrorize those in its path. Would Judah be decimated again? This irresistible invasion would not roll over God's people, for Jehovah would encamp about his house "against the army" (ASV) or "as a guard" (ESV). Inasmuch as the Lord decreed the burden against the land, so He ordained the protection of His people. Observe carefully: God would orchestrate these events, for He said, "I will cut off ... I will take away ... I will encamp" (vv. 6, 7, 8).

God Arises Against the North (9:1-4)

The burden of the word of Jehovah would come to the north of Judah. One by one, the hostile neighbors would fall to the invading force. The identification of the "land of Hadrach" is disputed. Perhaps "Hadrach" meant a location in Syria (Laetsch 450; Baldwin 158); or maybe the name was symbolic for the Medo-Persian Empire (Keil 325). Regardless, like the other domains north of Judah, Hadrach was marked for punishment by God. Damascus, a principle city of Syria, was a strategic target—the "resting place" for the burden. Then Hamath (which was north of Damascus) would likewise face judgment.

The burden of judgment was declared because "the Lord has an eye on mankind and on all the tribes of Israel" (ESV). The Lord saw; therefore He would act. If the ASV is preferred— "the eye of man and of all the tribes of Israel is *toward Jehovah*"— the sense would seem to be that the nations and Israel would see the Lord's judgment in these events and would realize that divine providence empowered this army.

The invading power would sweep down the Phoenician coast on Tyre and Sidon "because they are very wise" (ASV), that is, in their own eyes. Their worldly wisdom would be their undoing. Or, if the ESV is preferred, destruction came on them "though they are very wise." That is, in spite of their wisdom, nothing could save them from God's burden of punishment.

The description of Tyre's demise includes additional details. Her strategic location, strong defense, and vast resources—all the reasons for her pride—would not abate the foreboding burden. "Behold!" says the prophet, "the Lord will dispossess her" (v. 4). The Lord God would strip her of her wealth, strike down her defenses, and swallow her up by fire (v. 4; cf. Eze. 26; 28).

How would Judah digest Zechariah's proclamation? Who could believe that Tyre, that imposing fortress in the sea, would come to ruin? Certainly neither Judah nor Tyre could have known in ca. 500 B.C what was over the horizon. But God knew, for He changes the seasons. Though Tyre had withstood sieges in the past (e.g., a 13-year siege by Nebuchadnezzar), nothing can resist God's power when He decrees the removal of kings (cf. Dan. 2:21).

Did Tyre ever face such a destruction after the time of Zechariah? Indeed! The passing of two centuries would not alter the divine decree, and the divine inspiration of the Bible is confirmed by predictive prophecies like these.

When Alexander advanced through Syria and Phoenicia, he besieged the island city for seven months. The Greeks built their own road in the sea, 200 feet wide, from mainland Tyre to the island fortress. The debris from mainland Tyre was cast into the city, and the city was destroyed and burned. In his article, Tyre in Prophecy, Kyle Butt wrote:

> Eventually the Tyrians were defeated, their walls penetrated, and Alexander's forces entered the city and devastated it. Most of the men of Tyre were killed in continued fighting. Siculus recorded that approximately 2,000 of the men in Tyre who were of military age were crucified, and about 13,000 "non-combatants" were sold into slavery (17.46) (apologeticspress.com).

God Arises Against the South (9:5-7)

The burden of the word of Jehovah was also against Philistia. Verses five through seven describe the *reaction* of the cities and the *results* that would follow their destruction.

The emphasis is first on the reaction of the cities (what one experienced was indicative of what all would experience). Ashdod would see the unbelievable destruction of Tyre and fear. "If Tyre could not resist, how can we," the inhabitants would reason. Gaza also would be "sore pained," or "writhe in anguish." How intense the anguish of imminent terrors! Ekron's hopes (i.e., the expectation of help from Tyre or the hope that Tyrian resistance would halt the advance) went up in smoke with Tyre's destruction.

Zechariah also revealed that God's judgment of Ashkelon, Gaza, Ekron, and Ashdod—the cities of Philistia—would bring about unexpected results. Not only would the cities be destroyed, but the people would be dispersed and their ethnic identity would be lost. "A mixed people" would dwell there, and its cultural practices would cease (v. 7). Centuries of ritualistic idolatry would vanish as God altered the complexion of the landscape in a most dramatic and forceful way. God would "take away its abominations from between its teeth" (v. 7).

But note that the Lord had more than judgment in mind. The Philistine burden would pave the way for divine influence. There would be a remnant for God; they would be "brought into the fold." They would be like the family of Judah, as some of the Jebusites had been assimilated into Israel. Mark J. Boda's reflection on this text is worth noting:

> God's sovereign plan, however, should not be construed in an exclusively negative manner. Zechariah 9 echoes the end of Zechariah 8, namely, that God envisions a community that transcends Israel's borders and ethnicity. The surprising inclusion of the Philistines among the tribes of Israel is evidence of God's intention to bless all nations through Abraham's seed (428).

Some affirm that Alexander's campaign cannot be in view in these passages because the conversion of Philistines didn't immediately follow. We must consider, however, that (1) it is not known whether there were any proselytes at that time, and (2) it begs the question to say that the results *must immediately follow*. The effect of the invasion and the decimation of an idolatrous culture created fertile soil for divine influence—immediately, in inter-biblical times, and for the preaching of the first-century gospel (cf. Acts 8:40).

God Arises for His House (9:8)

In the likeness of David's words, God would also arise for his house (not against). That is, the same divine power and providence that brought destruction through the

Greeks would also defend his people. This overwhelming power would not destroy Judah because God would encamp at his house (around his people, not merely the temple) and protect them. Judah would not face conquest and exile as they had in recent times because "now I see with my own eyes." When God sees—that is when He determines to intervene to accomplish His purpose—His will shall be done.

Homer Hailey noted:

> Egypt, Assyria, Chaldea, and Persia had all oppressed them. And now Alexander the Great would invade the land, conquer the people, and impose the Grecian culture, philosophy, and religion upon them; but Jehovah would encamp about this people and through them fulfill His purpose (370).

The facts of history are: Alexander the Great mowed down all resistance in Palestine, but he did not assault Judah (Leupold 172). Why is that? Because God's divine purpose would certainly come to pass: the king would come.

THE KING SHALL ARRIVE

Zechariah 9:9-13 declared that the king would arrive in Jerusalem, and that is why Jehovah would arise through the ages and impose His will in the earth. Judah was encouraged to believe and trust in God. If the king must come to Jerusalem (regardless of how far in the future), then the Lord would defend her. Jerusalem must exist because her king was coming.

The King Arrives (9:9-10)

Zechariah 9:9 predicted the Messiah's arrival and thus foretold what would happen next. That is, after "God arises" against Judah's neighbors, the king shall arrive. The Holy Spirit confirmed that this scripture foretold the triumphal entry of Christ—when the Lord Jesus rode into Jerusalem on a donkey on the Sunday morning that preceded his death (Mat. 21:1-11; Mark 11:1-11; Luke 19:29-44; John 12:12-19). Although 300 years elapsed between the "burden of Jehovah" and the king's arrival, God's purpose in those conquests and realignment of the nations was preparatory to the Messiah's arrival (cf. Gal. 4:4). God wields His power over the land *because* the king must come to Jerusalem. What a glorious day!

The description of the king's arrival highlighted His adoration, attributes, and administration (vv. 9-10). His arrival would cause celebration because He would be recognized as the Messiah. He is righteous and brings salvation (or *has* salvation in the sense of divine empowerment [cf. Rom. 1:4; Heb. 5:7]). What a contrast to the conquerors who preceded Him! He would be humble and mounted on a donkey. What amazing prophetic details that were fulfilled in Jesus' life!

Verse ten describes his administration by outlining the following details. The king's reign would not be characterized by military conquest; rather, His influence would grow throughout the earth because He "would speak peace to the nations" (cf. Isa. 2:2-4). The Prince of Peace (Isa. 9:6) would rule over the nations "from sea to sea, and from the River to the ends of the earth" (Zec. 9:10). This passage identifies that the nature of Christ's conquest *at his first coming* was never intended to be a military or physical conquest of nations (For a refutation of the dispensational interpretation of this context, see Carver 137-139).

The Lord Arises Again (9:11-13)

The purpose of verses 11 through 13 are not hard to discern, although there is disagreement on the time period to which these passages allude. J. B. Coffman (139-141) affirms that these verses address the Christian Age, which follows the coming of the king. One might assume that these subsequent passages (vv. 11-13) follow *in time* Christ's coming since they follow in the text. But distant events are frequently compressed together in the prophets. A successive series of events does not necessarily follow in every chapter, or within the chapters. For example, in Isaiah 9:6 we have a Messianic prophecy. There is a great deal of prophetic material that follows this passage in the text that does not follow in time. Similarly, Isaiah chapters eight (the coming Assyrian invasion of the north) and nine (the coming of the Messianic king and his kingdom) appear like events near to each other but are separated by more than 700 years. Hermann J. Austel explained this prophetic style when he wrote:

In the first [oracle of Zec. 9-11], there is frequent alternation between near and far fulfillments, or telescoping, a frequent prophetic practice in which distant events are viewed from the standpoint of near events. The near and the far are often intermingled in such a way that they merge into one (697).

Zechariah 9:11-13 stresses that God is the one who will protect and defend His people—whether further return of exiled people was indicated or the future protection of vulnerable Judah through centuries of foreign domination.

Verse 11 states, "As for you also, because of the blood of my covenant with you, I will set your prisoners free from the waterless pit." This was intended to encourage those of Zechariah's day not to fear their humble position in Judah—nor should the generations to come— *because the king would eventually come.* God would preserve his people.

Even Coffman can't fail to see "a partial fulfillment" of verse 13 in the second century B.C. (141). Divine power and providence would guarantee the success of the "sons of Zion" over the "sons of Greece." But the point is not simply an isolated fact of history. Jehovah's purpose was that the king must come to Jerusalem. Therefore, in intervening time, God would empower his people; they would not be overrun by enemies.

THE LORD SHALL APPEAR

Zechariah 9:14-17 paints a vivid picture of the Lord's presence and purpose in the earth.

The Lord's Presence (9:14-15)

Jehovah would appear (the figurative language does not require a visible appearance); the Lord would manifest His power and protect His people. He would be with them. The Lord would shoot His arrow, sound His trumpet, and march forth in violent whirlwinds of the south. This divine power would enable God's people to resist aggression and prevail over her foes.

> With a series of graphic symbols, the efficiency of the Lord in assisting his people is emphasized. The intense figurative language pictures Israel as devouring their enemies and drinking their blood, like guzzling wine (v. 15; Num. 23:24) (Jackson 483).

Because *God* protects them, they would have overwhelming success (v. 15).

The Lord's Purpose (9:16-17)

But the presence of the Lord, protecting his people through the centuries, is for a divine purpose. "On that day" decreed by God—the day when the Lord's purpose would be fulfilled—salvation would be brought down. The purpose of the Lord is to save, as described in the peaceful administration of the king. He would speak peace and save them because He loves his people, and they are precious to him (v. 16). He would save them because He is great in goodness, and He would provide for their needs in abundance (v. 17).

THE PEOPLE SHOULD ASK

From the Lord's providential interventions for his glorious purpose, Zechariah transitions to an admonition. Blessings come from Jehovah, but burdens fall on idolaters.

Blessings From God (10:1)

Because God is the all-powerful creator and loving provider, the people should depend on the Lord. "Ask rain from the Lord," the prophet declares (10:1). The late, or spring, rain would ripen the crops. They must remember that it is Jehovah "who makes the storm clouds" (ESV). He gives the showers, therefore the food of the field is from him.

Burdens From God (10:2)

The difficult life in post-exile Judah was a *consequence* of the nation's failure to regard God as the source of all blessings. As Paul would later warn, "Do not be deceived: God is not mocked, for whatever one sows, that will he also reap" (Gal. 6:7). The household gods and diviners, on whom many had relied in the past, uttered nonsense, lies, falsehood, and empty promises. For their failure to honor Jehovah as the true and living God, the people had wandered like sheep without a shepherd and had been afflicted (v. 2). Why had they suffered? Because, "The eyes of the Lord are in every place, keeping watch on the evil and the good" (Pro. 15:3). They should rely on the Lord.

THE PEOPLE SHALL ASSEMBLE

But the Lord would not abandon His flock, for through them He would accomplish His glorious divine plan of the ages. Observe the emphasis on what God would do. When the Lord would set the cornerstone and redeem His people, He would: bring them back, gather them in, they would return, He would bring them home, He would bring them to the land, and they would walk in his name (vv. 6, 8, 9, 10, 12).

When Jehovah would established His house in the earth, he would demonstrate His care for the flock in many ways, and from Judah the cornerstone would come. When God "builds His house," the Lord's compassion would result in mighty conquests on behalf of His people.

God's Cornerstone (10:3-4)

When God builds his house, the people will be gathered. Thus, for the people to assemble, the cornerstone must be laid. Herein, we find another Messianic prediction of how Christ would accomplish the divine purpose in the world. Austel noted:

> It is of course true that Judah is seen here as the source of able, stable, and victorious leadership, but the One who exemplified all the highest qualities of leadership is God's Shepherd, the Messiah (698).

Rather than wandering aimlessly (v. 2), God would provide leadership and victory. He would punish the shepherds and the he-goats (faithless domestic leaders and/or foreign administrators who oppressed Judah [v. 3]). From Judah, the chief cornerstone, the nail and the battle bow would come. God would show His glory by providing out of weakened Judah His perfect and practical leadership for the betterment of the people.

Like the prediction of the king's arrival in chapter nine, the chief cornerstone out of Judah indicated the construction of *God's plan*. George L. Klein observed, "The cornerstone metaphor is an appropriate portrayal of the essential role the Messiah will play in building up the household of God, that is, the people of God" (294). As the king would bring about the divine purpose in the world, so God's house would require the chief cornerstone to be laid (cf. Isa. 28:16; Psa. 118:22; Mat. 21:42; Eph. 2:20).

God's Compassion and Conquests (10:5-12)

As in chapter nine (vv. 16-17), the Lord's merciful nature is emphasized (10:3, 6). He acts on behalf of His people because He cares for the flock and has compassion for His people. In as much as His people were scattered over the centuries because of their sins, so His mercy would result in the gathering of his people together and bringing them back to the land (vv. 6, 8, 9, 10).

This does not, however, refer to a literal return of Israel any more than Christ would be a stone or the Nile would dry up (v. 11). Furthermore, Zechariah said that there wouldn't be enough room for all those who would return (v. 10). This prophetic picture represents the success of God's plan in figurative language familiar to the exiles.

In reality, when God would lay the chief cornerstone and build His house— and when He would "restore the tabernacles of David"— this would involve the nations, not merely fleshly Israel (cf. 9:10; Amos 9:11-15; Acts 15:15-17). Through the preaching of the gospel, the Lord would whistle and many would return (v. 8).

As Isaiah described all nations flowing to the elevated mountain of the Lord's house to learn of His ways, Zechariah revealed the same experience in language appreciated by the people of his day. The sin consequence (i.e., exile, representing separation from God) is reversed when God builds His house and brings His people home. This is accomplished by Christ's first coming, and the assembling of his people figuratively represents salvation from sin. Accordingly, the result is "they shall walk in his name." That is, they will live according to God's will. Not all of Israel would participate in the compassionate homecoming, as Zechariah would later reveal. Many would reject the shepherd and suffer divine punishment (ch. 11). But those who follow God's leader will come home (return to fellowship with God) and walk in His ways.

Like the exodus from Egypt, so God would hear and remember His people. He would make them like mighty warriors and save them. He would make them strong, and they would rejoice in His divine fellowship and protection. What a beautiful picture of the restoration of mankind to fellowship with God—in the house of God, the church (cf. 1 Ti. 3:15-16; Gal. 6:14-16).

To summarize, we note the benefits from God's compassionate purpose. When God builds His house and calls for the scattered to return, they would be victorious, strong, saved, answered, full of joy, redeemed, a multitude, and they will live for Him. In language and images particular to the time, this depicts spiritual blessings that would be found in Christ (cf. Eph. 1:3).

But what would these distant events mean for the people of Zechariah's day? Simply this: because God's divine purpose would be accomplished through them, they should renew their efforts and find encouragement in the promise of divine protection and blessing throughout the ages. The king must arrive, the cornerstone must come; therefore God would encamp about His house, stir up the sons of Zion, and defend Judah throughout the centuries.

THE CHURCH SHOULD BE IN AWE

The church should read the prophets because they suffered in serving the Lord's cause, serve as an example to us, and helped bring us the saving word (cf. Matt. 23:37; 5:11-12; Jas. 5:10; 1 Pet. 1:10-12). The prophets are to be read, believed, obeyed, and loved (Luke 24:25; Rom. 15:4). Within them we find passages that stir the soul, like "ye shall run and not grow weary," and "like a lamb led to the slaughter" (Isa. 40:31; 53:7). "Though your sins be as scarlet, they shall be as white as snow" (Isa. 1:18). In the same way, we should love the words of Zechariah.

Zechariah is not the easiest prophet to follow. We find ourselves in unfamiliar territory, reading unfamiliar words in an unfamiliar style. Unfortunately, some assume that such a foreign text might be irrelevant to us. Some might think it is impossible to understand. This is not true. With a sincere desire and diligent study, the prophets represent a large body of inspired literature that is extremely rewarding. The impression made on the soul is forever.

Because of Who God Is

The church should be in awe because of who God is. God is our Creator, Judge, and Redeemer. As the Creator of heaven and earth, nothing is too hard for Him (Jer. 32:17, 27). Time is nothing to Him; a thousand years is like a day (2 Pe. 3:8). When He stands, His enemies are scattered. We ought to fall down and praise His holy name, for Almighty God is also infinite in goodness, love, and mercy. God sees, and He will act.

Because of What God Does

The church should be in awe because of what God does. God saves and strengthens His people. He is *the Lord of heaven and earth*. He governs this world according to His perfect holiness and consistent with His divine purpose. We need not concern ourselves with the times and seasons that are within God's own authority, but we do praise Him that He changes the times and seasons according to His will.

God imposes His will in the earth without suspending the laws of nature by a miracle. He creates changes in the course of history that would not otherwise happen without divine intervention. Should He desire to realign the nations or prevent harm to His people—in any age—He rules according to His own pleasure. Thus, these wonderful chapters remind us of God's power and special providence in nature, in the nations, and in nurturing His people. The Lord's omnipotence enforces His promise that not even the gates of hades shall prevail against the church. Thankfully, our inheritance is guarded by God's power (1 Pe. 1:5).

The church should be in awe because of what God does in revealing to us His plan. By prophetic passages like Zechariah 9 and its exact fulfillment, we know

God has confirmed the word of His servants and has provided evidence for the divine inspiration of the Scriptures. We ought to embrace the promises of the Lord's return because we see that the promises and prophecies of His first coming were fulfilled with minute precision. Thank God for his inspired word.

CONCLUSION

Throughout this study, we have followed God's work in the world—in the nations and on behalf of His people. But the focal point is, "Why?" Why did God move the nations and protect His flock? Because God was working an eternal plan to bring the king into the world so that the gospel of peace could be preached to all the nations. The coming of the king would result in the greatest conquest in world history: the conquest of the Son of God over Satan, of salvation over sin, of men over themselves, yielding their lives willingly to our gracious and loving God. Therefore, we can "return to God" and walk in His ways. We can enjoy the abundance and blessings that come from fellowship with God and that lead to everlasting life.

The church should be in awe as we look back over the ages and see what God purposed, prophesied, and brought to pass. We stand in awe of our great God and Savior, who fulfills all his promises. With great anticipation, we long for His glorious return! "Awesome is God from His sanctuary; the God of Israel—He is the one who gives power and strength to His people. Blessed be God!" (Psa. 68:35).

WORKS CITED

Austel, Hermann. J. *Baker Commentary on the Bible.* Walter A. Elwell, ed. Baker: Grand Rapids, 1989.

Baldwin, Joyce G. *Tyndale Old Testament Commentaries: Haggai, Zechariah, Malachi.* D. J. Wiseman, ed. Inter-Varsity Press: Downers Grove, 1972.

Boda, Mark J. *The NIV Application Commentary: Haggai, Zechariah.* Terry Muck, ed. Grand Rapids: Zondervan, 2004.

Butt, Kyle. "Tyre in Prophecy." ApologeticsPress.com. 2006. 28 Apr 2015. http://apologeticspress.org/apcontent.aspx?category=13&article=1790.

Carver, Everett I. *When Jesus Comes Again.* Phillipsburg: Presbyterian and Reformed, 1979.

Coffman, James Burton. *Commentary on the Minor Prophets: Zechariah and*

Malachi. Austin: Firm Foundation, 1983.

Hailey, Homer. *A Commentary on the Minor Prophets.* Grand Rapids: Baker, 1972.

Jackson, Wayne. *An Old Testament Commentary: The Prophets.* Stockton: Christian Courier, 2015.

Keil, C. F. and F. Delitzsch. *Commentary on the Old Testament in Ten Volumes.* Vol 10. Tr. James Martin. Eerdmans: Grand Rapids, 1978.

Klein, George L. *The New American Commentary: Zechariah.* E. Ray Clendenen, ed. Nashville: B and H Publishing Group, 2008.

Laetsch, Theo. *Bible Commentary: The Minor Prophets.* Concordia: St. Louis, 1956.

Leupold, H. C. *Exposition of Zechariah.* 1956. Baker: Grand Rapids, 1971.

CHAPTER 17

Zechariah 11:
"The Good and Foolish Shepherds"

Mark Hanstein

In the Old Testament, the term *shepherd* comes from a verb which means "to pasture" or "tend" a flock. From this, it is easy to see, then, what their work required. First, a shepherd was one who cared for a flock of sheep. So it is no surprise that we read of Abel as "a keeper of flocks" (Gen. 4:2). He was one who fed and protected the sheep. Second, a shepherd was one who sought the lost sheep. One of Jesus' parables conveys this very idea (Luke 15:3-7), and this was such a common occurrence in life that His hearers could easily identify with this illustration. Third, a shepherd was one who rescued the sheep that were attacked by predators. The prophet Amos speaks of the shepherd who "snatches from the lion's mouth a couple of legs or a piece of an ear" (Amos 3:12). David, "tending his father's sheep...rescued" some of them from the mouth of the lion or bear (1 Sa.17:34-36). Such was the work of a shepherd who labored in behalf of his sheep.

God is seen in the Scriptures as a shepherd. Jacob spoke of "the God who has been my shepherd all my life to this day" (Gen 48:15). This is also how David viewed God. "The Lord is my shepherd, I shall not want. He makes me lie down in green pastures; He leads me beside quiet waters" (Psa. 23:1, 2). And, "I fear no evil, for You are with me; Your rod and Your staff, they comfort me" (v. 4). Asaph called God the "Shepherd of Israel" (Psa. 80:1). Clearly, God cared for Israel as a shepherd would his sheep (Isa. 40:11). He fed and protected them (Jer. 31:10). God sought the lost (Eze. 34:12; cf. Mat. 15:24-26:22-28). He rescued them when the nation cried out to him in repentance (e.g. Jud. 6:6). Such was the work of God who labored in behalf of His sheep, Israel.

Jesus referred to Himself as "the good shepherd" who "lays down His life for the sheep" (John. 10:11). He is the one who "calls his own sheep by name and leads them out" (v. 3; cf. v.14). The Lord is the one who "goes ahead of them, and the sheep follow him because they know his voice" (v. 4). Clearly, Jesus cares for His people as a shepherd would his sheep (Heb. 13:30). He feeds and protects those who would follow Him (1 Pe. 2:25). He seeks the lost (Luke 19:10; cf. 13:34). He rescues those who come to Him for forgiveness (e.g. Luke 8:36-50; Heb. 7:25). He was struck down for the sake of the sheep (Mat. 26:31). Such was the work of God's "only begotten Son" (cf. John. 3:16) who labored in behalf of the sheep, those He came to save.

The term *shepherd* is used in Scripture to describe leaders among God's people. Moses was a shepherd when God called him to lead Israel out of Egypt (Exo. 3:1). David was a shepherd when God called him to be king over Israel (1 Sa. 16:1ff.). The shepherd's life perhaps was an excellent training ground for one who would be called on to lead God's people (cf. Amos 1:1). God expected these spiritual shepherds to be responsible for the well-being of the sheep. He expected them to lead the sheep in the right way. He expected them to act in behalf of the sheep and in their best interest.

In the New Testament the term *shepherd* refers to men who are elders in the Lord's church. They are to "shepherd the church of God which He purchased with His own blood" (Acts 20:28). From this it is easy to see what their work requires. Overseers in the church should feed and protect the sheep. Bishops should seek the lost sheep. Pastors should rescue the sheep from spiritual predators. Such is the work of an elder in the Lord's church who labors in behalf of "the flock, among which the Holy Spirit has made [them] overseers" (Acts 20:28).

This background serves to remind us of the kind of shepherd Zechariah was required to be when God called him to such a work. For far too long, God's people here were like their ancestors, as "sheep without a shepherd" (Num. 27:17; cf. 1 Ki. 22:17; Zec. 10:2). Spiritually, things were so out of order that God saw them as "the flock doomed to slaughter" (Zec. 11:4, 7) and facing a terrible calamity—the coming wrath of God (Zec. 11:1-3). The people needed good shepherds, but they had bad shepherds.

GOOD SHEPHERDS

What makes a good shepherd? From this section of the book of Zechariah, several things are evident.

First, a good shepherd obeys God's commands. The Lord told Zechariah to "pasture the flock doomed to slaughter" (Zec. 11:4). Zechariah obeyed the Lord for we find that he did what God ordered him to do (v. 7). He tried to lead the flock to be what God wanted it to be. To this end he took "two staffs" which he called "Favor" and "Union" and "pastured the flock." These reminded the people that God's favor was given to them as long as they followed Him, and that the scattered sheep of Israel were being brought together in unity and harmony through the work of their shepherd, Zechariah.

A shepherd in the Lord's church must do this same thing if he is ever to please the Lord. Obedience to God, among other things, means that the men themselves, as well as the churches that select them to be elders, make sure they are truly qualified (1 Ti. 3:1-7; Ti. 1:6-10; 1 Pe. 5:1-4). It takes a certain kind of man to be a bishop for God has been very specific regarding the work one is called on to do. How blessed are churches and the men who serve in this way when such is recognized and respected.

Obedience also requires a willingness to do the work God has given elders to do. How often is it that elders ignore what this God-given work is all about because they find aspects of it distasteful or requiring more of them than they are willing to give? How often is it that elders misunderstand what their work is all about because they do not study the Scriptures like they should? How often do elders think of themselves as nothing more than some sort of corporate board, charged with keeping the "right" people happy, making sure the treasury is not overspent, or seeing to it that the preacher doesn't offend anyone in his preaching and teaching? Have we forgotten that the Lord has given elders the task of "exercising oversight . . .according to the will of God" (1 Pe. 5:2)? Have we forgotten that we watch over "souls as those who will give an account" to God (Heb. 13:17; cf. 1 Pe. 5:4)?

Obedience to God means that an elder recognizes that this work involves being a pattern for others, exemplifying a life-style of godliness and spirituality (1 Pe. 5:3). Being the right example leads to credibility with others as they observe the integrity and sincerity in the life of one who serves as a pastor. Without credibility, what an elder professes is meaningless. To this end, elders need to make sure that their personal choices and habits enhance and do not damage their credibility. While credibility does not mean perfection, it does require consistency and putting spiritual things first by the one who serves in this capacity. Credibility gives power to the instruction shepherds must give the brethren. Elders are to illustrate with their lives what they teach others to do. They demonstrate to the spiritual flock—the church—how to live for God. Credibility is a powerful ally when shepherds must deal with spiritual problems in a church or lead a church through difficult matters such as church discipline. Brethren can support and trust leaders they respect, convinced that their shepherds are putting God's will first. I would like to think that in "considering the issue of their life" brethren can truly "imitate their faith" (Heb. 13:7). Good shepherds are legitimate examples and a blessing to the church, "the flock among which the Holy Spirit has made [them] overseers" (Acts 20:28).

Second, a good shepherd cares for the sheep under his charge. This was the case with Zechariah, for in the role of a shepherd the prophet cared for all of the flock just as God had commanded (Zec. 11:7). This included even the afflicted and the sick among the nation of Judah. Not one of God's sheep was ignored or overlooked.

In considering shepherds in God's church today, Sherman Cannon was exactly right when he pointed out that the work of the eldership is more a concern for the souls of men and the leading of an exemplary life before them than the measure of "rule" and/or "authority" one possesses. God has given elders the responsibility to "shepherd" His flock (1 Pe. 5:2). A shepherd in the Lord's church is required to do as Zechariah did (1 Pe. 5:2). This is not always easy, however. Members of the church can be difficult to work with. They can be unwilling to take good advice. They can rebel and be their own worst enemies. They can have many problems that take much of an elder's time as he tries to help them overcome their challenges. Sickness and loss can befall brethren, and they need elders to help them through these difficult times. Sin can overtake many, demanding much from an elder as he tries to reclaim the wayward. Good shepherds truly care for the spiritual welfare of all the people under their charge.

To this end, good shepherds strive to know the sheep they serve. How can a man truly be a shepherd if he doesn't take the time to know the members of the congregation? This requires, then, that an elder be out among the sheep. Doing so gives an overseer insight into how best to do their work. It builds trust between sheep and shepherds (cf. 1 Th. 5:12-15). Knowing the flock aids elders in helping them to mature spiritually. Knowing the flock assists elders in developing the members' talents for service to God. Knowing the flock enables elders to deal with and solve any problems members have because their needs and struggle are known.

Shepherds who know the sheep also know what to feed the sheep—a balanced diet of the Word of God. Pastors are involved in this teaching process personally (1 Ti. 3:2; Eph. 4:11), encouraging and admonishing (1 Th. 5:14), and exhorting in the sound doctrine (Tit. 1:9). This includes teaching their churches the truth on such matters as divorce and remarriage, instrumental music in worship, and the women's role, to name just a few issues. In a day and time when several elderships across the land are ignoring God's will on these and other matters of doctrine, or teaching something different than what the Bible actually says, a good shepherd will stand where God wants him to stand on matters of doctrine even if the brethren do not like it.

Shepherds guard the flock of God from evildoers, false teachers, and troublemakers. They battle wolves that seek to harm the church of God (cf. Acts 20:28-30). Good shepherds silence and refute those who contradict and deceive (Tit. 1:9-11) since they themselves are well versed in God's Word.

Shepherds personally seek sheep gone astray (cf. Luke 15:3-7), sacrificing their time and themselves to rescue and return lost sheep to the Lord for He holds those leaders accountable for the flock. Undoubtedly, the sheep are comforted and secure knowing that their elders indeed "watch in behalf of [their] souls." Good shepherds are legitimate shepherds.

Third, a good shepherd leads and instructs people toward God. This is what the prophet Zechariah attempted to do. To this end he "annihilated the three shepherds in one month" (Zec. 11:8). It is difficult to clearly identify who these false shepherds are. It appears that the Jews would have been familiar with their identity, given the presence of the definite article in this text. For the rest of us, it is not so easy. While commentators have offered some 40 different interpretations here, the best conclusion is that the "three shepherds" are the priests, elders, and scribes of Israel. Zechariah removed these leaders because of the way they mistreated His people. God was "impatient" with them due to their hypocrisy and self-centeredness (Zec. 11:5). His soul, literally, was "short" with them, showing the limits of God's patience toward those who are unrepentant and fail to live up to His expectations.

It must be recognized that ungodly leaders cause great harm to God's people in any age. Their lives and their work are not conducted in a vacuum. When leaders are motivated by power, recognition, or self-interest, rather than by a desire to please the Lord and a love for people, the effect of their influence can be devastating for the people they lead.

Such was the case in Zechariah's day. In spite of his best efforts, these obstinate people refused to follow God, so God gave up on them. He said, "I will not pasture you. What is to die, let it die, and what is to be annihilated, let it be annihilated; and let those who are left eat one another's flesh" (Zec. 11:9). They were abandoned and left unprotected in the face of their enemies—as sheep without a shepherd. Zechariah took his staff "Favor" and "cut it in pieces" (Zec. 11:10) symbolizing a breaking of the "covenant," or promise, God had made to restrain the nations from decimating Israel if they would consistently obey God (Deu. 28:1-14). Now the people no longer had the favor that comes from God. The "afflicted of the flock" certainly recognized that God's will was being fulfilled (Zec. 11:11). The headstrong, however, demonstrated what they thought of the shepherd's work among them was worth. Insultingly, they offered to weigh out "thirty shekels of silver as [his] wages" (v. 12)—the compensation price for a Hebrew slave wounded by an ox (cf. Exo. 21:32)—showing that they did not value God or His word. God rejected that "magnificent price" (Zec. 11:13) because the people had rejected Him. Zechariah responds by cutting in pieces his "second staff Union" (v. 14). Sadly, all that awaits the people now is destruction (cf. Zec. 11:5, 6). This raises the question, would the outcome have been different if the ungodly leaders of Israel themselves had been different and put God first?

From this, there is a lesson to be learned by all shepherds in the Lord's church. In elderships today there are far too many cowards. In elderships today, there are far too many who are unskilled in the Word and unable or unwilling "both to exhort in sound doctrine and to refute those who contradict" (Tit. 1:9). In elderships today there are far too many self-interested individuals. In elderships today there are far too many men who do not understand the times with knowledge of what the church should do (cf. 1 Ch. 12:33), men who fail to see the implications and consequences involved in the way they lead and teach the church. If this doesn't change, how can the effect on many of our churches be anything but devastating?

Shepherds in the Lord's church lead people in the way they should go. They do not drive them. Spiritual leadership means that elders understand that "managing" and "ruling" the flock has more to do with guiding and leading God's people. They realize that authoritarian, dictatorial, imperious rule is not spiritual leadership at all. Good shepherds know that they must lead honestly, lovingly, maturely, and patiently if sheep are to listen and follow. Spiritual leadership means the agenda of elders is motivated by spiritual concerns, not personal advantage or power. It has to do with pleasing God, loving people, and the salvation of souls.

Shepherds in the Lord's church are leading out in front of the flock. They are not careless or lazy. They approach their task "with eagerness" (1 Pe. 5:2). They never ask the sheep to do anything merely at their command or directive. Effective elders motivate the flock to go where they themselves have already gone.

Good shepherds today are faithful to God, regardless of the cost. Good shepherds today are true to His Word and do not give ground or compromise in any way. Good shepherds today are sacrificial when it comes to their money, their time, and themselves. Good shepherds today recognize that souls hang in the balance with the decisions they make, in the example they portray, and in the teaching they do.

FOOLISH SHEPHERDS

What is a foolish shepherd, an evil shepherd? Again, from this section of the book of Zechariah, several things are evident.

First, a foolish shepherd is indifferent toward the sheep (Zec. 11:16). He does not really care for them. The foolish shepherd's concern is not for "the perishing . . . the scattered" or "the broken." He does not even care to "sustain the one standing." As Zechariah observed, the concern of the foolish shepherd is for himself. He will "devour the flesh of the fat sheep, and tear off their hoofs." There is some similarity to the shepherds mentioned earlier in the chapter. They "wailed" because "their glory [was] ruined" (v. 3). They had "no pity" on the people they led (v. 5).

When elders in the Lord's church care more for themselves and their stature than they do God's people, something is wrong. This foolishness must change if the church is to be truly what God would have it to be in the world. Brethren should expect no less from their elders than what God expects from them.

Second, a foolish shepherd does not protect the sheep (Zec. 11:16). Rather he leaves them unguarded, as "food for every beast of the field" and "scattered" (cf. Ezek. 34:5). There is some similarity to the shepherds mentioned earlier who should have kept the sheep safe, but instead sold them out to others who would slay them (Zec. 11:5). Those shepherds enriched themselves at the expense of those they led and, at the same time, had the audacity to thank God for their good fortune.

When elders in the Lord's church refuse to stand firmly on the absolutes of Scripture, something is wrong. After all, for the church to be "the pillar and support of the truth" (1 Ti. 3:15), elders must be willing to confront and silence error. In doing so they protect the souls in their charge.

Third, a foolish shepherd does not seek the sheep that are scattered (Zec. 11:16) and leaves the flock (v. 17). The sheep suffer because, as in Jeremiah's day, shepherds were "destroying and scattering the sheep of My pasture" (cf. Jer. 23:1).

When elders of the Lord's church are not evangelistic and as seeking the wayward, something is wrong. The primary concern of elders should be the well-being of souls. When this is the case, the lost are found.

Fourth, a foolish shepherd is a worthless shepherd who will be punished (Zec. 11:17). As Zechariah described it, "a sword will be on his arm and on his right eye! His arm will be totally withered." The foolish shepherd will get what he deserves because he did not do the job a shepherd should do.

What others judgment can elders in the Lord's church expect when they fail to do what God has told them to do? James speaks of a "stricter judgment" for teachers (Jas. 3:1). Can such be any less for elders who refuse to carry out what God expects in this regard?

Because they rejected the good shepherd God had given them (Zec. 11:8), God's people received one who would do exactly the opposite of what a shepherd is expected to do. God raised up this "foolish shepherd" who would mislead, mistreat, and desert the sheep. Because of their obstinate attitude God's people were worse off than ever before.

Is it not often the case that churches get what they deserve when it comes to the leaders they have? When they are unaware or do not care about God's will in the matter of qualified shepherds, will they run the risk of appointing men who would mislead, mistreat, and desert them? Would such churches be worse off than ever before?

CONCLUSION

The Messianic thrust of this section of Zechariah (cf. Mat. 27:9, 10) must be observed, as well. Matthew associates this with the time of Christ (cf. Mat. 27:9,10). The reason the apostle attributes this to Jeremiah is that the writing of Zechariah would be in the collection of prophetic books headed by Jeremiah's book. A first century Jew, then, would easily recognize this fact.

Jesus is symbolically portrayed in Zechariah asking those He came to shepherd what they thought He was worth to them (Zec. 11:12). Derisively, the leaders offered 30 pieces of silver, the exact price Judas Iscariot was paid to betray the Lord (Mat. 26:14-16). The Jews of Jesus' day thought He was worth no more than a common slave. Throwing the 30 pieces of silver to "the potter" (Zec. 11:13) was fulfilled when the guilt-ridden Judas Iscariot went back and threw the money on the temple floor. Unwilling to put the "blood" money into the temple treasury, the priests gathered it up and "with the money bought a Potter's Field" (Mat. 27:3-10).

It is also worth noting that Jesus often confronted the hypocrisy of Israel's religious leaders during His ministry (cf. Mat. 23:1-36; Luke 11:37-54). Jesus' denunciations of the Jewish leaders were eventually followed by the destruction of Jerusalem and the whole nation of Israel in A.D. 70. God allowed Rome to invade and destroy Israel (Luke 19:41-44; 21:20-24). Roman armies killed some 1,100,000 Jews. In the great siege against Jerusalem, several starving citizens resorted to cannibalism in an effort to survive (cf. Jer. 19:9).

Their rejection of the Good Shepherd was devastating. The Jewish leaders had done much to contribute to this sad state of affairs for they did not lead the people in the right way.

The work of the good shepherds is not easy. There are the countless hours of planning, prayer, visitation, and labor that testify to this. Most of the effort elders put into their work is unseen and unknown by the congregation as a whole.

The duties of the good shepherds involve great responsibility. They are the ones who ultimately plan, oversee, and direct the work of the church. They are the ones given the responsibility to "keep watch" and "shepherd the flock of God." They are the ones who will give an account of their stewardship to God. This is why they must put the Lord's interests above their own.

Perhaps this is why the Lord reminds the church to "let [shepherds] do this with joy and not with grief, for this would be unprofitable for you" (Heb. 13:17).

Perhaps this is why the Lord reminds good shepherds that "when the Chief Shepherd appears, you will receive the unfading crown of glory" (1 Pe. 5:4).

CHAPTER 18

Zechariah 12:1–13:6: "The Future Israel's Future In Turning To The Lord"

Dave Chamberlin

few months ago, on a Wednesday evening, I was visiting a congregation out of state. I was told that the teacher of that class was teaching through the New Testament and had been teaching that class for a number of years but upon reaching the book of the Revelation would say something to the effect that it was too hard to understand and as a result it was being skipped. This particular behavior had been going on for a number of years with the result that few adults, in that congregation, knew anything about that great piece of apocalyptic literature.

The book of Zechariah, in the Old Testament, seems to have the same reputation among some individuals as does the Revelation in the New Testament. It is just too hard to study therefore we will just skip it. People who say that about either book are actually indicating a belief that God would allow an inspired work to be so difficult as to not be understood. Does that not bring into question the ability of God as the master communicator? Perhaps it is a lack of an effective study effort on the part of the teacher.

The book of Zechariah, especially in the section of chapters 12 through 14, can seem to be rather daunting to the casual reader but with a diligent determination that portion of the text will open a wealth of information for the serious Bible student. The nurturing process of God's love for His people is evidenced throughout Israel's history. The book of Zechariah is God's word, through the prophet, to a reunited Israel readying themselves for a future king and his kingdom. Israel has, at this point in time, survived the discipline of God's provision through the seventy years of Babylonian captivity. Idolatry had led to God's use of the Babylonians in a disciplinary role against Jerusalem and Judah but the result was seen in a people (Israel) who would, for the most part, attempt to maintain a proper relationship with their God. Idolatry would continue to be a problem for God's people, even into New Testament times, but not to the extent as evidenced in pre-exilic times.

God's love, for the recipient of Zechariah's message, is about to be manifested in the Messiah and his kingdom. Leupold writes:

Particularly prominent in the book is the Messianic element. With the exception of Isaiah, there is no other prophet whose book contains such a wealth and variety of this element, not only in proportion to the total amount of material offered, but also as a sum total of passages. New items in rich measure, presented in rich colors, appear at every juncture in the book. The emphasis of this feature, of course, rests entirely on the thought that for every situation developing in Israel's history there is nothing more necessary than faith in the Messiah of God. That faith is so many-sided and so entirely adequate to every situation that arises that, when new problems appear, all the nation needs is a fuller revelation of what the Messiah is and does and it will discover at once that its help lies entirely in Him (Leupold 4).

THE TEXT OF ZECHARIAH 12:1—13:6

A. Israel's Conflict 12:1—4

Verse 1

The inspired writer begins this section with the notation that this is "the burden of the word of the Lord concerning Israel." (v.1) The word burden (Heb. massa') contains within it the definition to carry a physical load but can be used figuratively of a spiritual load one is carrying as in Psalm 38: 4.

> *"For my iniquities are gone over my head:*
> *As a heavy burden they weigh too much for me."*

The word of the Lord is the source of the burden and is parallel to the first section of Zechariah (chapters 9—11) where the burden is "upon the land of Hadrach" which represents the hostile world power and here (chapters 12—14) where the burden is "concerning Israel" as indicated within the text as "Jerusalem and Judah." It would seem that the term "burden" carries with it the weight of God's word whether it is in reference to a scene of judgment or one of blessing.

Laetsch indicates:

The book of Malachi is called a *massa* (ch.1:1), yet it contains truly marvelous promises (ch.1:2, 11; chs.3 and 4). Finally, Jeremiah calls the utterances of the false prophets *massa* (Lam.2: 14), "false burdens." Yet these *massas* did not prophesy judgments, burdens, but peace, peace (cp. Jer.6: 14; 8: 11; 5: 12). The term *massa* therefore cannot denote only judgment prophecies. It is a synonym of prophecy, proclamation, prophetic utterance (Laetsch 294).

The use of the term "Israel" (as indicated in verse 2) would certainly be an all-inclusive term for God's people in light of a return of both those of the northern kingdom of Israel from Assyrian captivity and those from the southern kingdom of Judah and Babylonian captivity. The obvious assimilation of both groups into the Babylonian captivity is clear from prophecy as indicated in passages like Ezekiel 36 and especially Ezekiel 37 where verses 24 through 28 conclude with the future coming of the Messiah. The focus upon the usage of "Jerusalem and Judah" is quite natural since a major theme for both Haggai and Zechariah is in the rebuilding of the temple located in the city of Jerusalem within the environs of Judah.

The "One" who declares this "burden" is identified as the Creator of all that exists. His identifying characteristics are indicated as three verbs (stretches, lays, and forms) which are "participial forms in the original text, denoting characteristic, habitual action" (Laetsch 478). These mighty daily activities of God are noted for a people who need an "ever present Lord" if they are to remain faithful as they focus on the coming Messiah. This phraseology is also found in Isaiah 42: 1- 9 (especially in verse 5) where the context is decidedly Messianic.

Verses 2—4

It is inconceivable to the reader of the time, that insignificant Jerusalem would be powerful enough to cause an invading army to be repelled by a force of arms. In Zechariah's time Jerusalem was still in a period of reconstruction with a final repair to the walls some 60 to 70 years in the future. (Temple rebuilt—c.516 BC and walls rebuilt—c.444 BC) How could Jerusalem withstand another invasion like that of the Babylonians?

The answer to the question is found in the protective power of the Lord of verse one. For any invading foe, Jerusalem would become "a cup that causes reeling," in verse two, "a heavy stone" that will injure all who try to lift it in verse three and a striking of the enemy horses "with blindness" (horse always connected with war) in verse four. The message is clear. Jerusalem and Judah must remain faithful to God if they are to receive the security that only He can provide.

B. Israel's Victory 12: 5—9

Verse 5

Up to this point the prophet has made known the foes of Judah and their fate. In "that day" Jerusalem becomes "a cup that causes reeling," and "a heavy stone" that causes severe injury for all who attempt to lift it, the Lord will Himself strike all the "horses" of the enemy with blindness. It is not a powerful Jerusalem that brings about this great victory but rather the "Lord of hosts," the God of their salvation.

Then the clans of Judah will say in their hearts, 'A strong support for us are the inhabitants of Jerusalem through the Lord of hosts, their God' (Zechariah 12: 5 NASB).

The response by the clans of Judah in verse five is the result of the inhabitants of Jerusalem being a strong support. Leupold makes all of this a bit clearer when he notes:

> The confidence of Judah was expressed thus: "The inhabitants of Jerusalem are my strength" (lit. "strength to me," *'amtsah lî*). The literal statement removes much that might seem objectionable about their claim. They do not actually say: "are my strength," but, "afford strength to me." Again, they add the qualifying statement: "in the Lord of hosts, their God." This makes the Lord Himself the ultimate source of Jerusalem's strength and so, mediately, of Judah's chieftains ("clans" NASB dcc). We find the thought becoming still clearer as we notice some subsidiary material that the book of Zechariah offers. It is not only a harmless attitude that Judah's chieftains express; it is the only one possible and permissible after what preceded. This is one of the many indications that the two sections of the book mutually require one another: 1: 17 and 2: 12, as well as 10: 6, 12, indicate that God has chosen Jerusalem and will strengthen her. Therefore, because of God's choice, men should choose it also, and adhere faithfully to it (Leupold 231).

The reader of Zechariah, as well as the listener of Zechariah's day, will begin to notice a shift from the present (Zechariah's present) to the future. That future is confirmed through the activity of an Israel (Jerusalem and Judah) strengthened by the Lord. The Lord's promise follows in verses 6—9.

Verse 6

"In that day" of verse six is determined by the hearts of those of the clans of Judah in verse five. The strength for the clans of Judah is found in the example set forth by the inhabitants of Jerusalem. Jerusalem is the key to all the blessings that will befall Israel both in their present state and as found in the arrival of the Messiah and his kingdom. This restoration of Jerusalem, manifested in the reestablishment of worship in a restored Temple, is the key to the coming of the Messiah. This is also the thought expressed in Isaiah 2: 1—4, Micah 4: 1—3, and Zechariah 2: 6—13. The thought that is expressed is simple; no restoration—no Messiah.

"In that day" of verse six, the Lord will show His power by making "the clans of Judah like a firepot among pieces of wood and a flaming torch among sheaves." God's use of the clans of Judah is graphically portrayed in an unstoppable consuming fire whose source is the Lord Himself. This thought is a continuation of that expressed in Zechariah 2: 5.

"For I," declares the Lord, "will be a wall of fire around her, and I will be the glory in her midst."

The firepot that is indicated in this verse is the container (lit. *kiyyôr'esh, pan of fire*), usually bronze, used to transport hot coals from one area to another for the purpose of building a fire. The clans of Judah would be God's firepot, cleansing the land of all their enemies, "while the inhabitants of Jerusalem again dwell on their own sites in Jerusalem."

Verses 7—9

The work of the Lord continues to be noted as a part of "in that day of verse six. The emphasis of verse seven indicates that God's salvation of Israel will involve the saving of the tents of Judah first in order that the glory of the inhabitants of Jerusalem might not be magnified above Judah. Those living within Jerusalem had free access to the rebuilt Temple and the protection (eventually when Nehemiah's work was completed) of Jerusalem's walls. The possibility for tribal division was still present among those who lived in houses and those who continued in a more nomadic life-style. A boastful life-style is not needed at this point in time when so much depends upon a united Israel focusing on the coming Messiah. The attitude needed at this time was well expressed by Jeremiah in Jeremiah 9: 23, 24.

Thus says the Lord, "Let not a wise man boast of his wisdom, and let not the mighty man boast of his might, let not a rich man boast of his riches; but let him who boasts boast of this, that he understands and knows Me, that I am the Lord who exercises lovingkindness, justice, and righteousness on earth; for I delight in these things," declares the Lord.

Again, "in that day" verse eight, emphasizes the care that the Lord has for "the inhabitants of Jerusalem." They are seen as a strong encouragement (verse 5) for all Israel and their defense is assured by the Lord. The word of encouragement is seen in the fact that the most feeble will be like David, Israel's hero warrior and the "house of David," with a possible reference to the importance of the Davidic house as noted in 2 Samuel 7. The house of 2 Samuel 7 is God's response to David when he, David, desires to build a Temple for God.

Here in verse eight of Zechariah 12 is the comparison of the house of David to God. The translation of 'elohîm as God is misleading within the context. Leupold writes:

He, however, that is of "house of David" shall be as a supernatural heavenly being, 'elohîm—for this is the meaning of the term as it is in 1 Sam. 28: 13. Though 'elohîm usually means "God," here a climax is reached in "the angel of the Lord," so the preceding term is apparently used in this other well-established sense. Of course, the word order of this verse suggests that the climax would indicate that "the angel of the Lord" is divine as the Old Testament clearly teaches elsewhere, cf. Exod. 23: 20ff; Josh. 5: 13ff. Since "the angel of the Lord" usually functioned as the leader of Israel both in the days of the wilderness wanderings and also during the time of the conquest of Canaan (cf. the two passages just indicated) therefore, the expression here means: "the angel of the Lord before them (Leupold 233, 234).

Verse nine sums up this section of verses seven through nine by indicating that God, "in that day," will "destroy all the nations that come against Jerusalem." There is never, in all of this discussion about the destruction of Israel's enemies, any indication that Israel would ever raise a physical army of great force to deal with the problem. The thoughts expressed by God are consistent with the words of Jesus as He responds to Pontius Pilate in John 19: 36.

"My kingdom is not of this world. If My kingdom were of this world, then My servants would be fighting, that I might not be delivered up to the Jews; but as it is, My kingdom is not of this realm."

Those enemies of Jerusalem will destroy themselves as they attempt to destroy God's people. This thought is true in every generation where God's people are found. Babylon, Persia, Greece and Rome are all gone, smashed by the stone of Daniel 2: 44. God takes care of His children in every generation. An attempt, by an individual or a nation, to destroy God's children is tantamount to going after "the apple of His eye" (Zechariah 2: 8). The text of Zechariah 12: 10- 14 will give evidence to God's concern for those who belong to Him.

C. Israel's True Penitent Behavior 12: 10—14

Verse 10

The transition from the present time of Zechariah to the future coming of the Messiah becomes more evident with verse 10. The information that is provided in the verse in question is repeated in a shortened form by the inspired writer John in John 19:37. This verse, in John 19: 37, contains but a fragment of the thought expressed in the original. The point of this notation is to show that Zechariah 12: 10 is absolutely Messianic as proven by the context in which John uses it. As the transition from "chosen people" Israel to "chosen people" church is being made it behooves us to remember that God's plan for the foundational element of the church is bound up in a responsive Jewish element obedient to that first gospel preaching (Romans 1: 16). This same transition is apparent when making a study of the woman in Revelation 12 who initially gives birth to the Christ as God's "chosen people" Israel but later must flee the dragon as God's "chosen people" the church.

The context of Zechariah 12: 10 is certainly referencing the crucifixion of the Messiah but the message of this verse indicates that the Father is the one who is pierced as a result of the piercing of the Son. The difficulty of the thought "piercing" is that we isolate the thrust of a spear without taking into consideration the effect the act (of crucifixion) would have on the other members of the Godhead. This same affect is seen in the discussion between Saul of Tarsus and the resurrected Christ on the road to Damascus as recorded in Acts 9: 1—5). The point that is being made is that a persecution of Christians is a direct attack upon God. A piercing of the Son is a piercing of the Father and the Holy Spirit. This whole process of thought returns to the statement made in Zechariah 2: 8, "for he who touches you, touches the apple of His eye."

Leupold indicates:

> The result of the imparting of the Spirit is that those who have received Him look to Him whom they have pierced and mourn. The question very naturally arises, "Whom did they pierce?" The second member of the verse says very directly that it is He who will pour out His Spirit upon them. This clear statement must be retained. But if God is pierced, it is very obvious that the verb "they pierced" must be used in a figurative sense and not literally, for God cannot be literally pierced. A good parallel is Lev. 24:11, 16, where also a verb "pierced" is used (not *daqar* as here but *naqab*), and its object is the "name of God." But "to pierce God's name" must mean something like "profane His Name." The same meaning may, therefore, be assumed for the expression under consideration (Leupold 237).

In all of this one needs to carefully consider his or her relationship to God's children. To act in an unjustifiable way towards a child of God is to act in the same way towards God. To touch His child is the same as touching the "apple of His eye."

Verses 11—14

In that day of the event indicated in verse ten, there will be a great wave of mourning in Jerusalem when the gravity of the situation is finally realized. One can almost imagine the terror in the voices of those Jews who respond to the preaching of Peter in that first gospel sermon recorded in Acts 2: 37. "Now when they heard, they were pierced to the heart, and said to Peter and the rest of the apostles, 'Brethren, what shall we do?'"

The mourning that is expressed in verses 11—14 is described in verse ten "as one mourns for an only son" like "the bitter weeping over a first-born." The example in verse eleven makes reference to "Hadadrimmon in the plain of Meggido" where a great lamentation took place at the death of that greatest king of Judah, Josiah when he was slain by Neco (2 Chronicles 35: 22—25). Every family in the land will experience mourning for the One who was pierced in verse ten. All the families of Israel from the Messianic line through David including the lineage of Solomon (Matthew 1: 1—16) and the lineage indicated through Nathan as recorded in Luke 3: 23—38. From the greatest to the least of families the mourning is great. The priestly lineage of Aaron is indicated from Levi down to the family of the Shimeites; their mourning is also great. A final concluding statement emphasizing the gravity of the situation is noted in verse 14.

D. Israel's True Sanctification 13: 1—6

Once again the phrase "in that day" introduces the reader (and listener) to more information concerning that marvelous Messianic age noted in Zechariah 12: 10. The "fountain" of verse one will remind the reader of the "pouring forth of the Holy Spirit" as described in Joel 2: 28—31 and its fulfillment in Acts 2: 17—21 on the Day of Pentecost. The very promise of Jesus the Messiah concerning the (out pouring) baptism of the Holy Spirit (Acts 1: 4, 5; John 14: 16, 26; 15: 26) would usher in the birth of the church and salvation for those who would wash themselves in this "fountain" of Zechariah 13: 1. This cleansing of Israel is also likened to that of the promise of God to Daniel in Daniel 9: 24. Those six points in Daniel 9: 24 reference the work of the Messiah in bringing salvation to, not only Israel but also, the whole world. The shedding of the blood of the Messiah is the fountain that was opened for the removal of "sin" and "impurity" as indicated in verse one.

The rest of the verses of this section (two through six) are all connected to the phrase of verse two, "And it will come about in that day." In verse two this new age will result in cutting "off the names of the idols from the land" along with "the prophets" and "the unclean spirit." An emphasis on removing the prophets continues through to verse six leaving the impression that all prophecy from God is going to cease within the time frame of this new age. Hailey writes:

At the same time that Jehovah opens the fountain for sin and for uncleanness, idolatry will perish out of the land. This does not say "out of the earth," for it yet continues; but the names of the idols will be cut off out of the land of the Messiah's rule, the true spiritual Judah. That which had been the plague of ancient Judah would be unknown in the new. An apostate church could yield to forms of idolatry, but the true church would not. True prophets would pass out of the land but false prophets would not, for these may ever plague the church. True prophets would cease, for there would no longer be need for them (Hailey 391, 392).

CONCLUSION

This section of Zechariah (Chapters 12: 1—13: 6) should provide the true believer with a great confidence in the God Who watches over His children. For the people of Israel the thought of calamity not creating despair was prevalent in God's word through Zechariah. Israel's conflict was indicated in Zechariah 12: 1—4 but not all was lost in this time of calamity. A reliance upon the power of God was called for and the result of that power was seen in Israel's victory in chapter 12: 5—9. The sending of the Messiah and His resultant sacrifice prompted a penitent behavior from Israel in chapter 12: 10—14. The result of that penitent behavior was Israel's true sanctification.

Even though we are separated from the Israelite of Zechariah's day by many centuries, the application of that time is just as true today as it was then. True victory can only be found in the kingdom of the Messiah. God loves each of us to the extent that we are so precious that we can be referred to as was Jacob in Deuteronomy 32: 10.

> *"He found him in a desert land,*
> *And in the howling waste of a wilderness;*
> *He encircled him, He cared for him,*
> *He guarded him as the pupil of His eye'*

You are that precious in His sight.

WORKS CITED

Hailey, Homer. *A Commentary On The Minor Prophets*. Grand Rapids, Michigan: Baker Book House, 1972. Print.

Laetsch, Theo. *Bible Commentary The Minor Prophets*. Saint Louis, Missouri: Concordia Publishing House, 1965. Print.

Leupold, H.C. *Exposition of Zechariah*. Grand Rapids, Michigan: Baker Book House, 1971. Print.

CHAPTER 19

Zechariah 13:7–14:21: "Judgment Of Purification and Jerusalem's Future Glory"

Wayne Jones

The assignment for this chapter involves braving the proverbial waters of two important but challenging genres of Biblical literature – namely, prophetic and apocalyptic. Any text that features one of these writing styles presents unique challenges to Bible students. However, if a text has both of these styles intertwined it can lead to much speculation, assumption, and even false teaching due to poor interpretation. While space will not permit a full discussion of how properly to interpret such Bible texts, it should be noted that one can lose the overall picture by concentrating too much on the details. Not every symbol has a direct or specific correlation to a person or event in the future. Sometimes the intent of writings like this is to paint the overall picture and convey an overarching message. We would do well to remember this as we move through this section of Zechariah's prophecy.

While we may not be able to identify every symbol or agree on what everything represents, we can still appreciate the purpose of Zechariah's closing words. In chapter 11 God promises to raise up a Shepherd. In chapter 12 that Shepherd is pierced. In chapter 13 there is reassurance that God is in control, even of these events that will one day take place. In this chapter, the final chapter, God continues to offer assurance that He is fighting for His people, and they will be purified and victorious. Zechariah closes his written prophecy with the theme of Scripture – victory in Jesus!

There is one other note of explanation that needs to be considered before beginning our discussion of this challenging text. Chapter 14 is one of the most difficult chapters to interpret in all of Holy Writ. There are about as many different interpretations of its meaning as there are commentaries that have been written about them. Our contention is that the verses under consideration in this assignment are a prophetic look at spiritual Israel, the church, from the time of its establishment through the various persecutions that it has faced through the years. Space will not permit us to explain away every other theory of interpretation about this text. We are not suggesting that other views are necessarily incorrect (so long as they are consistent with the doctrine of the kingdom and Biblical eschatology). It is simply our studied opinion that the primary focus of the final 24 verses of Zechariah's prophecy is Christ, His cross, His church, and its perfection through suffering.

THE SCATTERING OF THE SHEPHERD'S FLOCK (13:7-9)

Beginning in 12:10, Zechariah discusses the "one whom they pierced." Bringing that discussion through chapters 12 and 13, he provides a poetic transition in these three verses from the Shepherd to the flock. The main character is the same, but the emphasis shifts to the future of the pierced one's flock and His protection over them in the face of persecution. In chapter 12 and the first six verses of chapter 13, we learn that salvation, grace, and a fountain will be opened at His piercing. The benefits are spiritual and eternal. However, in our current text, we are assured that suffering will also accompany the Shepherd's piercing. In the end, that suffering has a purpose. That purpose is the purification of the flock and the glorification of the Shepherd. Zechariah 13:7-9 gives an overview of these things in poetic language while chapter 14 gives fuller detail as to how and when this would take place.

We know that this passage is about Jesus because He quotes it and applies it to Himself (Mat. 26:31). There is also evidence within the context of this passage that proves the same thing. He is called "my shepherd." This is not a reference to the foolish, insensitive shepherd described in 11:15–17, nor the shepherds who would show no pity for the poor and oppressed (11:5). This Shepherd is Jehovah's. The word "my" is not about ownership, but partnership. He is not merely hired or appointed to the position. He is of, and He is like, Jehovah. Thus, He is also called "my companion" or "my associate" (NASB) or "the man who stands next to me" (ESV). This word "occurs only here and in Leviticus where it is usually rendered 'neighbor' It suggests one united to another by the possession of common nature, rights and privileges" (Smith np). Though He is a man, He shares in the nature and purpose of Jehovah. This "companion" is none other than Jesus Christ!

The prophet calls for the sword to awaken (i.e., become active) against Jehovah's companion. The sword was representative of judicial punishment (cf. Rom. 13:4) and punishment for sin (Exo. 5:21; Psa. 17:13). Both of these ideas are present in the death of Jesus. However, the sword was not to be the actual instrument of death by which the Shepherd would be struck.

When this occurs, it will affect not only the Shepherd, but also His sheep. They would be scattered, and not all of them would return to Him. As in every generation, there would be a remnant that would come through persecution stronger, but some would not make it. Some would not return to Him. Those who would return are discussed in the later part of verse seven through verse nine. Several things are said about them. First, His hand would be upon them (7b). Many versions including NKJV, NASB, and ESV use the word "against" in this passage. However, the ASV seems to capture the meaning of the phrase more accurately by using the word "upon." The promise is that even the "little ones" would be protected while scattered and by His hand they would be gathered back together at a later time. The Shepherd is not against those who are scattered, but He would seek their restoration and purification. Second, those scattered but remaining faithful would be tried by fire (Psa. 66:10; 1 Pe. 1:6-7). Third, in the midst of their trials they would not renounce His name, but rather they would call upon Him to save and sustain (Psa. 91:15). When they called, they would not only ask for help, but they would identify themselves with Him. They would claim the One that the world rejected, the One that was struck with the sword. This specific choice would determine which individuals make up the "one-third" of verse 8.

What would be the result? God would claim them just they had claimed Him (Hos. 2:1. 23; 1 Pe. 2:9-10). Victory would be theirs, and God would be their deliverer. During the days of Zechariah's ministry, the temple and its worship was restored. It is highly probable that the Jewish people were so satisfied with their accomplishments that they forgot about the future promise of a worldwide kingdom and a coming Messiah. Thus, the prophet opens the final section of his prophecy by reminding them that something better is coming, and the battle has not yet been won. God would win, and His people would join in the victory, but neither had happened just yet.

JUDGMENT AND DELIVERANCE (14:1-5)

"The day of the Lord" is a phrase used by Bible writers to indicate a time when God intervened in human affairs to accomplish His purpose. "Every judgment action of God in history was 'a day of Yahweh.' Each 'day of Yahweh' was a type, preview and warning of the final day of Yahweh, i.e., the final judgment of the wicked" (Smith np). This day belonged to God because it was a day wherein His power and purpose would be revealed. Trouble and difficulty inflicted upon God's people and their faithfulness in the face of it can be a powerful testimony to His worthiness to be served and His sovereignty over the world and its rulers.

The opening verses of chapter 14 seemed to be an extension of the discussion introduced at the end of chapter 13. The purging of the one-third who returned in 13:9 seems to be under discussion in this opening section. Verses 1 and 2 provide an overall picture of that purging process that includes a continual intense attack against Jerusalem (i.e., spiritual Israel, or the church). God either caused or allowed "all nations" to gather against His people so that their faith might be proved and that the infant church might grow to maturity. Daniel in 7:12 and John in Revelation 20:7-9 describe this time of testing and oppression. When the suffering and persecution had served its purpose, then deliverance would be granted. The language of verse two suggests the tragedy and loss that would be experienced in this time of trial, but one thing was promised – they would not be cut off from the city.

Verses three through five reveal that the church would overcome the world by her commitment to Christ and by Christ's commitment to her. One might get the impression from reading verses one and two that God was going to turn the nations loose on His church and leave them to fend for themselves. Nothing could be further from the truth. When the battle starts, Jehovah would be leading the charge "as He who fights in the day of battle." The ASV translates this phrase in the past tense -- "as when he fought in the day of battle." Billingsley notes that this phrase "stands for all previous battles and all future battle" (443).

Not only will He fight for His people, but He will also make a way of escape (4-5). He will do so by descending upon the Mount of Olives. This is not the first time this mountain is mentioned in the Old Testament, but is the only time it is mentioned by this name. There are many events in the life of Christ that are connected to this mountain, not the least of which is His glorious ascension. So, as New Testament readers look back at this prophecy they get a greater sense of significance for this promised deliverance. He would descend where He had ascended to provide a way of escape. When His feet hit, the mountain would be divided in half creating a new valley through which the remnant would pass and be protected.

Their fleeing would be like those had "fled from the earthquake in the days of Uzziah king of Judah" and they would flee as far as Azal. Little is known about either one of these references. This same earthquake is mentioned by Amos (1:1), but no other details are given. It must have been one of great destruction and magnitude for it to be a reference point for two different prophets. Micah mentions a place named Beth-Azel (1:18) and this could be the place Zechariah is referencing. His readers, no doubt, would have know this place and its location east of Jerusalem at the mouth of this divinely formed valley of escape. We would do well to remember that while we might not see the valley or know where we will end up, God will protect and deliver His people.

SALVATION (6-11)

Verses six and seven are extremely difficult to interpret. It is probable that Zechariah is not alluding to a specific event, but to the mood and atmosphere of the church during the time of intense persecution. The Hebrew verb translated "diminished" in the NKVJ and "dwindle" in the NASB "denotes "drawing together, thickening, solidifying, losing some of the characteristic attributes or functions. Thus, the luminaries grow dim. This gloominess is symbolic of the plight and persecution of the people of God" (Smith np). We must remember not every symbolic reference must be identified. Sometimes the prophet is trying to paint a picture. Zechariah wants his readers to feel the desperation and gloom without dismissing any chance for deliverance. It would be "neither day nor night." It will be unique. Nothing like this will have ever happened before. Even still, not all hope is lost. Just when night seems to be approaching "it shall happen that it will be light."

Zechariah highlights salvation in Christ through the exaltation of Jerusalem (i.e., the church). First, in that day and from that place, the fountain that had been opened (Zech. 13:1) would produce "living waters" (14:8) that are "fresh, pure, and perennial" (Spence np). Water symbolizes the deliverance offered through Christ as he fights for his people. It's pictured as flowing from Dead Sea to the Mediterranean Sea during both summer and winter suggesting that it be available to all men at any time.

Second, in that day and from that place, the Lord would rule over all the earth (14:9). Here we reach "the pinnacle of this discourse…God will be universally recognized throughout the whole world because of the living water proclaimed by the church. His name would be known from sea to sea and river to river to the ends of the earth…the name of the Messiah would be in the mouth of all the people" (Billingsley 445).

Third, in that day and from that place, the church would be prominent above all (14:10a). Sitting on seven high hills, physical Jerusalem already towered over the surrounding geographical areas. In spiritual Jerusalem, the exaltation would be further emphasized by the leveling of the surrounding regions.

Fourth, in that day and from that place, the church would be inhabited. Zechariah uses the boundaries of physical Jerusalem to illustrate the population of spiritual Jerusalem; from the far northern boundary (Benjamin's gate); the far eastern boundary (the first gate); the far western boundary (the second gate); and the far southern boundary (the king's winepress). "The various locations seem to indicate full length of the walls from east to west, and from north to south" (Hailey

398) "illustrating the growth and stability of the church by the figure of the earthly city of Jerusalem firmly ordered and built" (Smith np).

Fifth, in that day and from that place, there would be a guarantee of safety unlike physical Jerusalem had ever known. Their ancestors had watched as Jerusalem was destroyed. They had been responsible for rebuilding it. In the prophecy of Zechariah of the Messianic age, Jerusalem (spiritual) would never be destroyed. Bible students might liken this promise to the reality of Romans 8:1 which states, "There is therefore now no condemnation to those who are in Christ Jesus."

THE DESTRUCTION OF HER ENEMIES (12-15)

For this salvation offered through Jehovah to provide the safety that has was promised in verse 11, there must be a decisive victory over those nations who had set themselves against Jerusalem back in verse two. This next section of Zechariah's prophecy promises and details the eventual destruction of the enemies of the church.

Victory would come through plague (14:12, 15). By using this term in the opening and closing verses of this section, we can conclude that the point of these verses are to describe the various aspects of that plague and to show the complete destruction their enemies. Since Jerusalem is representative of the church, it must be noted that the details of this plague are merely representative of the coming destruction on the enemies of God's people. Much like the book of Revelation, this section of prophecy uses graphic and detailed physical terms to describe spiritual concepts. At numerous points in the history of Israel and its place among the nations, God used plagues as a means of punishment and in order to ensure victory. The most notable of these occasions was in Israel's exodus from Egypt.

Their flesh would decay while they were still alive and standing. Their eyes, which were being used to look with anger and malice at Jerusalem, would rot in their sockets. Their tongues, with which they had spoken evil about the God's people and blasphemed God, Himself, would dissolve in their mouths. They would turn on one another while the people of God would unite from all over the earth to fight against them. Their ruin would even affect their wealth and riches. Their beasts of travel, war, labor, and food would be taken from them. It would appear that God's destruction of the enemies of spiritual Jerusalem would suffer in a similar way to what Job suffered. The difference between the two is that these things would never be restored. They would answer for their treatment of the Savior and His precious body. Hailey offered this simple summation: "All the enemies of God's camp will go down in defeat" (399).

THE CONVERSION OF THE NATIONS (16-19)

Not everyone who opposed God's people would be destroyed. Some would be converted and as a result they, too, would worship God in an orderly and prescribed manner. One of the three yearly Jewish feasts, namely the Feast of Tabernacles, is used to represent worship under the new covenant. Under the Old Testament system, the Gentile nations would not have been invited to participate in this great feast, but in the New Covenant all are invited.

The Feast of Tabernacles is what is considered to be the most important of the three feasts under the Mosaic system. "This feast was a feast of rest, joy, praise, and thanksgiving" (Billingsley 448) and celebrated freedom from captivity. At this feast, it was common to pray for rains that might ensure a productive crop and harvest. Zechariah feeds off of this tradition and suggests that those who refused to worship would be denied rain. He does not mean that modern droughts are a divine punishment, but rather that those who refuse to worship will experience the drought of spiritual blessings that are only found in Christ (Eph. 1:3).

THE HOLINESS OF JEHOVAH (20-21)

The exclusion of the Canaanites is similar to Revelation 21:27 and 22:15. Not everyone can be in the church, and not everyone can go to heaven. Those who are unholy and refuse to be made righteous will be rejected. Since the shepherd has been struck and the fountain of life has been opened there is no reason to come to the gates of the city unholy. If one does, he will be like the Canaanites – rejected and shut out.

Everything in spiritual Jerusalem will be holy. The "bells of the horses" is a reference to "small metallic plates suspended from the necks or heads of the animals for the sake of ornament and making a tinkling noise when striking against each other. These plates may have had the names of the owners inscribed on them" (Smith np). On these bells was the name of Jehovah and a declaration of His holiness just like the attire of the priests (Exo. 28:26). In spiritual Jerusalem, that which was unholy is made holy.

Furthermore, in spiritual Jerusalem all temple vessels are equally holy. Such was not the case in physical Jerusalem and the physical temple. In fact, these pots to which Zechariah refers were considered the most basic of all temple vessels. Yet, "in the day of Messiah's reign they will be equal to the bowls before the altar which caught the blood of the victims for sprinkling before the Lord" (Billingsley 449-450).

Finally, in spiritual Jerusalem that which used to be common is now holy. "Every pot is Jerusalem and Judah." Smith's comments are especially helpful in explaining the words of Zechariah:

All distinction between sacred and secular shall be a thing of the past. Every vessel (possession) used throughout Messiah's realm would be devoted to the service of the king. Common, ordinary vessels would be suitable for sacrificial purposes. The basic idea here is that old Levitical distinctions in degrees of holiness in society (priests, Levites, people), temple (outer court, holy place, holy of holies), animals (clean, unclean) would disappear. All shall now be equally holy (np).

The principle expressed here is what God was trying to explain to Peter in Acts 10 regarding the Gentiles, that they are being included in the church. The distinctions made in the Mosaic system between common and holy were as much nailed to the cross as the law itself.

The purpose of this prophecy was not to excuse unholiness or to diminish the value of holy things. The message being conveyed is that in spiritual Jerusalem all who desire to be holy and righteous can be. Thanks be to God for that possibility!

The closing verses of this great book reveal a truth that has long been misunderstood – some of the greatest blessings are the result of the greatest adversities. The security and holiness that are enjoyed in the church is the direct result of the suffering of our Good Shepherd and the trials of this life that purify us. Zechariah leaves his readers wondering and longing for the day that spiritual Jerusalem would be established. Brethren, we live in that day. May we never take these wonderful blessings of the Messianic age for granted.

WORKS CITED

Billingsley, Rick. *Minor Prophets II: Nahum-Malachi:* Truth Commentaries. Bowling Green, KY: Guardian of Truth Foundation, 2007.

Hailey, Homer. *A Commentary On The Minor Prophets.* Grand Rapids, MI: Baker Book House, 1972.

Smith, James E. *The Minor Prophets.* Joplin, MO: College Press, 1994. Print. Old Testament Survey Series.

Spence-Jones, H. D. M., ed. *Zechariah.* London; New York: Funk & Wagnalls Company, 1909. Print. The Pulpit Commentary.

Holy Bible. *The New King James Version.* Nashville, TN: Thomas Nelson, 1982.

CHAPTER 20

Malachi 1:1–5
"An Opening Appeal To God's People"
Melvin Otey

The book of Malachi is one of three post-exhilic prophetic works (Haggai and Zechariah are the others), and it is the final installment in most arrangements of the Old Testament catalog. More than four centuries would pass after its writing before Christ entered the world in fulfillment of Jehovah's many promises. Hence, it is part of the last biblical window into the condition of God's people before John the Baptist began paving the way for Jesus' earthly ministry.

Excepting the superscription and conclusion, the book is arranged in distinct sections or "oracles." The first, along with the superscription, provides an introduction and foundation for the book (1:2-5). The second concerns the priests and their dishonoring of the Lord (1:6-2:9). The remaining sections address various aspects of popular disregard for Israel's covenant with Jehovah (2:10-16; 2:17-3:6; 3:7-12; 3:13-4:3). Here, we will address the book's introductory material.

THE SUPERSCRIPTION

"The burden of the word of Jehovah to Israel by Malachi" (all biblical quotations are taken from the ASV unless otherwise noted). With the first clause of this first verse, the writer establishes an air of gravity that demands reverent attention to all that follows. The words were not his own; rather they originated with the One who created the universe and all that is therein. Throughout the subsequent text, the writer explicitly and repeatedly (more than 25 times in the book's four brief chapters) attributed the content to the mouth of Jehovah.

While it is not an altogether novel designation for a communiqué from the Holy One (see, e.g., Zec. 9:1, 12:1; cf. Nah. 1:1; Hab. 1:1; Isa. 13:1, 15:1, 17:1, 19:1 *et al.*), "the burden of the word" is a notable phrase. The term "burden" sometimes refers generally to a message from Jehovah. John Calvin was probably correct in asserting that it was regarded as "ominous" and portended "some judgment of God" (461). It certainly can denote a weighty load, something heavy to bear along (see, e.g., Isa. 46:1-2). Of course, divine dispatches are ultimately intended to lighten humanity's load (see, e.g., Mat. 11:29-30; cf. Jer. 6:16). For the obstinate, however, the word of Jehovah can be a veritable millstone about their necks.

God's word might be a heavy load for at least two principal reasons. First, it is a psychological albatross in that sinful men committed to continuing in their sinful ways have long felt burdened by the word of God because they weary of being warned about Jehovah's displeasure and the consequences attending the same (Isa. 30:9-11; 2 Ti. 4:3-4). Second, while it is designed to save men's souls by provoking them to repentance and spurring them to righteousness, it ultimately condemns the unrepentant and unrighteous eternally (John 12:48; Rom. 2:12-16).

The Audience

This weighty message, of course, like the majority of preserved inspired material, was to "Israel," the descendants of Abraham, Isaac, and Jacob who were entrusted with the oracles of God (Rom. 3:2; Deu. 4:7-8; Psa. 147:19-20). Of course, this was not the comprehensive group of twelve tribes Moses led out of Egypt or over whom David and Solomon reigned during their national zenith. Much had transpired since those former days.

The kingdom of Israel was rent in two soon after Solomon's son Rehoboam took the throne, and the ten tribes of the northern kingdom, called "Israel," existed as a separate nation from the southern kingdom, called "Judah." The northern kingdom fell immediately into apostasy and continued unwaveringly in it until it was ultimately judged by Jehovah via the Assyrian conquest in 721 B.C. (2 Ki. 17:22-23). Consistent with their imperial practices, the Assyrians deported the majority of the northern inhabitants and replaced them with foreign colonists who knew nothing of Jehovah (2 Ki. 15:29: 17:23-26). This intermingling produced an amalgam of both pagan and Mosaic traditions and a mixed race of people; "Samaritans" rather than true Israelites (2 Ki. 17:27-41; Josephus, *Antiquities* 10.10.7).

After the fall of the northern kingdom, Judah held the only real claim to the designation "Israel," and Judah was sometimes referred to as "Israel" thereafter (see, e.g., 2 Ch. 21:2, 28:19). Following the division, Benjamin was the only tribe that wholly remained with Judah and the house of David in the south (see 1 Ki. 12:19-23; 2 Ch. 11:1-12). Additionally, priests and Levites migrated from the north into Judah and Jerusalem to avoid the apostasy instigated by Jeroboam in the north (2 Ch. 11:13-14). While Judah fared somewhat better than their brethren to the north, it also endured significant bouts of apostasy. Intermittent, albeit significant, efforts at spiritual reform extended its national life, but Judah was ultimately overcome by the Babylonians, and many of its inhabitants were deported into Central Asia about a century and a half after their brethren to the north (1 Ch. 9:1).

Notably, the Babylonians did not import foreigners into Judah (Josephus, *Antiquities* 10.10.7), and, after 70 years, exiles were permitted to return beginning in approximately 536 B.C. under the leadership of Zerubbabel the governor and Joshua the high priest (2 Ch. 36:20-23; Neh. 7:6-7, 12:1; Hag. 1:1-2). Ezra led a second wave around 458 B.C. (Ezra 1:1-3). By the time the book of Malachi was penned, then, "Israel" was represented chiefly by the remnant of the two tribes of the south, Judah and Benjamin, along with some smattering of exiles returned from Babylon, ostensibly from among all twelve tribes, but predominantly from Judah and Benjamin (see Ezra 7).

The Author

This prophecy came from Jehovah and was delivered "by Malachi," that is, by his hand as the instrument of Jehovah. "Malachi" simply means "my messenger." The designation is so generic that some have posited that it is not a proper name at all (Cashdan 335; see, e.g., Dummelow 612). If this view is correct, then this is surely a singular instance in Scripture, for there are no other occasions where such a designation is used for an anonymous prophet. There has long been a division of opinion among scholars regarding the matter, but, where none of the other literary prophets are anonymous, it is probably better to regard "Malachi" as a proper name (Harrison 958). Ultimately, the resolution to this matter is immaterial to the thrust of the prophecy where, as here, the message rather than the messenger is so clearly in focus.

In any event, it is notable that, while the Old Testament prophets typically offered little in the way of biographical information, the scantiness of the material here is striking. The writer does not even discuss his genealogy or place of birth; neither does he provide typical temporal markers for the period of his prophetic activity (e.g., the names of rulers). To be sure, he lived in post-exhilic Judah when the land was ruled by governors subject to eastern monarchs (Mal. 1:7-8), and he seems to have been active after Zechariah and Haggai since reconstruction of the temple occurred in their time during the reign of Darius king of Persia (see Ezra 5:1-2, 6:14-16; Zech. 4:8-9; Hag. 1:1-4), but it stood complete and sacrifices were being offered in it at the time of this writing (see Mal. 1:7-10, 3:8-10).

In our effort to place this work and its penman in the proper historical setting, we must observe the close affinity of its content with that contained in the book of Nehemiah. The two denounce the same prominent sins, including priestly apathy and carelessness (compare Mal. 1:6 and Neh. 13:4-9), adulterous intermarriage with foreign women (compare Mal. 2:11-16 and Neh. 13:23-27; see also Ezra 9:1-2), and popular neglect of tithes (compare Mal. 3:7-12 and Neh. 13:10-13). Among other things, this leads scholars to date the book around the time of Ezra and Nehemiah. Some suggest an early date around 470-460 B.C., just before Ezra's arrival (see, e.g., Arnold and Beyer 470). Others favor the slightly later period between 450-430 B.C. (see, e.g. Hailey 401; Harrison 961). Under all the circumstances, it is impossible to be exact, but the author certainly seems to have written in the second half of the fifth century B.C. to the second or third generation of people in Judah after the return from Babylonian captivity.

THE FIRST ORACLE

I have loved you, saith Jehovah. Yet ye say, Wherein hast thou loved us? Was not Esau Jacob's brother, saith Jehovah: yet I loved Jacob; but Esau I hated, and made his mountains a desolation, and gave his heritage to the jackals of the wilderness. Whereas Edom saith, We are beaten down, but we will return and build the waste places; thus saith Jehovah of hosts, They shall build, but I will throw down; and men shall call them The border of wickedness, and The people against whom Jehovah hath indignation for ever. And your eyes shall see, and ye shall say, Jehovah be magnified beyond the border of Israel (Mal.1:2-5).

This first oracle addresses God's divine love for the descendants of Abraham, Isaac and Jacob. It provides the prism through which the whole book is properly viewed. Indeed, this theme of love "is present throughout the Book, and is the motivating force that impels the prophet to rebuke the people for all their shortcomings which had made them unworthy of God's love" (Cashdan 335).

The exchange depicted in these verses also introduces one of the book's prominent structural features, that is, rhetorical questions and answers (see also Mal. 1:6, 2:17, 3:14). This format suggests an apology, that is, a public defense, where logical, reasoned explanations are arranged to directly confront anticipated objections by the masses. Scholars refer to this as a "dialectic" method, where an assertion or charge is made and a fancied objection is subsequently refuted (Lewis

83; Hailey 402). Objections in these exchanges are punctuated with the words "ye say" (see, e.g., Mal. 1:2, 1:6-7, 1:13, 2:14, 2:17, 3:7-8, 3:13).

Jehovah's Declaration

The opening declaration, in particular, provides the lens through which the entire book must be read. So much is said in so few words: "I have loved you, saith Jehovah" (Mal. 1:2a). "In this one word God sums up all his gracious dealings with [Israel]; love was the spring of all" (Henry 1595). Jehovah could rightly have appealed to Israel on the basis of His supremacy and authority, but he did so on the basis of His love. The subsequent verses make it clear that He was not referring to His general love of the human family, but rather to the peculiar disposition and display that moved Him to adopt them as His special people, distinct from all the other peoples of the earth (Exo. 19:5).

In so many ways, it was necessary and appropriate to begin this address and conclude the Old Testament library with a declaration of Jehovah's love. God is love, of course (1 Jn. 1:8, 16), and He did not adopt this attribute when He sent Jesus into the world. Rather, this is who He has always been, and this is the attribute that moved Him to send Jesus into the world in the first instance. God had formerly and consistently declared His love for Israel (Deu. 4:37, 7:8; Jer. 31:3). Moreover, He had prominently displayed it (Psa. 25:6). Love spurred him to redeem the people out of Egyptian bondage (Deu. 4:37, 7:7-8; Hos. 11:1), and love moved Him to protect the nation from those who would do it harm (Deu. 23:5).

Israel's Objection

Recognition of the post-exhilic setting enhances one's appreciation for the opening affirmation of Jehovah's love. Israel's lowly condition does not excuse or explain the insolent, ungrateful mindset of the people in the face of this tender declaration, but it depicts the atmosphere in which it festered. The people were at a dangerously low spiritual ebb and responded to the declaration of God's love with an outrageous, insolent retort in their hearts and minds (if not the mouths): "Wherein hast thou loved us?" (Mal. 1:2b). Having forfeited their full prosperity as a consequence of their rebellion, Israel implied via this question that it had "no tokens of God's love" (Jamieson, *et al.* 712).

Israel's terse objection illustrates the genesis of its spiritual degradation and the root of the various sins confronted in this book. Simply stated, the people were insensitive to Jehovah's love (cf. Deu. 6:4-5). Tokens of His love were abundant. For instance, Israel had been restored to the land of its heritage and allowed to rebuild the temple and resume its services. Yet, the people considered only what they had (rightly) lost and ignored what Jehovah had graciously given (Jamieson, *et al.* 712). Surely, "Only willful [sic] blindness, or stubborn refusal to consider the evidence or base ingratitude could produce the charge that God's love had not rested upon Jacob" (Goddard 381).

Jehovah's Refutation

While Israel had no reasonable grounds upon which to question Jehovah's love, His charity should have been all the more obvious when its condition was contrasted with that of its neighbors. The Lord invited the comparison when He reminded the people of the election He made between Jacob and Esau, patriarchs of Israel and Edom, respectively: "Was not Esau Jacob's brother, saith Jehovah: yet I loved Jacob" (Mal. 1:2b). This singular "pivotal illustration" was proof of the divine favor Israel enjoyed (Goddard 380).

While Jacob and Esau were twin brothers, Jehovah chose Jacob and determined that Esau, the first born, would serve him (Gen. 25:23). Because the election of Jacob was made and announced before they were born, it obviously was not impelled by the relative merits of either man. Rather, it was the gratuitous product of God's divine favor. Moses explained in Deuteronomy 10:15, "Only Jehovah had a delight in thy fathers to love them, and he chose their seed after them, even you above all peoples, as at this day." Because of His love, God favored Israel above other peoples, even above the other descendants of Abraham and Isaac (Rom. 9:10-13).

It can be rather startling initially that Jehovah describes His treatment of Jacob and Esau as "love" for the one and "hate" for the other (Mal. 1:2-3). Consequently, it is important to note that the terms are used relatively rather than absolutely here (Wilson 209; Lewis 84; see, e.g., Gen. 29:30-31; Deu. 21:15-16; compare Luke 14:26 and Mat. 10:37). Simply stated, He preferred Jacob and advantaged him above Esau in that He made a covenant with Jacob and did not do so with Esau.

Esau and Jacob here stand for the nations that descended from both men rather than the patriarchs themselves (Dummelow 613), and Jehovah's disposition of favor and regard toward Jacob continued with the respective nations. In fact, it seemingly applies even more so to their descendants. There is no indication of particularized divine hostility toward Esau, also called Edom (see Gen. 25:30, 36:1, 36:8), but his idolatrous descendants certainly drew Jehovah's ire, in part for their antagonism toward the descendants of Jacob (Eze. 35:14-15; Isa. 34:5; Oba. 1-14).

As evidence for His relative favor toward the descendants of Jacob and hatred of the descendants of Esau, Jehovah noted Edom's then-current condition and future prospects. The children of Israel were preoccupied with their own plight to the extent and degree that they seemingly did not appreciate that their circumstances could have been far worse. The Edomites, among other surrounding peoples, had been sacked by foreign powers as well. Per the prophecies of Isaiah and Jeremiah years before (Isa. 34:5ff; Jer. 49:7-22), Jehovah had "made his mountains a desolation, and gave his heritage to the jackals of the wilderness" (Mal. 1:3). In the 5th century, perhaps as Malachi wrote, the Edomites had been or were being expelled from the land of their heritage and replaced by an Arabian tribe, the Nabateans (MacDonald 20). Meanwhile, a faithful remnant in Israel was being preserved to facilitate the Messiah's entrance into the world.

God's love for Israel was evinced by the comparative fate of Edom. The people and their land had indeed been decimated and "beaten down," but they apparently intended to return and rebuild their land (Mal. 1:4a). Despite their expectations and efforts, God would not suffer Esau's descendants to rise again. He warranted to "throw down" that which they rebuilt (Mal. 1:4b). Esau's descendants would be a byword, for men would call them "The border of wickedness, and The people against whom Jehovah hath indignation for ever" (Mal. 1:b).

Edom was a prime example of a people whom Jehovah did not favor. Conversely, He had promised that Israel would return from captivity and build again (Jer. 24:4-7, 30:1-4), and the descendants of Jacob had indeed returned and done so. They had been recipients of the greater privilege for the Edomites had experienced none of these blessings. "To the Jews, the Babylonian invasion was a chastening, but to Edom, it was a judgment" (Wiersbe 479). Ultimately, the people would recognize this and know that Jehovah's power extended beyond their natural borders (Mal. 1:5).

CONCLUSION

While it is easy to wag the finger, as it were, at Israel because of its lack of appreciation for what God was continuingly giving it, we miss a grand opportunity if we stop there. Paul once wrote, "For whatsoever things were written aforetime were written for our learning, that through patience and through comfort of the scriptures we might have hope" (Rom. 15:4). Malachi's first oracle (and the rest of the book, for that matter) perfectly illustrates the verity of this precept. In one sense, it is ancient history. In another, with only a little updating, it could have been written yesterday.

To our own collective shame, God's people are still guilty of not appreciating His love at times. In one respect, we can never fully appreciate it (Eph. 3:18-19), but, like Israel, we are completely without excuse for disregarding it. Christians, too, are recipients of Jehovah's love in a special way, and we occupy this position of favor because of His love rather than our own merit (Rom. 5:8; 1 Jn. 4:10). We should draw every breadth, speak every word and take every step basking in the glow of His divine favor.

In America, in particular, we have far more material sustenance than we could ever need, including food, clothing, vehicles, homes and fine church buildings (cf. 1 Ti. 6:6-10). We have the freedom to worship the Lord as He directs and invite others to do the same. Dismissing these privileges because of what we do not have would be like Israel looking at its rebuilt cities and the restored temple and saying to God, "Wherein hast thou loved us?"

Truly, Christians are loved above all the peoples of the earth. Sometimes, we simply need to look around. Even when we suffer, we are in far better position than others because we have special promises of preservation through tribulations (Rev. 2:10; 1 Th. 5:9). While God still chastens us because He loves us (Heb. 12:6; Rev. 3:19), He will destroy those who do not know and obey Him (2 Th. 1:7-9).

This does not mean the church is insulated from challenges. In a sinful world, our efforts to live godly invite trouble (Mark 4:17; 2 Ti. 3:12). Furthermore, Christians make mistakes like everyone else, and we must endure the consequences of our misdeeds. Yet, none of our troubles can separate us from God's love (Rom. 8:32-39). Even when we forfeit the full measure of our earthly treasure here on Earth, we have abundant tokens of divine love.

WORKS CITED

Arnold, Bill T. and Bryan E. Beyer. *Encountering the Old Testament: A Christian Survey.* 2d ed. Grand Rapids: Baker, 2008

Calvin, John. *Calvin's Commentaries.* Vol. XV. Grand Rapids: Baker, 2003.

Cashdan, Eli. "Malachi: Introduction and Commentary." *The Twelve Prophets.* Ed. A. Cohen. New York: Concino, 1985.

Dummelow, J.R. ed. *A Commentary on the Holy Bible.* New York: MacMillan, 1975.

Goddard, Burton L. "Malachi." *The Biblical Expositor.* Vol. 2. Grand Rapids: Baker, 1994.

Hailey, Homer. *A Commentary on the Minor Prophets.* Grand Rapids: Baker, 1972.

Harrison, R. K. *Introduction to the Old Testament.* Grand Rapids: Eerdmans, 1979.

Henry, Matthew. *Matthew Henry's Commentary on the Whole Bible.* Peabody: Hendrickson, 1997.

Jamieson, Robert, A.R. Fausset, and David Brown. A Commentary on the Old and New Testaments. Vol. 3. Grand Rapids: Eerdmans, 1989.

Josephus. Josephus: The Complete Works. Trans. William Whiston. Nashville: Nelson, 1998.

Lewis, Jack P. The Minor Prophets. Grand Rapids: Baker, 1967.

MacDonald, Burton. "Edom." The International Standard Bible Encyclopedia. Ed. Geoffrey W. Bromily. Grand Rapids: Eerdmans, 1982.

Wiersbe, Warren W. The Bible Exposition Commentary: Prophets. Colorado Springs: Victor, 2002.

Wilson, William. Wilson's Old Testament Word Studies. Peabody: Hendrickson, n.d.

CHAPTER 21

Malachi 1:6–2:9
"The Priests Warned"

Bud Woodall

"It pleases me." Those three words set me back. I knew that it was true, but hearing someone put their motivations into such a matter-of-fact statement was not what I expected. He was a young man, well beyond high school, but not yet 30 years old. He was deeply entangled in the world of sin, though his mother had pled with him and prayed for him to turn from that life. His health was completely ruined. The people in his life of immorality left him feeling cold and unloved – he told me that. "Why do you do it?" I asked, unsure of the answer I would receive. He did not blink or stutter: "It pleases me."

At the end of the day, isn't that the attitude behind sin? How many marriages have ended because one spouse or another did what "pleased them" in a given moment, selfishly filling a desire that would break the heart of their mate? How many souls have been lost because someone walked the path labeled: "It pleases me?" It is not a new problem; in fact, the book of Malachi shows us that God's priests had begun to abide by "it pleases me" rather than "it honors God."

As we open our Bibles to the first chapter of Malachi we find a warning from the God of heaven – for His own priests! The priests in the Mosaic system had myriad responsibilities:

> The chief duty of the priests was to offer or present offerings and sacrifices to God. Sometimes they had to kill the victims (Lev. 16:11) and always to sprinkle and pour out their blood, and burn their carcasses, or part of them, on the altar. They had charge of the altar and the sanctuary… Their duties were not, however, confined to the performance of the rites and ceremonies of that worship; for the law being committed to their custody, they, with the Levites, were entrusted with the religious instruction of the nation: "He shall teach Jacob Thy judgments, and Israel Thy law" (Deut. 33:10); and the people were exhorted to seek knowledge at the priests' lips (Brown 85-86).

Given these duties, imagine God's own priesthood failing to offer sacrifices as they should, failing to instruct the people, and failing to honor God! That is precisely what we find in Malachi 1:6—2:9, as we see God's warning for His priests.

THE INDICTMENT OF A FAILED PRIESTHOOD (MALACHI 1:6-9)

God's prophet wastes no time in bringing vital issues to light. The priests – those men who should have served on behalf of the people – had slipped into a spiritual malaise that had to be addressed. They had dishonored God through paltry sacrifices and needed to be reminded that such so-called sacrifices were in no way acceptable in the sight of heaven. God's indictment of his priests falls into two parts: the indictment itself and the reason for the indictment.

The Indictment – They Despised God (1:6-7).

Imagine the situation that has risen when the God of heaven must ask of any of His people, "Where is My honor... where is My respect?" (v. 6). These words are addressed to the priesthood (note the repetition of "O priests" in Mal. 1:6 and 2:1). What had they done? They "despised" God's name. The word "despised" is a recurring theme in this warning to the priests (1:6 – twice; 1:7; 1:12; and 2:9) and means "to do that which implies contempt; to slight, neglect, make little account of, to treat contemptuously and proudly... it is opposed to the act of esteeming, appreciating, or caring for" (Wilson 119). The priests – men anointed and set apart for serving God – held God in contempt! We would do well to remember another instance in which God's priests did not properly esteem Him:

> Now Nadab and Abihu, the sons of Aaron, took their respective firepans, and after putting fire in them, placed incense on it and offered strange fire before the LORD, which He had not commanded them. And fire came out from the presence of the LORD and consumed them, and they died before the LORD (Lev. 10:1-2).

Like Nadab and Abihu, the priests in the days of Malachi chose to follow convenience and self-will rather than the will of God. While these priests did not face an immediate judgment by fire, God was no less displeased with them. They despised God's name (1:6), the table of the LORD (a reference to the altar, 1:7), and the food of the altar (the sacrifices, 1:12). Therefore they would be "despised and abased before all the people" (2:9).

The Reason for the Indictment – Faulty Sacrifices (1:8-9).

The inspired prophet elaborated on the specific means by which the priests had despised Him: they offered the "blind," the "lame," and the "sick" animals in sacrifice (1:8). The situation was laughable. God asked, "Why not offer it to your governor? Would he be pleased with you?" They knew the answer. Their governor would never allow such a practice! In the book of Leviticus God had specifically stated what He expected in the sacrifices of His people:

> for you to be accepted--it must be a male without defect from the cattle, the sheep, or the goats. 'Whatever has a defect, you shall not offer, for it will not be accepted for you. 'When a man offers a sacrifice of peace offerings to the LORD to fulfill a special vow or for a freewill offering, of the herd or of the flock, it must be perfect to be accepted; there shall be no defect in it (Lev. 22:19-21).

Instead of offering sacrifices that were "without defect," the priesthood had begun to allow the people to bring any flawed animal that they wanted. In reality, God's own people had sunk to the level of bringing leftovers before the God of heaven – and He would not stand for it!

THE ATTITUDE OF A FAILED PRIESTHOOD (MALACHI 1:10-14)

The failure of the priesthood to offer proper sacrifices to God indicates the condition of their hearts. We may recoil in shock at the blunt indictment God laid against the priesthood, but when we take a look at the underlying attitudes behind the actions of the priests, we will understand God's indignation. Consider the three effects of the priests' attitude.

Their Attitude Undermined The Worship of God (1:10-11).

Take a moment to fully appreciate God's view of the sub-standard sacrifices. Their worship had become tainted and futile! "'Oh that there were one among you who would shut the gates, that you might not uselessly kindle *fire on* My altar! I am not pleased with you,' says the LORD of hosts, 'nor will I accept an offering from you'" (1:10). Although the people had not turned after idols again, their attitude was much like the description found in Jeremiah 5:23: "...this people has a stubborn and rebellious heart; They have turned aside and departed." The beautiful elements of Psalm 96: "Sing to the LORD, bless His name... Tell of His glory... great is the LORD and greatly to be praised... Splendor and majesty are before Him... Ascribe to the LORD the glory of His name... Tremble before Him..." were foreign to the priesthood in the days of Malachi. God's expressed desire is that the doors of the temple would simply be shut:

> As long as it was not serving as a meeting place for God and man, why should any perfunctory and self-deceiving rituals go on in it? Not only were the sacrifices ineffective, but the priests and the people were lulled into thinking that their deeds were winning God's approval. So why not shut the temple doors and be done with what was for the priests merely a nuisance? The thought may be applied to present-day churches that have ceased to be places where people worship in spirit and in truth and are merely meeting places and nothing more. It would be better for them to close down than to continue misleading those who think that what they are doing pleases God (Gaebelein 713).

In Mal. 1:11 we find three of the eight times God's "name" is mentioned in this section of the book of Malachi. God tells us that His name "will be great among the nations" two times in this verse. This seems to be an indication of the Messianic kingdom, which was foretold in Isaiah 2:2 (among many other passages): "Now it will come about that in the last days the mountain of the house of the LORD will be established as the chief of the mountains, and will be raised above the hills; And all the nations will stream to it." Indeed, that is precisely what happened, for the gospel of Jesus Christ is "the power of God for salvation to everyone who believes, to the Jew first and also to the Greek" (Rom. 1:16). The Jewish priests of Malachi's day may have despised God's name and invalidated their worship, but one day even the Gentile nations would give God the honor due His name!

Their Attitude Profaned God's Name (1:12).

As surely as God's name would be "great among the nations," the priests addressed by Malachi were "profaning" God's name. While they were the men who should have emphasized the holiness of God to the Jewish people, they were instead guilty of trampling the holy name of Jehovah! By "going through the motions" and offering sacrifices that were blemished, the priests were not maintaining some sense of God's holiness among an ungodly people – they were instead encouraging a low view of God, dragging the God of heaven down to the level of a man who could be cheaply dismissed. They lost sight of the fact that it was not the act of offering something in sacrifice to God, but it was offering the sacrifice that God commanded with a humble and obedient heart (see 1 Sa. 15:21-22; Amo. 5:21).

Their Attitude Cheated God (1:13-14).

Malachi shows the depths to which the priesthood had degenerated. He pointed out that they viewed their service as "tiresome," and they would "sniff" at it with disdain. They were bored with the worship of God! It meant nothing to them. Malachi then described the sacrifice of a blemished animal as the action of a "swindler," a word meaning "...crafty, deceitful, knavish" (Harris 2: 579). They should have remembered God's command to "...do no wrong in judgment, in measurement of weight, or capacity. You shall have just balances, just weights, a just ephah, and a just hin; I am the LORD your God, who brought you out from the land of Egypt" (Lev. 19:35-36). If they were to be honest and upright in their dealings with men, how much more honest should they have been in their sacrifices to God? The prophet records God's return to rhetorical questions with, "Should I receive that from your hand?" (1:13). Through their contempt for God the priests cheated God – not merely of the sacrifices, but of the devotion and honor that should have been behind the sacrifices.

THE REBUKE OF A FAILED PRIESTHOOD (MALACHI 2:1-9)

As we turn to the second chapter of Malachi we find a return to the phrase, "O priests," (found in 1:6) reminding us that our context has not changed. God is still addressing those priests who had allowed the sacrifices to be cheapened. Here we find the warning for those priests. What they had done was no small matter, and they would face consequences if they refused to turn back to God.

God Wanted Them to Hear His Words (2:1-5).

With no uncertain terms God called the priests to action: "If you do not listen, and if you do not take it to heart to give honor to my name... then I will send the curse upon you and I will curse your blessings" (2:2). They had abdicated their responsibility to the people and to God with their inferior sacrifices; if they failed to heed God's warning, He would judge them – harshly. Verse three indicates the righteous anger of Jehovah toward His priests, as He told them, "I will spread refuse on your faces, the refuse of your feasts; and you will be taken away with it."

We may at first see only a disgusting image, but it the message actually goes far deeper. Homer Hailey's comments regarding this refuse are telling:

> According to the law the dung of sacrifices was to be burned "without the camp" (Exod. 29:14; Lev. 4:11-12; 16:27), but Jehovah says He will spread it on the faces of the priests, "even the dung of your feasts." The Lord refuses to recognize the feasts as His, but rather, they are "your feasts." To speak of spreading dung on the faces of the priests is strong language, indeed! It indicates an ignominious humiliation in which the priests are treated as dung, making them unfit for the service of the Lord, and fit only to be carried away without the camp from His presence. The priests will be swept away as dung (412).

As severe and harsh as God's language is, He is not yet finished. Malachi brings them Jehovah's desire in all of this: "…that My covenant may continue with Levi" (2:4). Levi (the priestly tribe) had received God's covenant and should have held Jehovah in reverence because of it. God wanted His priesthood to listen to Him and turn back to that reverence.

God Wanted Them To Instruct His People (2:6-9).

Built into God's warning to the priesthood was a reminder of another part of their duties. While the priests were responsible for offering the sacrifices for the people, they also should have maintained an instructional role among the people of God. That function of the priesthood was explicitly laid out when Nadab and Abihu profaned God's commands by offering strange fire before Jehovah. Jehovah told Aaron (the high priest) that the priesthood was to "…make a distinction between the holy and the profane, and between the unclean and the clean, and so as to teach the sons of Israel all the statutes which the LORD has spoken to them through Moses" (Lev. 10:10-11). Malachi reminds the priests of this role with the words, "For the lips of a priest should preserve knowledge, and men should seek instruction from his mouth; for he is the messenger of the LORD of hosts" (2:7). The result is found in verse 9. The priests had despised His name (1:6), so God made the priests despised and abased before the people. Instead of holding the honor and respect of the people, the priests were contemptible and brought low in the eyes of the populace. Malachi 2:5-6 combine to show us what God expected of His priests: a display of life and peace, reverence for Jehovah, true instruction before the people, and a life of uprightness. In their failure, the priests were cursed and despised by God; "… indeed, I have cursed them *already*, because you are not taking *it* to heart" (2:2).

A MESSAGE FOR ALL CHRISTIANS

Although this message through the prophet Malachi (1:6—2:9) was penned centuries before Christ and aimed at a Jewish priesthood, it provides powerful instruction (Rom. 15:4) for Christians today. We are not the people of Judah who have come out of captivity, nor are we the Levitical priesthood. That old law, with its priesthood, has been done away (Rom. 7:1-4; see also Heb. 7:11ff), and "… we have a great high priest who has passed through the heavens, Jesus the Son of God…" (Heb. 4:14). Therefore the apostle Peter wrote to Christians, "But you are a chosen race, a royal priesthood, a holy nation, a people for God's own possession, so that you may proclaim the excellencies of Him who has called you out of darkness into His marvelous light" (1 Pe. 2:9). Christians are God's priests today! For this reason, as we examine Malachi 1:6—2:9, let us note the following applications for God's priesthood today.

Let Us Displace The Idol of Self.

The priests of Malachi's day presented the "blind… the lame and sick" for their offerings (1:8), and then thought they could "entreat God's favor, that He may be gracious…" (1:9). The response in the second half of verse 9 is withering: "With such an offering on your part, will He receive any of you kindly?" Those priests were focused on themselves and what they could get from God, rather than on God, and what they should give to Him. How can we go about displacing the idol of self?

Deny yourself. Jesus said, "If anyone wishes to come after Me, he must deny himself, and take up his cross and follow Me. For whoever wishes to save his life will lose it; but whoever loses his life for My sake will find it" (Mat. 16:24-25). We must renounce ourselves and live for Jesus Christ (Gal. 2:20)! If we wish to see an example of self-denial, look to Moses as pictured in Hebrews 11, for he "…refused to be called the son of Pharaoh's daughter, choosing rather to endure ill-treatment with the people of God than to enjoy the passing pleasures of sin" (Heb. 11:24-25). Deny yourself.

Control yourself. Too many have fallen into the "I feel it, so I should do it" mode of thinking, ignoring the words of Solomon who proclaims: "Like a city that is broken into and without walls is a man who has no control over his spirit" (Pro.

25:28). Closely akin to that error is, "I feel it, so I should say it!" Again, the book of Proverbs corrects the behavior, telling us that "He who guards his mouth and his tongue, guards his soul from troubles" (Pro. 21:23; we would be wise to apply this same teaching to our postings on social media, texts, and other electronic communication as well). May we never forget what our lives should look like: "But the fruit of the Spirit is love, joy, peace, patience, kindness, goodness, faithfulness, gentleness, self-control; against such things there is no law" (Gal. 5:22-23; see also 2 Pe. 1:5-8). The word for "self-control" in this passage is egkrateia, a word identified by Thayer as "the virtue of one who masters his desires and passions, especially his sensual appetites" (Grimm and Wilke 167). Make every effort to exercise self-control in your life.

Give yourself If we will truly displace the idol of self in our lives, there is no substitute for having fully submitted ourselves to our Lord as "a living sacrifice" (Rom. 12:1). Consider the inspired commendation of the Christians in Macedonia regarding their giving:

> Now, brethren, we wish to make known to you the grace of God which has been given in the churches of Macedonia, that in a great ordeal of affliction their abundance of joy and their deep poverty overflowed in the wealth of their liberality. For I testify that according to their ability, and beyond their ability, they gave of their own accord, begging us with much urging for the favor of participation in the support of the saints, and this, not as we had expected, but they first gave themselves to the Lord and to us by the will of God (2 Co. 8:1-5).

These Christians were in deep poverty, yet they had given "beyond their ability" to aid their brethren. The reason for this is found in verse 5: "They first gave themselves to the Lord and to us by the will of God." That is the cure for the idol of self! We must come to see who we are in the sight of God and submit to God because "It is He who has made us, and not we ourselves" (Psa. 100:3). Give yourself to God, and the idol of self cannot survive!

Let us be careful of what we teach.

Among those charges that God made against His priests in Malachi is one regarding their teaching: "For the lips of a priest should preserve knowledge, and men should seek instruction from his mouth; for he is the messenger of the LORD of hosts. But as for you, you have turned aside from the way; you have caused many to stumble by the instruction; you have corrupted the covenant of Levi" (Mal. 2:7-8). In a day in which we are told that "doctrine" should be avoided in our teaching and preaching because it is boring and ineffective, every child of God must stand even more firmly for the proper teaching of the New Testament. In 1 Timothy 4:16 Paul wrote, "Pay close attention to yourself and to your teaching; persevere in these things, for as you do this you will ensure salvation both for yourself and for those who hear you." The word for "teaching" in this passage is translated "doctrine" in the New King James Version. An aversion to doctrine is an aversion to teaching – and such an attitude is foreign to the will of God (see Tit. 1:8-9 for the importance of elders "holding fast the faithful word" so they can meet false teaching; also, Heb. 5:12-14 for the need to grow and train our senses to discern good and evil).

Regarding the need for knowledge – to be "transformed by the renewing of your mind" (Rom. 12:2) – one writer has stated:

> Anyone who has struggled with bad habits knows that you don't become transformed by just willing the old habits to go away. This is why preaching that centers too much on exhortation without instruction is ineffective. According to Paul, the key to change is the formation of a new perspective, the development of fresh insights about our lives and the world around us, the gathering of the knowledge and skill required to know what to do and how to do it. And this is where the mind comes in. Truth, knowledge, and study are powerful factors in the transformation of the self and the control of the body and its habits for a healthy life in the kingdom of God (Moreland 78).

It is past time for Christians to stop basing their appreciation for a sermon or Bible class on such shallow matters as whether the lesson made them "feel good," the brevity of the preaching/teaching, the oratory skills of the teacher, whether or not the lesson came from a favorite passage, or even that the lesson covered a favorite topic! Instead, let us ask, "Was this lesson true to the teaching of the Scriptures and properly applied to the lives of Christians today?" Preachers and Bible class teachers, we would do well to use that same criteria in preparing Bible classes and sermons. Our heavenly Father is intensely interested in the content of our teaching!

Let us give God His proper place.

This is the matter at the heart of Malachi 1:6—2:9 and the reason for God's warning to the priests. They had not shown honor and respect to God (1:6). They despised His name (1:6). They offered defiled sacrifices that were blind, lame, and sick (1:7-8). They profaned His name (1:12). They were weary of worship offered to God (1:13). They had failed to instruct the people in God's Word (2:8). Notice that all of these failures revolve around a single concept – they had removed Jehovah from the place that is rightfully His, and placed other matters ahead of serving the God of heaven.

Let every Christian know the truth and proclaim it with all our ability: God is incomparably great, perfect in all His nature, and worthy of every ounce of devotion we have! The glory that we give to God is "due" Him (Psa. 29:1-2) because He is "majestic in holiness, awesome in praises, working wonders" (Exo. 15:11). Every Christian should meditate on the words of Psalm 33:8, "Let all the earth fear the LORD; Let all the inhabitants of the world stand in awe of Him." We stand in awe of Him for a reason! Let the words of the 24 elders around the throne of God tell us why we stand in awe: "Worthy are You, our Lord and our God, to receive glory and honor and power; for You created all things, and because of Your will they existed, and were created" (Rev. 4:11). By your words every day, give God the place of honor that He deserves!

As our words give honor to God, let us be sure that the life we lead does the same. "Let your light shine before men in such a way that they may see your good works, and glorify your Father who is in heaven" (Mat. 5:16). As the apostle Paul instructed Christians to "flee immorality," he provided the reason: "do you not know that your body is a temple of the Holy Spirit who is in you, whom you have from God, and that you are not your own? For you have been bought with a price: therefore glorify God in your body" (1 Co. 6:18-20).

May we never be guilty of neglecting to give God the honor and reverence that belong to Him! Learn from the failure of the priests in Malachi's day, and "Set your mind on the things above, not on the things that are on earth" (Col. 3:2). If we will do this, the idol of self will not trouble us because we will be filled with reverence for the God of heaven, and there will be no room for an idol. Likewise, when we give God the honor that is due Him, we will teach His Word carefully and lovingly to a lost and dying world and to our brothers and sisters in Christ – because God is great, and we want everyone to know His majesty and love. Be one of His people, a Christian (see Acts 26:28-29), and be faithful to Him (1 Jn. 2:4-5). Give God His proper place in your life!

WORKS CITED

Brown, William. *The Tabernacle: Its Priests and Its Services.* Updated ed. Peabody, Mass.: Hendrickson, 1996. Print.

Gaebelein, Frank E. *The Expositor's Bible Commentary: Daniel and the Minor Prophets with the New International Version of the Holy.* Grand Rapids: Zondervan Pub. House, 1992. Print.

Grimm, Carl Ludwig Wilibald, and Christian Gottlob Wilke. *The New Thayer's Greek-English Lexicon of the New Testament: Being Grimm's Wilke's Clavis Novi Testamenti.* Peabody, Mass.: Hendrickson, 1981. Print.

Hailey, Homer. *A Commentary on the Minor Prophets.* Religious Supply, Inc. 1993. Print.

Harris, R. Laird. *Theological Wordbook of the Old Testament.* Vol. 2. Chicago: Moody, 1980. Print.

Moreland, James Porter. *Love Your God with All Your Mind: The Role of Reason in the Life of the Soul.* 2nd ed. Coloradp Springs, CO: NavPress, 2012. Print.

Wilson, William. *Wilson's Old Testament Word Studies.* McLean, Va.: MacDonald Pub. Print.

CHAPTER 22

Malachi 2:10–4:6
"The People Warned"

Will Hanstein

The book of Malachi was written during a time of unrighteousness and spiritual disillusionment for Israel. Likely written around 432 BC, the temple in Jerusalem had been rebuilt and the walls around the city had been restored by Nehemiah. Nevertheless, the people had slipped into old sinful habits. The priests themselves, who should have led the people to obedience to God, had instead led them into unrighteousness by neglecting and perverting their own duties.

The people had developed a mindset of ritualism and cynicism. Although God commanded righteousness and obedience, they lived as a law unto themselves. Israel maintained an attitude that questioned the worth of obedience to God. They uttered philosophical affirmations like, "Everyone who does evil is good in the sight of the Lord..." (Mal. 2:17). They asked questions like, "...What is the profit of our keeping his charge or of walking as in mourning before the Lord of hosts?" (Mal. 3:14). From their point of view, since evil men were not punished but instead blessed, there was no reason to obey the Lord's commandments. Godly men lived worse lives and evil men lived better ones.

Thus, Malachi wrote to shake Israel from their sinful and cynical mindset. After rebuking the priests specifically in Malachi 1:1-2:9, he turns to the nation as whole with a call to repent. God, through Malachi, warns the people about four matters in 2:10-4:6: (1) staying faithful to their spouses (2) living faithful lives (3) faithful giving to God (4) the coming faithful judgment of God. These words of Malachi will be the last words from God for four hundred years.

THE PEOPLE WARNED ABOUT UNFAITHFUL MARRIAGES (2:10-16).

First, Malachi warns the people about infidelity to their marriage vows. The people to whom Malachi wrote had become cynical toward marriage and their wives. God commanded Israel, "You shall not intermarry with them, giving your daughters to their sons or taking their daughters for your sons" (Deu. 7:3). Yet, Malachi rebukes the people, "For Judah has profaned the sanctuary of the Lord, which he loves, and has married the daughter of a foreign God" (Mal. 2:11). Their foreign wives had led the men of Israel into worshipping foreign gods, which Moses also predicted would happen (Deu 7:4).

Additionally, many in Israel abandoned their Israelite wives to do this (Mal. 2:13-16). Many Israelite men, after tiring of their Israelite wives, would divorce them and marry a Gentile woman who had greater appeal. This abominable treatment of their Israelite wives coupled with marrying ungodly, Gentile wives had another consequence-- unfaithful children. "Did he not make them one, with a portion of the Spirit in their union? And what was the one God seeking? Godly offspring. So guard yourselves in your spirit, and let none of you be faithless to the wife of your youth" (Mal 2:15). Their utter disregard for God's laws on marriage had brought about an ungodly influence in the lives of their children. Instead of teaching their children how to be godly Israelites, these ungodly Gentile women taught their children how to be ungodly pagans.

Yet, from the cynical point of view of Israel, why not do this? Since God not only refuses to punish the wicked, but even rewards them, why not do what makes a man feel good? Why should a man care about anyone other than himself, his wife and children included? Since the godly have a poorer lot in life than the wicked, it only makes sense for a person to do all he can to satisfy his desires.

Malachi points out two consequences of their actions. First, God rejected the Israelites, as His people. "Have we not all one Father? Has not one God created us? Why then are we faithless to one another, profaning the covenant of our fathers?" (Mal. 2:10) Members of a family have particular expectations regarding how they are to be treated by other family members. Family should always treat other members of the family with respect and dignity, never with contempt and abuse. Malachi, in much the same way, tells people that they are part of the same family, with the same Father and creator, who made the same covenant of behavior with the ancestors of this family. Malachi essentially said, "Members of our family do not treat each other like this." Their actions meant they had given up their heritage as Israelites and been rejected as children of God. "May the Lord cut off from the tents of Jacob any descendant of the of the man who does this, who brings an offering to the Lord of hosts" (Mal. 2:12).

Secondly, God was rejecting their worship. "And this second thing you do. You cover the Lord's altar with tears, with weeping and groaning because he no longer regards the offering or accepts it with favor from your hand" (Mal. 2:13). Incredibly, the Israelites had no idea why God would reject their worship (Mal. 2:14). They foolishly believed that going through the motions of temple worship was all that was necessary to satisfy God, but Malachi reminded them that God cared about their obedience. God demanded they worship him alone and obey his laws concerning marriage. "You shall not go after other gods, the gods of the peoples who are around you (Deu. 6:14). A man cannot worship something other than God and still be pleasing to God, nor can he violate God laws on marriage and expect God to accept his worship.

Malachi's admonition to Israel still rings true today. Single Christian men and women should make godliness the greatest priority in the selection of a mate. Yet, all too often, worldly criteria and physical desire win the day. A husband or a wife is chosen based mainly on physical appearance, income level, reputation in the community, etc. While the New Testament does not condemn a Christian marrying a non-Christian, a tremendous lesson can be learned from observing the outcome of Israelites marrying pagans in the Old Testament. It is much easier for a non-Christian to pull a Christian "down" to their spiritual level than it is for a Christian to pull a non-Christian "up" to their level. When Israelite men married pagan women, it was the idolatrous wife that pulled her husband away from God and into idolatry. Similarly, it is far more likely a Christian will be pulled into unfaithfulness by their non-Christian spouse than they will pull their non-Christian spouse into conformity with God. This says nothing of the ungodly influence upon their children.

Additionally, married Christians should make fidelity to their marriage vows of utmost priority. Yet, many married Christians cast their spouses aside when they tire of them or find someone that appeals to them more. Adopting rationalizations like, "God just wants me to be happy," Christian men are "faithless to the wife of (their) youth" (Mal 2:15). Yet, just like God rejected Israel for treating their wives this way, God will reject Christian men and women who do the same. Also, Christian men and women who do this impact their children in a horrible way. Just like divorce hindered Israelite children from faithfulness to God, Christians who divorce impact their children in a horrible way. Children in this situation are subjected to the ungodly influence of their Christian parent's actions, as well as the ungodly influence of that parent's new mate. While the world may act this way, may it never be said of the Lord's people! Single Christians should choose a spouse based on the godliness of that person. Married Christians should always hold their spouse in honor and treat them accordingly.

THE PEOPLE WARNED ABOUT UNFAITHFUL LIVES (2:17-3:5).

Secondly, Malachi warns the people about living unfaithful lives. Once again, cynicism and unrighteous living were the hallmarks of the day. The Jews cynically asked why they should serve God when the godly are humbled and the evil prosper. Malachi admonishes the Jews when he wrote, "You have wearied the Lord with your words..." (Mal. 2:17). The Jews again have no clue why God would be tired of what they are saying. Malachi's reply is that they weary the Lord with their cynicism. "...By saying, 'Everyone who does evil is good in the sight of the Lord, and he delights in them.' Or by asking, 'Where is the God of justice?'" (Mal. 2:17). Incredibly, not only did the Jews believe that evil men prospered and good men suffered, they believed God delighted in rewarding evil men and in punishing righteousness! Thus, the Israelites lived however they wanted to live because righteousness and obedience did not matter.

God's response to these false statements is that he will expose them as lies. He tells them that that He is coming to make things right. "Behold, I send my messenger, and he will prepare the way before me. And the Lord whom you seek will suddenly come to his temple; and the messenger of the covenant in whom you delight, behold, he is coming, says the Lord of hosts" (Mal. 3:1). The messenger spoken of is John the Immerser, who would prepare the way of the Lord about 400 years after the writing of Malachi (Mat. 11:10; Mark 1:2; Lk. 7:27). As Malachi mentions, this messenger, John the Baptist, would call the Levites to repentance. John would convict the Levites of failing in their duty as leaders of God's people (Mal. 3:2-4). While not all of the Levites were convicted of their sin and thus repented, many in John's time were. "But when he saw many of the Pharisees and Sadducees coming to his baptism, he said to them, "You brood of vipers! Who warned you to flee from the wrath to come? Bear fruit in keeping with repentance" (Matt. 3:7-8). As Malachi stated, John would act like a refiner's fire and fuller's soap (Mal. 3:2-3). He would separate the Levites who would repent from the Levites that refused.

After this occurs, the Lord himself "...will draw near to you for judgment. I will be swift against the sorcerers, against the adulterers, against those who swear falsely, against those who oppress the hired worker in his wages, the widow and the fatherless, against those who thrust aside the sojourner, and do not fear me, says the Lord of hosts" (Mal. 3:5). Contrary to the thinking of Malachi's Israel, the day would come when the Lord would judge everyone and convict them of their sin. Malachi lists five classes of people that would be exposed to the judgment of God in this verse. Those in Israel who were guilty of these sins would need to repent while they still had time. Thus, Malachi admonishes them to live faithful lives that are in obedience to God's laws.

This is a wonderful passage foretelling of the beginning of the Messianic kingdom. It tells of John the Immerser preparing the way for the ministry of Jesus. It also tells how the teachings of Jesus will convict men of sin and call them to obedience to God. The Jews of Malachi's day believed that evil prospered and God didn't care about justice. Thus, they could live however they wanted. Even though Jesus would not come for over 400 years, Malachi reminds the people that God does care about justice and the day will come when every sinner will meet it.

Current circumstances can lead the Christian to doubt God's justice. When non-Christians and even evil people prosper so much, Christians can be tempted to believe that, "Everyone who does evil is good in the sight of the Lord" (Mal. 2:17). A "what's the use in standing for godliness" attitude may result, which would then lead to the Christian giving up on living a godly lifestyle altogether. When the Christian sees that he is wandering down this path, he must remember the words of Malachi. The day will come when the Lord's justice will be executed. Lest we wander into sin because of our cynicism, let us remember that the Lord will draw near to *us* for judgment one day (Mal. 3:5).

THE PEOPLE WARNED ABOUT UNFAITHFUL GIVING (3:6-12).

Malachi also warns the people about faithless giving. He begins by reminding them that God could have judged them already, but He has withheld that judgment from them for now. The reason is a very simple one. "For I the Lord do not change; therefore you, O children of Jacob are not consumed" (Mal. 3:6). God is the same compassionate God he has always been since the creation of the world and is giving them time to "…return to me…" (Mal. 3:7). While the Jews have repeatedly disobeyed God's commandments since the time of Moses, God will return to blessing them if they will return to Him.

However, the Jews give a curious response to God's plea. They ask how they can return to God (Mal. 3:7). God sternly answers them, saying, "Stop robbing me" (Mal. 3:8). While they had no understanding of the import of their actions, their refusal to tithe of their harvest in effect robbed God. Moses told Israel, "Every tithe of the land, whether of the seed of the land or of the fruit of the trees, is the Lord's; it is holy to the Lord" (Lev. 27:30). Since tithes already belonged to God, those who refused to pay them robbed God of what He rightfully owned. It seems the cynical mindset of the Jewish people had reached the point where they felt it was of no benefit to tithe because it brought no blessings and left less in their pocket.

The consequence of this was dire. "You are cursed with a curse, for you are robbing me, the whole nation of you" (Mal. 3:9). God had cursed the land so that it would not bear the produce needed to sustain the people. Yet, there is a way to rectify this situation. God tells them that the way to return is to simply pay their tithe, or what they owe Him. If they give to God first, He will then bless them beyond what they can imagine. He says, "...I...will open the windows of heaven for you and pour down for you a blessing until there is no more need" (Mal. 3:10). God will make their soil fertile again and make sure they have plenty to eat, to the point where the nations around them will speak of the great prosperity of Israel (Mal. 3:12).

How easy it is for modern Christians to develop the same mindset as the people of Malachi's day. Christians today may overlook the blessings God has given them and wonder about the efficacy of giving to God. While we are no longer commanded to tithe, God does command us to give as we have been prospered on the first day of every week (1 Co. 16:1-4, et al). While the Christian may not realize it, by neglecting his giving or by giving less than he has prospered, he restricts the amount of blessings he will receive from God. It may appear that there is more money in his pocket if he restrains his giving, but he is missing the tremendous blessings that God gives to those who give to him first (Mal. 3:10-12). It is impossible to "out-give" God. God will always give more to us than we can ever give to Him and will reward our generosity with even greater generosity.

THE PEOPLE WARNED ABOUT UNFAITHFUL JUDGMENT (3:13-4:6).

Finally, the people are warned about unfaithful judgment. As has been mentioned earlier, the cynical attitude of the Jews in Malachi's day prompted them to speak hard words against God (Mal. 3:13-15). They made rash statements claiming it was useless to serve God and repent of sin. Evildoers prospered and God was incapable of exercising justice against their misdeeds.

Upon hearing these arrogant statements from many of their countrymen, some of the people spoke with one another and committed themselves to repentance and righteousness (Mal. 3:16). God responds to them first and writes their names in a book so He would remember whom they were when he comes in judgment (Mal. 3:16). He promises to make them his treasured possession and spare them from the judgment of the wicked (3:17-18).

Next, God responds to the unrighteous and warns them that His judgment is faithful. While He may not mete out His judgment according to their timeframe, when the time is right God will faithfully, or assuredly, render judgment on everyone, both the righteous and unrighteous. "For behold, the day is coming, burning like an oven, when all the arrogant and all evildoers will be stubble. The day that is coming shall set them ablaze, says the Lord of hosts, so that it will leave them neither root nor branch" (Mal. 4.1). When God decides the time is right, His judgment will be swift and terrible. Yet, the righteous will be spared and be victorious over all those who mistreated them. "And you shall tread down the wicked, for they will be ashes under the soles of your feet, on the day when I act, says the Lord of hosts" (Mal. 4:3).

Christians, once again, are not much different than the Jews of Malachi's day. Just like them, Christians can fall into a belief that it is useless to serve God and that God is powerless to bring judgment on the wicked. Through human eyes, it may appear that this is the case. News stories recount how some rich and powerful in this country flaunt the law and are not punished. Evolution is the order of the day and creationism is ridiculed and punished. Rape, murder, abortion, theft, homosexuality, drug abuse, etc. run rampant and those who practice such are excused or even praised in some cases. Leaders are elected who are not penitent about their sinful deeds but even celebrate them. The Christian may ask, "Where is God's justice?" As a result, it may seem more advantageous to join them, since it seems they cannot be beaten.

The Christian must never forget Malachi's warning. While it may not appear so in a given moment, the time will come when God will judge all those who have ever lived on this earth (2 Co. 5:10). His coming in judgment is faithful, or certain. Those who obey God and persevere against unrighteousness will be rewarded with an eternal home in Heaven. Those who succumb to the mindset that serving God is useless and that God cannot judge anyone will be assigned an eternal place in hell. Everyone will believe in God's faithful judgment at some point. The question is, "Will they believe while they still have time to be saved?"

CONCLUSION

Malachi closes, not only his book, but the entire Old Testament, by giving two admonitions. First, remember to obey God's law (Mal. 4:4). The nation of Israel had refused to obey it. Second, He is sending a prophet to help the people remember and repent (Mal. 4:5). While Malachi refers to him as Elijah, this simply means he will be a prophet like Elijah, calling the people to return to God. The New Testament says that this prophet like Elijah was John the immerser, as mentioned earlier (Mat. 11:14, Mark. 9:11-14; Luke. 1:17). Only by heeding God's law and with the help of this prophet would they avoid the terrible judgment God was bringing upon them (Mal. 4:6).

The people of Malachi's day may have thought this was to occur soon. However, God would give the Jewish people over 400 years to reflect and meditate on these two admonitions. He gave them over 400 years to return to Him and be saved. God is giving us opportunity right now to do the same. God has given us almost 2,000 years since John, the prophet like Elijah, and Jesus Christ, God's Son, preached this message of judgment to the Jews. Modern man has had the message of judgment from Jesus' apostles for the same length of time. We must heed God's warning. God will assuredly come in judgment. We must heed His law if we are to triumph over unrighteousness.

S ECTION **3**

Principles From The Prophets

CHAPTER 23

"The Lord Is Good"
(Nahum 1:7)

Gary Hampton

Those who doubt, or deny, God's existence often have focused their attention on examples of God's judgment as it was carried out on people in the Bible. They cannot see how a good God could punish a part of His creation. Nahum gives us the solution to the seeming dilemma.

NAHUM 1:7

Nahum may have been written around 630 B.C. God, in His goodness, had spared the Assyrians for approximately 150 years after Jonah had delivered the message, "Yet forty days, and Nineveh shall be overthrown" (Jon. 3:4). [Scripture references are from the NKJV unless otherwise noted]. It was appropriate for Nahum to write, "The Lord is good, a stronghold in the day of trouble; and He knows those who trust in Him" (1:7). "God's slowness to anger had been demonstrated to the Assyrians when He changed His mind about destroying Nineveh in the days of Jonah" (Roper 247). However, God's "long-suffering is not to be interpreted as indifference or as lack of power" (Lewis 57).

Israel experienced the goodness of God through the deliverance from Egyptian bondage and the giving of His word (Neh. 9:13, 20). "And they took strong cities and a rich land, and possessed houses full of all goods, Cisterns already dug, vineyards, olive groves, and fruit trees in abundance, so they ate and were filled and grew fat, and delighted themselves in Your great goodness" (Neh. 9:25). There is a sense in which all of this was accomplished because Abraham, their father, trusted God and faithfully followed him (Gen. 15:13-21).

It is important to note that Nahum indicated that God's protection is promised to those who He knows trust in Him. David's words of praise following the defeat of the four Philistine giants remind us of Nahum's words. "The Lord is my rock and my fortress and my deliverer; the God of my strength, in whom I will trust;

my shield and the horn of my salvation, my stronghold and my refuge; my Savior, You save me from violence" (2 Sa. 22:2-3).

GOD DEALS WITH EVIL

"God's goodness does not mean inactivity in the face of evil. On the contrary, his goodness leads him to deal with it for the sake of his seekers. The 'overwhelming flood'" could be understood as being a part of either verse 7 or verse 8, "or both, so that the flood becomes both his action of protection and of making an end of Nineveh" (Matheny). "Even in the manifestation of His wrath God proves His goodness; for the judgment, by exterminating the wicked, brings deliverance to the righteous who trust in the Lord, out of the affliction prepared for them by the wickedness of the world" (Keil 11).

There are several instances in scripture where God powerfully punishes his enemies and uses that punishment to protect his own people. "The very action that brings destruction to some means salvation for others. Goodness and severity, then, are not opposite poles of God, but manifestations of his unity....God is good, and his goodness means severity toward evil" (Matheny).

The best known instance of this is the flood. Peter wrote, "when once the Divine longsuffering waited in the days of Noah, while the ark was being prepared, in which a few, that is, eight souls, were saved through water" (1 Pe. 3:20). God used the water of the flood to float the ark, saving Noah and his family. Peter's second epistle contains a further important observation. God "did not spare the ancient world, but saved Noah, one of eight people, a preacher of righteousness, bringing in the flood on the world of the ungodly" (2 Pe. 2:5).

GOD IS GOOD

Jesus' encounter with a ruler gave Him an opportunity to underscore the fact that He is God. He achieved this by calling attention to a unique characteristic of deity. "Now a certain ruler asked Him, saying, 'Good Teacher, what shall I do to inherit eternal life?' So Jesus said to him, 'Why do you call Me good? No one is good but One, that is, God'" (Luke 18:18-19; Mat. 19:16-22; Mark 10:17-22). "Jesus informs him that the good is not something esoteric but is God himself and his commandments" (Lewis Mat. 69). The young man "had addressed Jesus by a title which belongs only to God, and he had asked Jesus the question concerning that of which God alone was fitted to speak" (McGarvey 544). David's song of thanksgiving contains the words, "Oh, give thanks to the Lord, for He is good! For His mercy endures forever" (1 Ch. 16:34). A song attributed to him says, "Good and upright is the Lord; Therefore He teaches sinners in the way" (Psa. 25:8). He further sang, "Oh, taste and see that the Lord is good; Blessed is the man who trusts in Him!" (Psa. 34:8). The shepherd king was also said to have written, "For You, Lord, are good, and ready to forgive, and abundant in mercy to all those who call upon You" (Psa. 86:5).

The Lord challenged the young ruler to realize that he had "unwittingly confessed the divinity of Jesus, and thus startled him into a consideration of the marvelous fact which his own mouth had stated. This is done because the young man would need to believe in the divinity of Jesus to endure the test to which he was about to be subjected" (Ibid). In other words, "If the young man applied the adjective 'good' to the Teacher, was he willing to take the expression to its limit and acknowledge the 'good teacher' as divine—with total submission to him?" (Jackson 45).

GOD KNOWS THOSE WHO TRUST HIM

There is substantial evidence that God "knows those who trust in Him." The Psalmist said, "For the Lord knows the way of the righteous" (1:6a). "The Lord knows the days of the upright, and their inheritance shall be forever" (37:18). Noah lived in an age when "the Lord saw that the wickedness of man was great in the earth, and that every intent of the thoughts of his heart was only evil continually.... But Noah found grace in the eyes of the Lord" (Gen. 6:5, 8). God saved Noah and his family (Heb. 11:7).

Abraham heard the Lord say, "Because the outcry against Sodom and Gomorrah is great, and because their sin is very grave, I will go down now and see whether they have done altogether according to the outcry against it that has come to Me; and if not, I will know" (Gen. 18:20-21). Abraham pleaded with God to spare the cities if ten righteous men could be found, but the depravity overwhelmed even that small number. Yet, God "delivered righteous Lot, who was oppressed by the filthy conduct of the wicked (for that righteous man, dwelling among them, tormented his righteous soul from day to day by seeing and hearing their lawless deeds)" (2 Pe. 2:7-8).

Rahab placed her trust in the God of Israel whom she recognized was "in heaven above and on earth beneath." She asked the spies to show her kindness just as she had shown them kindness. The Lord who gave Israel the land protected Rahab and her family (Jos. 2:8-21; 6:17, 22-23; Heb. 11:31). Hezekiah, when threatened by Sennacherib king of Assyria, placed his complete trust in God and was delivered (2 Ki. 19). The prophet Hosea reported that God's people would live in exile without a king. "Afterward the children of Israel shall return and seek the Lord their God and David their king. They shall fear the Lord and His goodness in the latter days" (3:4-5). The affliction the Lord brought upon his people would "drive them to seek the Lord and His goodness which is inseparable from Himself (Keil 73). Jeremiah delivered similar words from the Lord, saying, "Therefore they shall come and sing in the height of Zion, Streaming to the goodness of the Lord—For wheat and new wine and oil, For the young of the flock and the herd; Their souls shall be like a well-watered garden, And they shall sorrow no more at all" (31:12).

GOD'S GOODNESS PROMOTES A PENITENT SPIRIT

"A perpetual penitent spirit is the product of daily reflection upon the goodness of God" (Chesser 35). David, a man after God's own heart (1 Sa. 13:14; Acts 13:22), was moved by such reflection. "Have mercy upon me, O God, According to Your lovingkindness; According to the multitude of Your tender mercies, Blot out my transgressions. Wash me thoroughly from my iniquity, And cleanse me from my sin" (Psa. 51:1-2).

"Discerning the badness of sin is dependent upon beholding the goodness of God" (ibid., 36). Paul asked the saints at Rome, "Or do you despise the riches of His goodness, forbearance, and long-suffering, not knowing that the goodness of God leads you to repentance?" (Rom. 2:4). "Pondering God's goodness is the fuel upon which penitence runs. It flows through the veins of the heart, keeping it alive, tender, humble, and contrite" (Ibid).

"Meditating upon the goodness of God short-circuits sin. It derails its progress. It disrupts its onward flow. It joins the intent of God's law through Moses, enabling man to discern the exceeding sinful nature of sin" (Ibid). Paul explained it from his own experience. "Has then what is good become death to me? Certainly not! But sin, that it might appear sin, was producing death in me through what is good, so that sin through the commandment might become exceedingly sinful" (Rom. 7:13).

GOD'S GOODNESS IS SEEN IN HIS PROVIDENTIAL CARE

The Ruler of creation is worthy of our praise. "For the word of the Lord is right, And all His work is done in truth. He loves righteousness and justice; the earth is full of the goodness of the Lord" (Psa. 33:4-5). He has made ample provision for those who walk according to his will. "Bless the Lord, O my soul; and all that is within me, bless His holy name! Bless the Lord, O my soul, And forget not all His benefits" (Psa. 103:1-2). Israel experienced his provision in wonderful ways. Isaiah said, "I will mention the lovingkindnesses of the Lord And the praises of the Lord, according to all that the Lord has bestowed on us, and the great goodness toward the house of Israel, which He has bestowed on them according to His mercies, according to the multitude of His loving kindnesses" (63:7).

"When perilous times come and trouble like a mighty river overflows, Jehovah is an impregnable stronghold to all who flee to Him....In love and protective care, He knows fully those that take refuge in Him. His power is as great to protect as it is to destroy" (Hailey 255). The singer of Israel gave thanks for God's providence as seen in the nation's deliverance. "Oh, that men would give thanks to the Lord for His goodness, and for His wonderful works to the children of men! For He satisfies the longing soul, and fills the hungry soul with goodness" (Psa. 105:8-9).

GOD'S GOODNESS IS THE SOURCE OF SALVATION

Paul's words to Titus are a powerful reminder of the importance of God's goodness in reference to the salvation of our eternal souls.

For we ourselves were once foolish, disobedient, led astray, slaves to various passions and pleasures, passing our days in malice and envy, hated by others and hating one another. But when the goodness and loving kindness of God our Savior appeared, he saved us, not because of works done by us in righteousness, but according to his own mercy, by the washing of regeneration and renewal of the Holy Spirit (Tit. 3:3-5 ESV).

The apostle first identifies with his readers by saying "we ourselves were once foolish. "Foolish" describes the lost "because he lacks understanding of God's truth. Sometimes it is because he has not been taught (Romans 1:14). Sometimes the person was taught, but he didn't listen (Luke 24:25)" (Reese 395). One can also be described as foolish "because his mind has been darkened (Ephesians 4:18)" or "he has been 'bewitched'" (Ibid).

The act that made salvation possible arose out of the "goodness" of our "Savior" Father in designing a plan for His Son to come to earth and offer Himself for lost mankind. "Goodness" describes "an attitude towards others that expresses itself by trying to do good to those others....[It] is a spirit which is always ready and eager to give whatever gift may be necessary. This is one of God's attributes. He is benevolent, benign, essentially generous" (Ibid., 398).

Salvation, then, is not the result of man's meritorious works but God's mercy, which "is kindness or pity for those in need or distress and that kindness manifests itself in action more than in words" (Ibid., 400). Our loving Father extends his mercy through the "washing of regeneration." "Regeneration" is defined as "new birth, reproduction, renewal, re-creation" (Thayer 474), an obvious reference to baptism. Paul pictured it in his letter to Rome, when he asked, "Or do you not know that as many of us as were baptized into Christ Jesus were baptized into His death? Therefore we were buried with Him through baptism into death, that just as Christ was raised from the dead by the glory of the Father, even so we also should walk in newness of life" (Rom.6:3-4). The source of the new birth is baptism in which participation in the death of Christ results in contacting the blood he shed in his death (John 19:31-35).

REMAIN FAITHFUL TO EXPERIENCE GOD'S GOODNESS

The importance of remaining faithful can be seen in Paul's words to the brethren at Rome. "Therefore consider the goodness and severity of God; on those who fell, severity; but toward you, goodness, if you continue in His goodness. Otherwise you also will be cut off" (Rom. 11:22). God's severity was seen in the punishment of sinful Israel, portrayed as the breaking off of the branches of the olive tree. The goodness of God was seen in the grafting in of the Gentiles, represented by Paul as branches from a wild olive tree.

"The conditional clause in this verse, 'if thou continue in his goodness', is a reminder that there is no security in the bond of the gospel apart from perseverance. There is no such thing as continuance in the favour of God in spite of apostasy" (Murray 88). Man is required to faithfully serve God in order to continue receiving the wonderful benefits of God's goodness. Paul does go on in this promise with a "note of *severity* in the way by which the alternative is expressed: 'otherwise thou also shalt be cut off', a severity with the same character and decisiveness as that mentioned in the earlier part of the verse" (Ibid., 88-89).

GOD'S GOODNESS COMPELS US TO PREACH

We have already seen how Paul emphasized God's goodness in saving the Gentiles and his severity in punishing the Jews (Rom. 11:22). Earlier verses in the same epistle make it clear that he was concerned for all the lost, both Jew and

Gentile, and did everything in his power to proclaim the gospel as the ultimate means of accessing the Father's goodness (Rom. 1:14-16; 9:1-3; 10:1).

Paul was fully aware of a coming day in which all would stand before the judgment seat of Christ to receive the harvest of their deeds (2 Co. 5:10). "The apostle had developed a fear (reverential awe) of the Lord (combined with 'love' [v. 14]), and on this basis he persuaded men to either yield to the gospel or to concede his personal integrity" (Jackson 351). He also encouraged others to remember and proclaim the goodness of God available through the gospel. Timothy was instructed, "And the things that you have heard from me among many witnesses, commit these to faithful men who will be able to teach others also" (2 Ti. 2:2).

The apostle's desire for all people to experience the Lord's goodness led him to take steps some might consider extraordinary.

> For though I am free from all men, I have made myself a servant to all, that I might win the more; and to the Jews I became as a Jew, that I might win Jews; to those who are under the law, as under the law, that I might win those who are under the law; to those who are without law as without law (not being without law toward God, but under law toward Christ), that I might win those who are without law; to the weak I became weak, that I might win the weak. I have become all things to all men, that I might by all means save some. Now this I do for the gospel's sake, that I may be partaker of it with you (1 Co. 9:19-23).

All of us who have experienced God's goodness in salvation from the eternal consequences of our sins ought to similarly use every means at our disposal to reach the lost.

CONCLUSION

Men may deny it, but Nahum's declaration that, "The Lord is good," is a repeated theme of scripture. Israel experienced God's goodness even through the punishment of others, like Egypt. In fact, the Lord used the punishment of others, as in the case of the flood, to bring about the salvation of faithful Noah. Goodness is so much a part of the nature of deity Jesus indicated to the rich young ruler that calling him "good" made him God. The Father is well acquainted with those who trust in him and fully blesses them. Those demonstrating a penitent spirit will experience the goodness of God in their forgiveness.

The Sovereign of the universe lovingly provides for His people. All who obey his voice experience the joy of being set free from their sins. He likewise rewards those who remain faithful. The initial and ongoing experience with the Almighty's saving hand motivates His children to go into all the world proclaiming the good news and urging others to obey the gospel to experience His goodness.

May we all remember "the Lord is good" every moment of our lives. May that remembrance result in a thankful spirit and drive us to tell the world of God's greatest act of goodness in sending His Son to walk among men, die a cruel death and shed His saving blood in that death!

WORKS CITED

Chesser, Frank. *Thinking Right About God.* Huntsville, AL: Publishing Designs, 2014. Print.

Hailey, Homer. *A Commentary on the Minor Prophets.* Grand Rapids, MI: Baker Book House, 1972. Print.

Jackson, Wayne. *A New Testament Commentary.* Stockton, CA: Christian Courier Publications, 2012. Print.

Keil, C. F. *MinorProphets.* Vol. XX. Grand Rapids, MI: William B. Eerdmans, 1978. Print. Commentary on the Old Testament in Ten Volumes by C. F. Keil and F. Delitzsch.

Lewis, Jack P. *The Gospel According to Matthew Part II 13:53-28:20.* Ed. Everett Feruson. Austin, TX: Sweet, 1976. Print. The Living Word Commentary.

Lewis, Jack P. *The Minor Prophets.* Grand Rapids, MI: Baker Book House, 1966. Print.

McGarvey, J. W., and Pilip Y. Pendleton. *The Fourfold Gospel.* Cincinnati, OH: The Standard Publishing Foundation, N.d. Print.

Matheny, J. Randal. "Protection and Destruction in the Same Phrase." Web log post. *Walking with God.* N.p., 20 Feb. 2015. Web. 24 Feb. 2015.

Murray, John. *The Epistle to the Romans: The English Text with Introduction, Exposition and Notes in Two Volumes.* Grand Rapids, Mich: Eerdmans, 1980. Print.

Reese, Gareth L. *New Testament Epistles 1 Timothy Titus 2 Timothy: A Critical and Exegetical Commentary.* Moberly, MO: Scripture Exposition, 1999. Print.

Roper, Coy D. *The Minor Prophets, 2: Obadiah, Jonah, Micah, Nahum, Habakkuk, Zephaniah, and Haggai.* Ed. Eddie Cloer. Searcy, AR: Resource Publications, 2013. Print. Truth for Today Commentary.

Thayer, Joseph H. *Thayer's Greek - English Lexicon of the New Testament.* Grand Rapids, MI: Baker Book House, 1977. Print.

CHAPTER 24

"The Righteous Will Live By Faith"
(Habakkuk 2:4)

Ron White

We get sick of hearing shocking news. Somebody needs to do something. Injustice, scams, violence, riots, threats from terrorists, perversion protected by statute, provoke the righteous. We question, what's the hold up; when will God strike? We're "fed up".

Read Habakkuk. The key to life is tucked away in this short book. Volumes have been printed searching for the meaning of seven simple (English) words recorded by this obscure prophet. His expression pops up in several Bible verses. New Testament writers cite this crucial principle from Habakkuk in Rom. 1:17, Gal. 3:11, and Heb. 10:38. God encourages this distressed prophet to remain faithful even while witnessing injustice and facing a gloomy era.

Since Habakkuk predicts a coming Babylonian invasion (1:6) he probably was alive near the end of Josiah's reign (609 BC), or even in Jehoiakim's reign (609-598 BC). Rival superpowers jockeyed for dominance. Babylonians under Nabopolasser and Nebuchadnezzar, at the battle of Carchemish (605 BC) defeated the last Assyrian king and chased the Egyptians, an Assyrian ally, back to their border (Jer. 46). Habakkuk possibly lived to see the Babylonians attack Judah in 597 BC, or even witness the fall of Jerusalem in 587 BC. Some commentators seem distressed by Habakkuk's ability to foresee the future. They are disinclined to believe the Holy Spirit inspired him so they date his work after the Babylonian exile (Taylor 975).

We commonly overlook original settings of Old Testament verses quoted in the New Testament. Where is the original mention of, *You shall love your neighbor as yourself?* It is recorded in that crusty old book Hebrew priests had to study (Lev. 19:17-18). What circumstance does its original context depict? In that text, a believer who walks in love should rebuke an erring brother rather than remain mum and watch him become lost! By recalling its original usage, we enhance our understanding of the saying telling us how love behaves. The same is true with understanding New Testament quotes from Habakkuk.

Let us observe the original context of Habakkuk's famous statement, "At the righteous will live by faith" (2:4). Habakkuk wishes to sort out confusion troubling his mind and that of fellow believers. He feels a growing sense of alarm brought on by injustice, international instability, and threats to his country. God seems inactive. The prophet wants to know how long before God acts. He appeals directly to God for insight instead of making an inquiry of a think tank, "brain trusts" (Baxter 213). He respectfully submits his questions to God, not against Him. Since God controls the destinies of nations, the prophet submits his question to Him and patiently waits for an answer. God graciously grants him an enlightening interview.

God's revelation to Habakkuk needs to be written on "tablet" so the populace might read them (Hab. 2:1-2; cf. Luke 1:63). Conveying God's message on that medium, which a runner might carry, indicates "it may be read at a hurried glance" (Lewis 63). The prophet learns God is going to punish Judah for her sins, an expression of justice Habakkuk can understand. He laments the evil behavior happening right in front of his eyes (1:2-4). In their history citizens in Judah did worship foreign gods, apparently supposing neighboring superpowers must have powerful gods (2 Ch. 25:14-16). Yes, Habakkuk can admit King Manasseh was wicked as stated by God's servants, the prophets (2 Ki. 21:10-15). Perhaps he recognizes more recent evil in the reign of Jehoiakim (2 Ki. 23:36-24:4), "a selfish, covetous, tyrannical ruler. His was a hardened and reckless character. He opposed the whole prophetic movement. He murdered the prophet Uriah. All the vices of the time of Manasseh came trooping back again" (Calkins 89). Understandable to Habakkuk, sin must be punished.

We like the spunk of this prophet because Habakkuk represents us well. Like people in our time, he is left confused by God's tactic for administering judgment (the theological "problem of theodicy"). So he asks God, why will you use a more wicked nation than we to punish Judah? Surely God cannot hold his "peace when the wicked swallow up the man that is more righteous than he" (1:13). The prophet stations himself like a man on a fortress wall, looking into the distance to see what response God will bring him. Habakkuk gets his answer. Oh, God says after He uses "that bitter and hasty nation" to purge Judah, He will judge those invaders too, not yet, but in due time when the He chooses (2: 3, 16).

> The Lord informs him, "Yes, your estimate of the Chaldean is quite right; his soul is all wrong; but though I use him to chastise My people, he himself shall be brought to woe in the end; and although in the present painful process the righteous suffer with (and by) the wicked, yet the righteous shall never perish in the end like the wicked, but shall live because of his faith, as will yet be seen, for the earth shall yet be filled with the knowledge of the glory of the Lord (Baxter 211).

That wicked nation, especially "he" (2:4), apparently the Babylonian king, is rapidly building his nation on unstable footing. God knows Babylon's supporting foundation for growing wealth contains defective elements, a flawed, mixed composition - pride, greed, theft, extortion, plunder, and blood. Warnings and woes come from the mouth of the Lord against such (2:4-20). "Woe to him who builds his realm by unjust gain" (2:9). So what is Habakkuk's immediate application? An unjust Chaldean will die clinging in faith to his power and lifeless idol (2:18-20). In contrast, "the righteous will live by his faith" clinging to the Almighty Living God (2:4). That is the believer's duty. Remain steadfast in an evil world. In time the righteous will be vindicated!

What does this faith phrase mean and practically imply? The prophet expresses a sentiment which reminds me of an observation made by one of our country's founders: "Indeed I tremble for my country when I reflect that God is just, that His justice cannot sleep forever". (attributed to Thomas Jefferson, 1774). Both felt certain that God will come in judgment in a time of His own choosing to address injustice. When judgment falls on a nation, "... it is an invariable law of God that the righteous must suffer along with the guilty" yet... "God will bring [the righteous] through the ordeal at hand and destroy the destroyer@ (Hailey 280, 282).

What's happening in the world? Someone says he's a Christian and gets beheaded or shot for it. Music lovers, perhaps you have heard George Jones' old song using these casual lyrics – "God's gonna get'cha for that! God's gonna get'cha for that! There's no place to run and hide, for He knows where you're at! " In contrast to that true but homely rhyme, Habakkuk uses high poetic eloquence in his prayer/psalm. Chapter 3 records "some of the best in Hebrew literature" (Calkins 89). As an exhibit of displeasure, God will judge evil and display heads of wicked warriors upon their own staves (3:13-14).

Habakkuk emphasizes how important it is to keep a childlike faith in God. Let's face this -humans cannot plumb the depths of God's mind or administrative arrangements! We do not understand why He still allows a place among men, for present-day brutal, corrupt, authoritarian rulers and unfair, baffling systems. How does He manage to superintend affairs of nations, still allow human free will, and then maneuver those who will serve as His instruments of justice? In the midst of all of that, believers trust God will still preserve righteous remnants who at times seem to be on the verge of extinction, people who escape by the skin of their teeth. Understanding such things was "beyond the scope of the prophet's mental horizon. Running the universe is God's business (Lewis 63-64). Our intellect is not greater than Habakkuk's. We must attain a state of mind where we recognize that many of the ways of God are too high for us to comprehend. At times our view of events on earth differs from heaven's. "Little children" (1 Jn. 2), our Father has given us enough reason to trust him.

For believers to behave as we are taught, "be anxious for nothing" (Phi. 4:6), requires trusting our loving Father is taking care of His children. A toddler does not worry about his next meal, clothing, and security at night, or where a father is carrying him (Mat. 6). Father knows what he is doing. If dad is on a rooftop and tells his little boy to climb on up, ascend that 20-foot ladder, the prospect of such an elevation might scare the youngster. But if dad calls down instructions and keeps saying, "You can make it. Just hang on and take one step at a time! Look up here, not down," a youngster with a sufficient faith in dad will ascend that 20-foot ladder (cf. Col. 3:1).

Some situations believers experience in this world puzzle us. An unborn infant living comfortably in mom's womb does not worry about lack of oxygen, keeping fed, or hydrated. When birth pains strike, that unborn child feels squeezed hard, his body twisting, his skull deforming. He is terribly constricted getting shoved through a birth canal. Surely the warmth and comfort enjoyed through nine months was good enough. Why does he have to go through this ordeal? Then baby emerges into a different world full of lights, smells, tastes, and opportunities that never could have been imagined before. That reminds me of our passive predicament when believers transition from this life into the world to come, completely in God's hands (cf. Watkins, 34 min). We cannot grasp what awaits us over there (1 Jn. 3:2)!

So, Habakkuk will not be anxious. The prophet's questions were answered. He will try to keep calm even when days of tribulation draw near. "I heard, and my body trembled, my lips quivered at the voice; rottenness entered into my bones, and I tremble in my place; because I must wait quietly for the day of trouble, for the coming up of the people that invades us" (Hab. 3:16). He now realizes, God knows what is occurring among the nations and has everything under control. "Yet I will rejoice in Jehovah, I will joy in the God of my salvation. Jehovah, the Lord, is my strength; and he makes my feet like hinds' feet and will make me to walk upon my high places (Hab. 3:18-19).

By responding to Habakkuk's queries, God gives modern believers reading Habakkuk reason to keep faith in Him. To benefit, we must be readers of our beloved Bibles! Moderns rehash questions already addressed by the prophets. Bible students become full of Bible answers to our concerns, not burdened with worrisome questions fretted over by uninformed people. We enjoy hindsight. The rise and fall of nations occurred just as God divulged to Habakkuk. God is faithful. Nations the Chaldeans spoiled did rise up and plunder the Babylonian empire (2:8). "This was fulfilled against the Chaldeans by Cyrus, ruler of the Medes and Persians, who entered Babylon in October, 539 BC, twenty-three years after the death of Nebuchadnezzar (562 BC). The execution against nations of today is by those whom Jehovah raises up for the purpose" (Hailey 284-85). Habakkuk ensures us our faith in God rests on solid evidences. We read in history how the Medes and Chaldeans joined to destroy Nineveh, then the Medes turned on the Chaldeans the "bitter and hasty" nation that made captives of Judah did not last a century (Gray 830). Do not nations who threaten people more righteous than they are, still arise? In news reports, we see them fighting among themselves, much like what occurred with the Assyrians, Egyptians, Babylonians, Persians, Grecians, etc. At Hebrews 10:37-39, "As the writer of Hebrews saw the Roman invasion approaching, and realized a parallel destruction of the Jewish order in his day, he appealed to this passage" (Hailey 283). Purging of nations is "no new thing under the sun" (Ecc. 1:9). No wonder living by faith eliminates anxiety (Mat. 6).

What does Habakkuk's phrase mean theologically? Certain reformers (e.g. Calvin, Luther) camped out on the word "faith." Segments of their writings seem to conclude God said there is no need for human action for one to be accounted just in God's eyes. Anyone regenerated, it is sometimes alleged, passively gets shoved into the kingdom. So, one "gets saved" solely by God choosing to elect him. Such a view makes Bible verses appear to clash. Luther's "justification by faith only... introduces a new idea that is neither in Habakkuk nor in Paul from whom Luther took his cue" (Lewis 66). Scripture does teach us saving faith includes action although human deeds do not merit our salvation -even when we behave quite well. "This principle stated by Habakkuk became the foundation argument of Paul's gospel against the Jewish contention of salvation by works of the law," (Rom. 1:17; Gal. 3:11) (Hailey 283).

Augustus Strong, a Calvinist theologian, understands saving faith has an intellectual element, an emotional element, and a voluntary element. Then he represents Campbellite Disciples as advocates of faith that "is merely intellectual belief in the truth, on the presentation of evidence" (Strong 837-40). We are not Campbellites even though we respect some of the insights Disciples discovered. Perhaps Strong winced at the potency in Campbell's writings which exposed errors of Calvinism. So, Strong shied away parroting Calvin and branding God's special call "irresistible, "preferring "efficacious" (Strong 792).

Restoration preachers did use reason to counter rabid Calvinists who supposed the Holy Spirit had to directly zap with faith an un-regenerate person to jolt him out of unbelief, his brain engaged or not. Actually, those vilified preachers disputed some forms of Protestantism that supposed faith was, "mere intellectual assent to a set or system of tenants" instead of" direct personal reliance upon Christ." (B. Smith, 336). Justifying use of his intellect to understand God's revealed truth and dismiss creedal systems enshrining religious error, Alexander Campbell wrote, "In the controversy about the body of Moses, Michael reasoned, but did not slander nor revile: while Satan reviled and did not reason. Ever since error was believed among men, it has been sustained by the same means... (Campbell 3). There is a place for reason (Isa. 1:18; 1 Pe. 3:15). Faith does not slight well-founded reason. God understood Habakkuk's reasons for concern about God's reputation (1:13). By graciously responding, the Lord bolstered both the faith of that prophet and ours.

New Testament writers commonly quoted from the Greek translation of their Hebrew Scriptures (Septuagint). At Rom. 1:17, Paul trims off the pronoun found in Habakkuk. The Hebrew text of Hab. 2:4, as translated in the American Standard Version, includes the possessive pronoun "his" faith. The Septuagint translation reads "my faith." When Paul quotes Habakkuk, he eliminates both of those possessive pronouns. Paul concisely wrote, "the righteous out of faith shall be living" (Gill).

Of added interest, the Hebrew word definition for faith (emunah), is from the verb which includes, "to be firm, steadfast," as when Aaron and Hur steadied Moses' raised arms during a battle (Exo. 17:12). It is used of "faithfulness" in marriage. In our time some interpret Paul's use of "faith" in Romans to mean "that single act of faith by which the sinner accrues forgiveness and justification" (G. Smith 142), while in context, Habakkuk speaks of enduring faith, fidelity, remaining trustworthy. The Hebrew writer also uses Habakkuk's broader, enduring, loyal, steadfast meaning in his application at Heb. 10:37-38 – "but my righteous one shall live by faith: and if he shrinks back, my soul has no pleasure in him. "So, instead of faith being an initial spasm followed by perpetual inactivity, it stirs one to steadfastly obey God (Heb. 11:1-12). This constancy of "the righteous" does not fizzle out.

Habakkuk's famed commendation of faith speaks of benefits beyond our physical existence and embraces life of our souls. We suggest the prophet refers to souls because he mentions that very word in his contrast: a puffed up soul (2:4) of a proud Chaldean. Nebuchadnezzar, the Babylonian ruler, speaking of himself, "was at rest in my house, and flourishing in my palace . . . The king spake and said, 'Is not this great Babylon, which I have built for the royal dwelling place, by the might of my power and for the glory of my Majesty?'" (Dan. 4: 30). So God humbles the proud King. "You shall be made to eat grass as oxen; and seven times shall pass over thee until you know that the Most High rules in the kingdom of men, and gives it to whomsoever he will" (Dan. 4:32). "In contrast to the character of the proud, and in the face of his swaggering arrogance, 'the righteous shall live by his faith'" (Hailey 283).

Similar to Habakkuk, but distinct because it was personal, Job wants to know what God was doing allowing so much evil to befall him. Job wants to interview God and fire questions at the Lord. Here is what strikes me about Job wanting to put his nose in heaven's business: if God had revealed to Job accusations Satan had made about him and agreements arranged in heaven prior to Job's trial, would Job have behaved the same? No! Job had to be kept in the dark in order for his integrity to be proven. In the case of Habakkuk, God allowed him some insight.

As we have seen, Christians at times also wonder why God seems to be doing nothing when evil abounds in the world. The question is not new. We "walk by faith, not by sight" (2 Co. 5:7). Like Job, you might be "put to grief in manifold trials, that the proof of your faith more precious than gold" can be exposed. Even "though now you see him not" you love Him. You anticipate the "end of your faith, even the salvation of your souls. "You who walk in faith are like Old Testament prophets who "sought and searched diligently..." trying to figure out what heaven was up to when those ill-treated ancients only received glimpses into the mind of God (1 Pe. 1:6-12). From our human perspective we notice that sin has in itself the seeds of self-destruction. Wisdom literature asks, "Can a man take fire in his bosom and his clothes not be burned?" (Pro. 6:27; also Ps. 73). On the other hand, "the righteous shall live" noticing in his service to God, blessings 'a hundredfold now in this time". .. "and in the world to come eternal life" (Mark 10:29-30).

Abraham walked by faith. God lets him experience puzzling situations which teach him spiritual lessons that enhance his faith. Regarding Sarah having a child in old age, God compels Abraham to consider beforehand, "Is anything too hard for Jehovah?" (Gen. 18:14). Prior to angelic messengers appearing to Abraham and speaking about the looming doom of Sodom, God says, "their sin is very grievous" (Gen. 18:20). So, does God really need those angels to go roam around town in order to detect wickedness, or does he speak with Abraham to provoke, stir up, get him to utter words of faith? Says Abraham, "Will you consume the righteous with the wicked" (Gen. 18:23)? The patriarch cannot believe that. Abraham perceives that harming the righteous is not God's ambition. "Shall not the judge of all the earth do right?" (Gen. 18:25). As Abraham proceeds to contemplate what number of righteous people in Sodom would allow it to be preserved, thinking maybe 50, 45, clear down to ten people, both Abraham and we perceive how precious every upright soul is to God. Surely the bargaining conversation between Abraham and the messengers was not done to manipulate God so much as to enhance our understanding of God. He will do right!

Even those believers slain for the word of God cry out, "How long, oh Master, the holy and true, do you not judge and avenge our blood on them that dwell on the earth?" (Rev. 6:10). People today sometimes wonder if an earthquake will crack off part of California and dump it in the ocean. We are shocked when we hear deeds of those who suppose they promote Islam by beheading children, kidnaping and enslaving girls, burning a man alive in a cage. How can God let it continue? Lot was also "sore distressed by the lascivious life of the wicked.. vexed his righteous soul from day to day with their lawless deeds" (2 Pe. 2: 7-8). Then in a little while, judgment fell on them. We learn from Habakkuk and other heroes of faith, God knows what is going on down here on planet Earth!

Though we might speak of God as if He is maneering nations like pawns, humans with free will are not lifeless things. Still, God's goals will get done. When God allows Daniel the privilege of seeing what will develop among nations in the future, remember how he felt? He lost his strength, trembled, lost his breath, just felt rotten (Dan. 10). Apparently humans do not have a constitution that can hold up trying to understand the complexities of God=s interventions, maneuvers, providences, timing of judgments on men and nations, or all the factors that will determine when he will bring this world to a halt. So, let us not "get all bent out of shape" over such things!

God told Pharaoh Necho to go to a battle against the Babylonian ruler, Nebuchadnezzar -at least that's what Pharaoh claimed. Even though he lived in a small buffer state between two superpowers, good King Josiah decided he would intervene and cut off the Egyptian. Sadly, Josiah died as a result (2 Ch. 35:20-24). We wonder why. Was it proper for Josiah to have disguised himself and stuck his nose in this event? Had God really talked to Pharaoh? Was Josiah trying to mess with a turning point in history that God had arranged, the famed battle of Carchemish on the Euphrates? We don not know such things.

Let those who are inclined to criticize God's administration heed Habakkuk's warning to those who practice treachery, violence, and injustice: "Jehovah is in his holy temple, let all the earth be silent before Him"(2:20). He may suddenly strike like lightning, thunder and an earthquake (Rev. 16:18). "In anger you march through the earth; in wrath you tread down the nations. You go forth for the salvation of your people; for the salvation of your anointed. (Hab. 3:12-13).

What central lesson do New Testament penmen learn from Habakkuk? Inspired writers recognize God expects humans in every age of human history to walk by faith. Even prior to the arrival of inspired insight given under Moses' law, the covenant under which Habakkuk lived, "Abraham believed God, and it was reckoned unto him for righteousness" (Gen. 15:6; Rom. 4:3). "By faith Abraham, being tried, offered up Isaac" (Heb. 11:17). Abraham, David, Habakkuk and other inspired writers recognize this faith principle as New Testament books declare.

Though King David lived under the law of Moses, later in history than Abraham, he also sought the blessing upon a man whom God reckons righteous apart from trusting in personal deeds (Rom. 4:6-8). A man who seeks God in submissive trust, instead of placing confidence in his perfect obedience, somehow God accepts. On what basis? Such a believer as Abraham perceives a just God will provide a means to cover his sins so they are not taken into account.

Recall Abraham about to offer his son, Isaac asks him, "Where is the Lamb?" Abraham responds, "God will provide himself the lamb for a burnt-offering, my son" (Gen. 22:7-8). God did provide the substitute, "a ram caught in the thicket by his horns" which became "a burnt-offering in the stead of his son" (Gen. 22:13). That event foreshadows things to come. Paul declares God "preached the gospel beforehand unto Abraham" (Gal. 3:8) regarding Gentiles being justified by faith. In his seed, "shall all the families of the earth be blessed" (Gen. 12:3). The patriarch recognized God will provide. So, it came about by the merit of "the Lamb of God who takes away the sin of the world" (John 1:29) we are "justified freely by his grace through the redemption that is in Christ Jesus: whom God sent forth to be a propitiation, through faith, in his blood to show his righteousness because of the passing over of the sins done aforetime, in the forbearance of God; for the showing, I say, of his righteousness at this present season: that he might himself be just, and the justifier of him that has faith in Jesus" (Rom. 3:24-26).

The book of Habakkuk we label a "minor prophet", but its grand, inspired insight wields a powerful influence on our understanding of faith. Both that prophet and we feel a growing sense of alarm brought on by horrifying world events. From our earthbound perspective, God seems inactive. Wrong! Habakkuk learns, an orderly sequence of international events are in the pipeline. God has everything under control. Is that not still true? God repeatedly has given righteous people reason to maintain hope. Abraham knew, "God will provide himself the lamb"-and he did. "He that spared not his own Son, but delivered him up for us all, how shall he not also with him freely give us all things?" (Rom. 8:32). God "begot us again unto a living hope by the resurrection of Jesus Christ... reserved in heaven for you, who by the power of God are guarded through faith unto a salvation ready to be revealed in the last time" (1 Pe. 1:3-5). Recognize, "it is God who works in you both to will and to work, for his good pleasure. Remain steadfast. Do all things without murmurings and questioning.." (Phi. 2:13-14). "And the world is passing away, and the lust of it; but he who does the will of God abides forever" (1 Jn. 2:17). God still takes care of us. Let's embrace this faith!

WORKS CITED

Baxter, J. Sidlow. *Explore the Book*, 6 vol. in 1, Zondervan, 1967. Print.

Campbell, Alexander, editor. *The Millennial Harbinger*. v. II, 1831, Harbinger Book Club, undated. Print.

Calkins, Raymond. *Modern Message of the Minor Prophets*. Harper, New York, 1947. Print.

Gill, Clinton R. *Bible Study Textbook, Minor Prophets -Micah through Malachi*, v.2. College Press, 1988. E-Sword.

Gray, James Comper and Adams, George M. *Biblical Encyclopedia*, v.3. Doran, 1903. Print.

Hailey, Homer. *Commentary on the Minor Prophets*. Baker, Grand Rapids, 1973. Print.

Lewis, Jack P. *The Minor Prophets*. Baker, Grand Rapids, 1967. Print.

Smith, Benjamin Lyon, editor. *Millennial Harbinger Abridged*, v. 2. article by Robert Richardson. Print.

Smith, George Adam. *Book of the Twelve Prophets*. v.II . Harper, New York, 1928. Print.

Strong, Augustus Hopkins. *Systematic Theology*. The Judson Press, 1967. Print.

Taylor, Charles L., Jr. Interpreter's Bible, Habakkuk, v. VI. Abington, Nashville, 1956. Print.

Watkins, Bill. "Walk This Way: Unitedly." www.wetrainpreachers.com/chapelcast/. Web. 20 Sept. 2014.

CHAPTER 25

"The Lord Is In His Holy Temple"
(Habakkuk 2:20)

Jill Jackson

Idolatry has been a serious problem in ancient and modern times, even for God's chosen people. In this study we will examine four observations God makes about idols in Habakkuk 2:18-19. Then we'll contrast those observations with the Lord himself who is in His holy temple (20). After affirming that God is the only one deserving of worship and honor, we'll consider three actions we must take to abstain from modern-day idolatry and submit to God's reign in the heart.

WHAT ARE IDOLS ANYWAY?

Is it not extremely important to reflect on what idolatry is? In Habakkuk 2:18-19, God presented four rational observations about idols for Habakkuk and the people to consider. He asked:

> What profit is an idol when its maker has shaped it, a metal image, a teacher of lies? For its maker trusts in his own creation when he makes speechless idols! Woe to him who says to a wooden thing, Awake; to a silent stone, Arise! Can this teach? Behold, it is overlaid with gold and silver and there is no breath at all in it.

Idols Don't Profit

Absolutely no benefit is found in serving an idol. It's absurd to think that a metal object shaped by its maker can benefit the one who made it. Jeremiah said idol worshippers "went after things that do not profit" (Jer. 2:8). Similarly, Isaiah addresses the foolishness of one who gives gold and silver to a goldsmith to fashion a god that a person would fall down and worship. He drives home this foolish behavior by pointing out that these man-made idols have to be carried, cannot move, and do nothing to answer cries of the afflicted or save one from troubles (Isa. 46:6-7). The ESV Study Bible says:

> Created gods are dependent on their creators. **they carry it.** If a god has to be carried, how can it unburden its worshippers? **it cannot move.** If a god cannot move, how can it intervene? **it does not answer or save.** Gold and silver are lavished on the god, to no benefit (Dennis 1325).

Idols Don't Engender Confidence

Idols are not worthy of confidence; they are teachers of lies. These inanimate objects produce spiritual blindness. Their followers fail to see how irrational it is to believe and trust in something created by their own hands—therein lies a lie (Isa. 44:9-20). They worship idols because they are led astray by a deluded heart. Homer Hailey said, "The idol is a teacher of lies; it promises what it can never produce; it leads away from Jehovah and to destruction" (228).

Idols Don't Speak

Idols are mute and offer no comfort—no answer to cries of despair. Idols are unable to teach—no instruction or direction for life are offered. Isaiah said that cries to an idol go unanswered (Isa. 46:7). It is a ridiculous notion that one can call on a inanimate object, expecting an answer. God said, "Woe to him who says to a wooden thing, Awake; to a silent stone, Arise!" (Hab. 2:19). Idols don't speak or answer the prayers of the people who cry to them.

Idols Don't Breathe

Idols are merely metal objects, wooden things, and silent stones—objects with no breath in them. "There is no breath at all in it" (Hab. 2:19). It's absurd to think there is life and potential salvation in a breathless object crafted from the hands of man. The reality is: idols are nothing more than an avenue of destruction for those who serve them.

BUT THE LORD IS IN HIS HOLY TEMPLE

After noting the ridiculousness of putting confidence in idols, we read: "But the Lord is in his holy temple; let all the earth keep silence before him" (Hab. 2:20). J. Ronald Blue expressed the sense of the passage when he wrote:

> From dumb, man-carved idols, attention shifts to the living Lord, the self-existent, eternal, holy Sovereign who rules the universe from His holy temple, that is, heaven. Instead of shouting, "Arise! Awake," the whole earth must stand in silent awe and worship before Him (1516).

We must stand in awe—hushed silence—and worship Him because of who He is and what He has done for us.

Keep Silence Because God Profits Those Who Serve Him

In contrast to idols, our God profits the ways of those who love His ways. He blesses the righteous and covers them with favor as a shield (Psa. 5:12). He hears the cries of the afflicted (Exo. 3:7). He is our deliverer (Psa. 34:19). He's the giver of all good and perfect gifts (Jas. 1:17). He cares for us (1 Pe. 5:7). He loved us so much he gave us His Son (John 3:16). A relationship with God provides us with immeasurable benefits!

Keep Silence Because God Is Worthy of Confidence

In contrast to idols, our God is worthy of our confidence as the Creator. He is the Creator of the world and all the things in it—the giver of life and breath and everything (Acts 17:24-25). Man became a living creature when God breathed into his nostrils the breath of life (Gen. 2:7).

Paul said those who serve idols fail to honor God because they worship the created rather than the Creator. He wrote:

> Claiming to be wise, they became fools, and exchanged the glory of the immortal God for images resembling mortal man and birds and animals and reptiles . . . they exchanged the truth about God for a lie and worshipped and served the creature rather than the Creator (Rom. 1:22-23, 25).

God alone is worthy of our worship and honor! There is no other beside Him; He alone is sovereign (Isa. 45:18).

Keep Silence Because God Speaks and Teaches

In contrast to idols, God has spoken to mankind from the beginning. In the garden He spoke to Adam and Eve (Gen. 3:9-19). He spoke through His chosen prophets (Heb. 1:1). He spoke through visions (Acts 11:5-9). He speaks through His Son (Heb. 1:1). Though His ways for communicating to His creation have differed through the years, our God is not speechless. He continues to speak to us today through His inspired word, giving us the tools to build our faith (1 John 5:13). Through his word we receive teaching, reproof, correction and training in righteousness (Rom. 10:17; 1 Ti. 3:16).

Keep Silence Because God Is Alive

In contrast to idols, our God is alive and all-powerful. Nothing is too hard for the Lord (Gen. 18:14). He can do all things and nothing He purposes to do can be thwarted (Job 42:2). Jehovah is alive and His presence is ever at work in those who seek His ways (Phi. 2:13).

IS THERE A GOLDEN CALF IN YOUR HOME?

We learn from Habakkuk 2:20 that we must put our faith and confidence in God, and no other, because He is the one in control. The Lord is in His holy temple. Keep silent and worship Him because He profits the ways of those who love Him. Reverence Him because He is the Creator and worthy of confidence in His promises. Honor Him because He continues to speak to us through His word and direct our paths. Stand in silent awe because He lives!

When we consider these and other scriptures about idolatry, we might recall Aaron's golden calf or Nebuchadnezzar's golden image. With these accounts in mind, some may fail to see the idolatry within their homes and personal lives because they haven't fashioned an image with their hands. They don't have golden calves in their homes, so they see no modern-day application when reading, "You shall have no other gods before me" (Exo. 20:3).

Matthew Henry's helpful definition of "other gods" shows that idolatry is a modern-day problem. He said, "Whatever is esteemed or loved, feared of served, delighted in or depended on, more than God, that (whatever it is) we do in effect make a god of" (studylight.org).

Idolatry is simply being attached or devoted to someone or something more than God. We don't have to have a golden calf in our homes for there to be idols in our hearts. A lack of whole-hearted faithfulness to God is idolatry.

God's command is clear: worship and serve him alone (Mat. 6:33). As the Creator, he has absolute authority over us. He has the right to require and receive our faithfulness (Mic. 6:6-8). He has the right of rule in our lives (Psa. 100).

CHOOSE THIS DAY WHOM YOU WILL SERVE

Joshua instructed the Israelites to "choose this day whom you will serve, whether the gods your fathers served in the region beyond the river, or the gods of the Amorites in whose land you dwell. But as for me and my house, we will serve the Lord" (Jos. 24:15).

Serving God means submitting to his will. According to Joshua, submission isn't a passive action—it's a proactive choice. The Israelites had a choice to make: serve lifeless gods or the one true God.

Just like the Israelites, we live in a world full of influences that seek our hearts and minds. We're surrounded by customs, trends, viewpoints and people in opposition to God. Just like the Israelites, we must choose whom we will serve. When God is in His rightful place as the ruler of our hearts, we will submit to His will and have no other gods before Him.

Consider three proactive choices the Christian—who chooses to serve the Lord as Joshua did—will make.

Choose To Worship God's Way

Choose to serve the Lord by submitting to His will for acceptable worship (John 4:24). For worship to be acceptable, God must be the object. The psalmist said, "Exalt the Lord our God; worship at his footstool! Holy is he!" (99:5).

Second, the worshipper must have a proper disposition (Jos. 24:14). The worshipper must have reverence and awe for the Creator (Heb. 12:28).

Finally, acceptable worship must be offered according to the authorized pattern—in truth (John 4:24; 17:17; 1 Co. 4:6; Col. 3:17).

Sadly, individuals and congregations who practice unscriptural worship are not hard to find. It's commonplace to hear of those in the Lord's body who have decided to introduce an instrument, a choir, or to reject the authorized leadership roles for men and women in the church.

Is this a church choosing to serve God? No, but this does reflect those who have no reverence for God's word and believe they have found a better way. This reflects those who have no interest in honoring God, but who make worship about their own preferences (1 Ki. 12:33). This reflects modern-day idolatry within the heart, because God is not worshipped according to His word.

Shouldn't we learn the lesson of history? Many have rebelled against God and have sought to change His rules for worship to their own liking. Jeroboam feared the people of his kingdom would turn back to the house of David. He didn't want them to go offer sacrifices in the temple of the Lord because he feared their hearts would return to the Lord. If that happened, he would lose his kingdom—and potentially his life—to King Rehoboam of Judah.

To prevent that, he devised a plan—a system of worship to fulfill his purpose, to keep the people in close proximity to him, to keep their hearts from returning to the Lord, to keep his kingdom intact. So he made two golden calves and placed one at Dan and the other at Bethel. He said to the Israelites, "Behold your gods, O Israel, who brought you up out of the land of Egypt" (1 Ki. 12:28). He made high places, appointed false priests, and changed the time of the sacred feast (vv. 31-33). The people followed right in line with him (1 Ki. 13:33; 2 Ki. 17:22). Because of their outright disobedience, God eventually removed the Israelites out of his sight, and they were taken captive by the Assyrians (2 Ki. 17:7-8, 23).

They kindled the anger of the Lord because they served idols and violated His command when He said, "You shall have no other gods before me" (Exo. 20:3). Despite the Lord's instructions and the warnings of the prophets, they refused to listen and despised His ways. They became false, abandoned the Lord, and followed the ways of the world around them (2 Ki. 17:11-18).

Acceptable worship doesn't add to or take away from God's words (Deu. 4:2; Lev. 10:1; Col. 3:17). Acceptable worship doesn't seek one's personal agenda, but seeks to do what is pleasing to God (1 Sa. 15:22). When God is the object of our worship, when our disposition is right, and when we follow the pattern authorized by God for worship, we're showing our submission to His right of rule in our lives. We're choosing, as Joshua, to serve the Lord.

Choose to Sacrifice

Choose to serve the Lord by being an individual willing to sacrifice. The choice to serve the Lord isn't always an easy road. Jesus said, "If anyone would come after me, let him deny himself and take up his cross and follow me" (Mat. 16:24). There's a cost to Christianity, but the cost should pale in comparison to the eternal gift that awaits us! When God is in his rightful place as the ruler in our lives, our self-denial and submission to his will is apparent, despite the "crosses" to bear.

But there are Christians who look at the world with longing eyes (Gen. 19:26; Luke 17:32). They esteem and love the ways of the world more than the ways of

God, and it manifests itself in the things they wear, the places they go, the movies they watch, the music they like, the books they read, and the companions they keep. These "idols" prevent them from serving God with wholehearted faithfulness.

Many hearts of Christians have become desensitized by worldly companions and cultural customs, creating a huge disconnect (1 Co. 15:33)! This disconnect allows one to be at peace with dividing loyalty between God's ways and the world's ways (2 Co. 6:14). If this wasn't true, these problems wouldn't plague the church. We wouldn't see young women dressed more appropriately for "clubbing" than worshipping the Creator. We wouldn't have men who are put in an uncomfortable situation when passing out the Lord's supper because some women expose inches of cleavage that is impossible not to notice. We wouldn't have Christian women getting together to go see "Magic Mike" or reading Fifty Shades of Grey. We wouldn't have teenagers and college students who believe purity isn't for the Christian culture today. We wouldn't have Christian people—aware of the sacrifice Christ made on their behalf—who are unwilling to completely sacrifice for him.

In Luke 18:18, we see this unwillingness to sacrifice depicted when the rich ruler asked Christ what he must do to inherit eternal life. Jesus told him to keep the commandments—don't commit adultery, don't murder, don't steal, don't bear false witness, and honor his parents. He told Christ he had kept these commandments from his youth. Jesus loved him, but knowing his heart, he required him to do the one thing he lacked: sell his possessions and give to the poor, and in exchange he would have treasure in heaven. But the man was very rich and loved his wealth. His possessions were his idols—esteemed, loved, delighted in, and depended on more than God. He went away sorrowful because he wasn't willing to sacrifice.

Was he a good man? Given the information provided we have reason to think so. He came to Christ with an interest in eternal life. He told Christ he had kept the commandments from his youth. There were some things he was willing to do to receive eternal life, but he was unwilling to fully devote himself to God, and that hindered his ability to claim eternal reward.

This is a problem that continues to plague many Christians. Some people don't want to give of their means because money is just too tight; yet money is always available for their children's sports or entertainment. Like the rich man, money can be an idol that prevents one from giving their whole heart in submission to God (cf. Luke 12:20).

Some people don't want to be faithful to every assembly. We once had a member of our congregation—who has since fallen away—tell us after his baptism that he'd be at worship unless the 49ers were playing. He was like the rich, young ruler—unwilling to fully give his life to Christ. His favorite game and team were his idol that prevented him from giving his whole heart in submission to God.

Devotion to God should be reflected in our speech, our interactions with others, the entertainment we choose, the clothes we wear, etc. God help us to be like Shadrach, Meshach and Abednego who, when confronted with a choice to serve the one true God or Nebuchadnezzar's golden image, said: Our God whom we serve is able to deliver us from the burning fiery furnace, and he will deliver us out of your hand, O king. But if not, be it known to you, O king, that we will not serve your gods or worship the golden image you have set up (Dan. 3:17-18).

Their reverence and devotion to the Creator was so complete they were willing to sacrifice their very lives before they would serve a man-made god—a speechless metal image, a teacher of lies, with no breath at all. And seeing their wholehearted faithfulness and God's deliverance, King Nebuchadnezzar blessed the name of the Lord. He said Shadrach, Meshach and Abednego trusted in God so much they set aside his command and yielded up their bodies rather than serve and worship any god except . . . God (v. 28). Do those outside of the body (and within) bless the name of the Lord because they see that we serve no other gods? This is the sort of compliment for which all Christians should aspire!

If our actions do not glorify God, there's only one other alternative—they glorify the ways of the world. If our actions don't depict a willingness to sacrifice, there's only one other alternative—they reveal an idol within the heart (cf. Col.3:5).

Choose to Have a Home Where God Dwells

Choose to serve the Lord by building a home that glorifies God in all times and circumstances. Our homes will never be what they need to be unless the individuals within them choose to serve only the Lord.

Homes that reflect a devotion to the Lord, and not the world, do not happen by accident. Homes that glorify God exist because parents choose to make eternal matters the strongest influence within the walls and beams that frame their homes. They demand that the world remains on the other side of the front door, because they have made the choice to build their house upon the Rock. Such parents recognize, with an awe-inspired silence and reverence, that the Lord is in His holy temple.

Choose, like Joshua, to have a home that serves the Lord. Our homes must be built upon the solid foundation that God's standards are the only standards to live by despite time and circumstances. As parents, our job is to ensure only things that glorify God will take place in our homes. We must show our children that our joy comes from submitting to the Father, because we value the blessings of being in a right relationship with Him (cf. Deu. 6:20-25). Wherever we are, whatever circumstances we encounter, we have to demonstrate that our home serves the Lord with dedication. There is no other way to live—no unworthy sacrifice—because we're a family that serves God!

Are there attitudes and activities taking place in your home that would bring shame upon the church? I've known Christians who have allowed their grown, non-Christian children to smoke and drink in their homes and who have kept alcoholic beverages in the refrigerator for their visiting adult children. What's so bad about that as long as they didn't participate? They loved their children. They had a good relationship with them. But they didn't love God and His ways more.

The reality is they didn't love their children enough to help them spiritually by providing an example different than the world (1 Jn 2:15). Sometimes parents seek ways to justify the behavior of their children when they sin. Love for family can be blinding and prevent one from seeing the harm in showing "love" (cf. 1 Ki. 1:6). Worst of all, it can prevent one from seeing that sometimes the greatest love—for God and our family—is shown when we say, "We'll not tolerate that in our home."

Can family become the modern-day idol? It can if those within the home choose family over Jesus (Mat. 10:37). It can if those within the home sit among sin or allow it to take place within the home while turning a blind eye (cf. 1 Sa. 2:27-29). We must understand that wanting harmony in our family more than harmony with God is idolatry.

CONCLUSION

Modern idolatry may not look like the ancient kind, but it's still a serious problem in the lives of many Christians. Choose this day whom you will serve! Choose the Lord and worship Him as He has directed. Choose God by sacrificing what He requires. Choose the true and living God by building a home in which the Lord's standards are obeyed any time and place. Choose God over idols because He has the right of authority in our lives, is the only one worthy of worship and honor, and because His ways provide the only avenue to everlasting life!

WORKS CITED

Blue, J. Ronald. *The Bible Knowledge Commentary: Old Testament.* John F. Walvoord and Roy B. Zuck, eds. Colorado Springs: Victor, 1985.

Hailey, Homer. *A Commentary on the Minor Prophets.* Grand Rapids: Baker, 1972.

Henry, Matthew. Exodus. n.p., 1706. *Matthew Henry Complete Commentary on the Whole Bible.* studylight.org. Web. 28 Apr. 2015.

Dennis, Lane T. et al., eds. *The ESV Study Bible.* Wheaton: Good News Publishers, 2008.

CHAPTER 26

"Seek The Lord"
(Zephaniah 2:3)

David Sproule

When Zephaniah came on the scene as the prophet of God to the Southern Kingdom, the nation of Judah had been rebelling against the Lord for the better part of two centuries. Following the death of Jehoshaphat, most of his successors to the throne (with only a few exceptions, like Hezekiah) "did evil in the sight of the Lord" (2 Ch. 21:6; 22:4; 33:2, 22), when they "served wooden images and idols" (2 Ch. 24:18), "sought the gods of Edom" (2 Ch. 25:20), "turned away from following the Lord" (2 Ch. 25:27), "transgressed against the Lord" (2 Ch. 26:16), "made molded images for the Baals" (2 Ch. 28:2; 33:3), "burned [their] children in the fire" (2 Ch. 28:3; 33:6), "sacrificed and burned incense on the high places" (2 Ch. 28:4), "became increasingly unfaithful to the Lord" (2 Ch. 28:22), "sacrificed to the gods of Damascus" (2 Ch. 28:23), "shut up the doors of the house of the Lord" (2 Ch. 28:24), "made high places to burn incense to other gods" (2 Ch. 28:25), "made wooden images" (2 Ch. 33:3), "worshiped all the host of heaven and served them" (2 Ch. 33:3), "practiced soothsaying, used witchcraft and sorcery" (2 Ch. 33:6), "consulted mediums and spiritists" (2 Ch. 33:6), "set a carved image…in the house of God" (2 Ch. 33:7), "sacrificed to all the carved images" (2 Ch. 33:22), "trespassed more and more" (2 Ch. 33:23), "seduced Judah and the inhabitants of Jerusalem to do more evil than the nations whom the Lord had destroyed before the children of Israel" (2 Ch. 33:9), and "did much evil in the sight of the Lord, to provoke Him to anger" (2 Ch. 33:6). [All Scripture references are taken from the New King James Version, unless otherwise noted.] Take a moment and digest all of that. This is what the kings of the nation of Judah (i.e., God's people) were leading the people to do in rebellion against the Lord.

What an increasingly distressing history to read and to explore! At every turn of the page, Judah continually "provoked to anger the Lord God" (2 Ch. 28:25). How long would the Lord endure this behavior against Him? Or, maybe a better question, why was the Lord enduring this behavior against Him? In the midst of this rebellion against the Lord is this interesting verse (note the first word),

"Yet He sent prophets to them, to bring them back to the Lord" (2 Ch. 24:19). Although Judah had given up on the Lord, the Lord had not given up on Judah. He continued to send prophet after prophet, pleading with His people, that they might hear, remember and return.

The history of the Divided Kingdom and the prophets sent by God (especially the writing prophets) paints a portrait of the nature of God for us that is certainly "written for our learning" (Rom. 15:4). We learn about the holiness of God—that He cannot be associated with evil and sin (Hab. 1:13; Psa. 5:4; 1 Jn. 1:5). We learn about the righteousness of God—that His way is right and He determines what sin is (Hos. 14:9; Gen. 18:19; Psa. 145:17). We learn about the justice of God—that He demands that penalty be paid for sin (Zep. 3:5; Psa. 89:14; Heb. 2:2). We learn about the love of God—that He paid the penalty for our sins, satisfying His justice (Isa. 53:4-6, 10-12; Rom. 3:21-26). We learn about the mercy of God—that He forgives sins and longs for His people to return to Him (Jer. 31:31-34; Mic. 7:18; Psa. 86:5).

When we understand the appalling nature of sin and then, in turn, understand the awe-inspiring nature of God, we will grow to have a new and greater appreciation for all things spiritual, and we will truly begin to see all things from God (even His commandments) as gifts from above.

Consider again the condition of Judah for the 200 years following the death of Jehoshaphat. Consider how sinful they had become. Consider how rebellious they had been. Consider how much they had provoked the Lord to anger. What did they deserve? What did the justice of God demand? Now ask this question: What would have been the most precious gift that God could have given to them, when He sent His prophet Zephaniah to them after 200 years of wickedness (with only a few bright spots along the way)? What they deserved is not what they received! They deserved the full vengeance of God without any mercy! What they received was a precious gift—the gift of repentance! We may not see repentance as a gift, but God does (cf. 2 Ti. 2:25). The death of Christ was designed "to give repentance to Israel" and to grant "to the Gentiles repentance to life" (Acts 5:31; 11:18). Repentance—the opportunity to turn and to seek the Lord—is a gift from above. Let us examine and grow in our appreciation for this gift, as it was offered to Judah through Zephaniah.

THE CALL FOR REPENTANCE AND SEEKING THE LORD

According to Zephaniah's timestamp in the first verse, he prophesied "in the days of Josiah the son of Amon, king of Judah." The exact timing is uncertain, but it appears to fit best in the years preceding the wide-sweeping reforms of Josiah. In the first chapter, Zephaniah pronounces God's judgment upon the world, with an emphasis on "the day of the Lord" soon to come upon Judah. In the second chapter, beginning with verse four, Zephaniah pronounces judgment on the heathen nations surrounding Judah. In the third chapter, Zephaniah assures Judah that it will not be spared the judgment of God, but salvation for the remnant is foretold.

Right in the midst of these declarations of punishment and judgment, the Lord cries out through Zephaniah for His people to repent and seek the Lord. Read the first three verses of chapter two, which will be investigated in the next two points:

> Gather yourselves together, yes, gather together, O undesirable nation, before the decree is issued, or the day passes like chaff, before the Lord's fierce anger comes upon you, before the day of the Lord's anger comes upon you! Seek the Lord, all you meek of the earth, who have upheld His justice. Seek righteousness, seek humility. It may be that you will be hidden in the day of the Lord's anger (Zep. 2:1-3).

Look at those first three words of verse three: "Seek the Lord!" What a blessed privilege! What a blessed hope! What a blessed gift! Oh, that everyone would long for the opportunity to seek the Lord!

THE CONDITIONS OF REPENTANCE AND SEEKING THE LORD

In order to appropriately and effectively repent and seek the Lord, there were definite conditions specified that must be followed. As these are examined, recognize that these same conditions are required of us today, as we are called upon to repent and seek the Lord.

Repentance and Seeking The Lord Requires A Sense of Shame.

Judah is called to "gather together," and Zephaniah calls her a "nation without shame" (2:1 NASB). As openly sinful as Judah had become in her rebellion against the Lord, she "[knew] no shame" for her behavior at all (3:5). Jeremiah, a contemporary of Zephaniah, cried out, "You refuse to be ashamed" (3:3), noting that "they were not at all ashamed; nor did they know how to blush" (6:15; 8:12). For one to effectively turn (repent) from sin and seek the Lord, he must be ashamed of his sinful ways; otherwise, he will never turn from them (cf. 2 Co. 7:9-10; 2 Th. 3:14). After getting caught up in his sins and falling before God in repentance, King David understood that prerequisite to true repentance and seeking the Lord "are a broken spirit, a broken and contrite heart" (Psa. 51:17).

Repentance and Seeking The Lord Requires A Heart of Humility.

Zephaniah called upon Judah, "Seek the Lord, all you humble of the land," and then he went on to say, "Seek humility" (2:3, ESV). Judah needed to be brought low, in order to be brought back to the Lord. Jesus came with a similar message. After John the Baptist and Jesus had been preaching repentance (Mat. 3:2; 4:17), the first words of Jesus' Sermon on the Mount were, "Blessed are the poor in spirit, for theirs is the kingdom of heaven" (Mat. 5:3). Then, near the end of His ministry, He reiterated, "He who humbles himself will be exalted" (Mat. 23:12). Until we take our eyes off of self, there is no way that we can put our eyes on the Lord!

Repentance and Seeking The Lord Requires A Desire To Do Right.

Zephaniah called upon Judah, "Seek the Lord, all…who do his just commands," and then he went on to say, "Seek righteousness" (2:3, ESV). The people of Judah needed to examine the direction and purpose of their lives. Jesus emphasized this same principle in the Sermon on the Mount, when He taught, "Blessed are those who hunger and thirst for righteousness" (Mat. 5:6). Then, in the next chapter, "Seek first the kingdom of God and His righteousness" (Mat. 6:33). And, again, in chapter seven, He taught, "Not everyone who says to Me, 'Lord, Lord,' shall enter the kingdom of heaven, but he who does the will of My Father in heaven" (Mat. 7:21). In the last verse of Hosea, the prophet said, "The ways of the Lord are right; the righteous walk in them" (14:9). It is the Lord who is righteous and the Lord who decides what is right; we must live in accordance with His character and His principles of righteousness. We will never stop doing wrong and start doing right, until we long to seek and obey the righteousness of God.

Repentance and Seeking The Lord Requires A Sense of Urgency.

Zephaniah used the word "seek" three times in 2:3, "Seek the Lord," "Seek righteousness," "Seek humility." He used another word three times in the verse right before this one to emphasize that the time to repent is right now! The prophet urged God's wayward people to gather together and seek the Lord, first of all, "before the decree takes effect" (2:2, NASB). That "decree" points back to the verdict that God had announced in the first chapter, especially in verses 2 and 3, "'I will utterly consume everything from the face of the land,' says the Lord; 'I will consume man and beast; I will consume the birds of the heavens, the fish of the sea, and the stumbling blocks along with the wicked. I will cut off man from the face of the land,' says the Lord."

Secondly, the prophet urged God's wayward people to gather together and seek the Lord "before the Lord's fierce anger comes upon you!" No doubt, again, he must be pointing back to chapter one, and perhaps especially verses four through six, for these are directed straight at Judah:

> I will stretch out My hand against Judah, and against all the inhabitants of Jerusalem. I will cut off every trace of Baal from this place, the names of the idolatrous priests with the pagan priests—those who worship the host of heaven on the housetops; those who worship and swear oaths by the Lord, but who also swear by Milcom; those who have turned back from following the Lord, and have not sought the Lord, nor inquired of Him.

Note how he calls out, as recipients of the Lord's anger, those of divided loyalty (swearing by the Lord and swearing by Milcom, an Ammonite god), those who turned away from the Lord and those "who do not seek the Lord" (NASB).

Thirdly, the prophet urged God's wayward people to gather together and seek the Lord "before the day of the Lord's anger comes upon you!" Again, this is referencing the first chapter, especially verses 7-18. The word "day" is found fourteen times in those last twelve verses of chapter one, warning of impending judgment and doom upon Judah. The prophet warned that "the day of the Lord is at hand" (1:7), and then emphasized, "That day is a day of wrath, a day of trouble and distress, a day of devastation and desolation, a day of darkness and gloominess, a day of clouds and thick darkness" (1:15).

The doom of the nation was fixed, but the individuals in the nation could make an individual decision about their own individual actions. As a later prophet would say, "When I say to the wicked, 'You shall surely die,' if he turns from his sin and does what is lawful and right...he shall surely live; he shall not die" (Eze. 33:14-16). The fate of our world today is fixed; the day is coming when it will pass away, but if we do the will of God, we can abide forever (1 Jn. 2:17). But, we must have a sense of urgency, understanding that "now is the accepted time; behold, now is the day of salvation" (2 Co. 6:2).

Repentance and Seeking The Lord Requires Action.

A shamed, humble, urgent desire to do right is not enough. True repentance is a change of mind that leads to a change of life. Those who seek the Lord must "turn from their wicked ways" (2 Ch. 7:14), "diligently seek Him" (Heb. 11:6) and "seek Him with all your heart and all your soul" (Deu. 4:29). The regret (or "sorrow," 2 Co. 7:10; cf. Mat. 21:29) leads to a resolution (or "I will," Luke 15:18), which leads to reformation (or "turn," Acts 26:20), which leads to restitution (or "restore," Eze. 33:14-15; Luke 19:8), and ultimately brings about results (or "works befitting repentance," Acts 26:20). John the Baptist warned the Jews that they must "bear fruits worthy of repentance" (Mat. 3:8-10). That change of mind must lead to action in changing one's daily life.

THE CONSEQUENCES OF REPENTANCE AND SEEKING THE LORD

As Zephaniah called the nation of Judah to repentance and seeking the Lord, he was quick to reveal the promised reward for such action: "…it may be that you will be hidden in the day of the Lord's anger" (2:3b). That's an interesting way to express it, for Zephaniah's name means, "Jehovah has hidden." If there was anyone who knew the joys and blessings of being hidden by and with the Lord, it was Zephaniah. And, now that same blessed promise is made to all who would "seek the Lord," "seek righteousness" and "seek humility."

"The day of the Lord's wrath" was "near" (1:18), but Judah could be sheltered from that wrath, if they would only turn and seek the Lord. For those who have been converted to Christ, through repentance and immersion (cf. Acts 2:38), take comfort in the reality that you share the same blessing that God promised more than 2,600 years ago—"your life is hidden with Christ in God" (Col. 3:3).

The consequences of seeking the Lord are abundant, for it is promised that the Lord "will hear from heaven, and will forgive their sin" (2 Ch. 7:14), and they will be "blessed" (Psa. 119:2), "not lack any good thing" (Psa. 34:10) and will "not [be] forsaken" (Psa. 9:10). Simply stated, the Lord said through Jeremiah, "And you will seek Me and find Me, when you search for Me with all your heart" (29:13; cf. 1 Ch. 28:9). "Seek" the Lord and "you will find" Him (Mat. 7:7)! What a blessing!

THE CATALYSTS FOR REPENTANCE AND SEEKING THE LORD

What is it that ultimately drives someone to repent and seek God? Some factors have already been noted in this study, like shame, regret, sorrow and a desire to be hidden in the Lord. All of these could be listed in this section of study, as well. However, there are at least three major motivating factors that ultimately lead a person to repent and seek the Lord. Two of these are found very plainly in the book of Zephaniah; the third is seen more in an overview of the book.

The Wrath of God Is A Major Motivation That Leads To Repentance and Seeking The Lord.

The first chapter of Zephaniah is a reflection of this truth in an extreme way. The very first words of the prophecy are definitive, straightforward and cutting. The first two words, "I will," are found ten times in the first chapter: "I will utterly consume everything...I will consume man and beast...I will consume the birds of the heavens...I will cut off man from the face of the land...I will stretch out My hand against Judah...I will cut off every trace of Baal from this place...I will punish the princes and the king's children...I will punish all those who leap over the threshold...I will search Jerusalem with lamps and punish the men who are settled in complacency...I will bring distress upon men..." (1:2, 3, 4, 8, 9, 12, 17). The word "punish" is found three times, the word "wrath" two times, and the word "against" five times. These punishments will come with: "a mournful cry," "a wailing," "a loud crashing," "cut down," "cut off," "bitter noise," "cry out," "trouble," "distress," "devastation," "desolation," "darkness," "gloominess," "blood shall be poured out," "flesh like refuse," "devoured," "fire," "riddance" (1:10, 11, 14-18). After reading that chapter about the wrath of God, the honest heart should be more than motivated to repent and seek the Lord! Reading about the wrath of God against the heathen nations around them (in chapter two) should just cement their resolve!

The Reward of God Is A Major Motivation That Leads To Repentance and Seeking The Lord.

The second part of the last chapter of Zephaniah is a reflection of this truth in an extreme way. Chapter two previewed the exciting promise of chapter three, when Zephaniah spoke of "the remnant of the house of Judah" (2:7, 9), whom God would cause to "return" and "possess" the lands of the enemies who would be overthrown. To fulfill His promise of the coming Messiah, God assured through the prophets that a remnant of His people would survive and return from captivity. Just as verses 14-17 of chapter one were some of the most bitter in regard to the wrath of God, verses 14-17 of chapter three are some of the most beautiful in regard to the reward of God. Savor each of these lines:

Sing, O daughter of Zion!

Shout, O Israel!

Be glad

And rejoice with all your heart, O daughter of Jerusalem!

The Lord has taken away your judgments,

He has cast out your enemy.

The King of Israel, the Lord, is in your midst;

You shall see disaster no more.

In that day it shall be said to Jerusalem: "Do not fear; Zion,

Let not your hands be weak.

The Lord your God in your midst,

The Mighty One, will save;

He will rejoice over you with gladness,

He will quiet you with His love,

He will rejoice over you with singing."

Then, just as the two words, "I will," ring with terror 10 times in the first chapter, the book closes in chapter three with the two words, "I will," ringing with triumph nine different times: "I will restore to the people a pure language...I will take away from your midst those who rejoice in your pride...I will leave in your midst a meek and humble people...I will gather those who sorrow over the appointed assembly...I will deal with all who afflict you...I will save the lame...I will appoint them for praise and fame...I will bring you back...I will give you fame and praise..." (3:9, 11, 12, 18-20). The word "rejoice" is found three times, "glad" two times, "save" two times, "in your midst" four times. This is something to "sing" and "shout" about! After reading that chapter about the reward of God, the honest heart should be more than motivated to repent and seek the Lord!

The goodness of God is a major motivation that leads to repentance and seeking the Lord. The whole book of Zephaniah is a reflection of this truth in an extreme way! On the one hand is the wrath of God, of which every accountable person is deserving, but God provides a way to escape from it! On the other hand is the reward of God, of which every accountable person is not deserving, but God provides a way to experience it! The very opportunity to repent and seek the Lord screams the goodness of God and ought to motivate each person to action.

The Christian needs to be reminded that "the goodness of God leads you to repentance" (Rom. 2:4). "The riches of His goodness," in that verse, is reminiscent of "the riches of His grace" (Eph. 1:7), which gives to us "redemption through His blood, the forgiveness of sins." It doesn't get any richer than that! "The riches of His forbearance" (in Romans 2:4) is reminiscent of when God's "forbearance…passed over the sins that were previously committed" (Rom. 3:25). It doesn't get any richer than that! "The riches of His longsuffering" (in Romans 2:4) is reminiscent of the fact that "the longsuffering of our Lord is salvation," for He is "not willing that any should perish but that all should come to repentance" (2 Pe. 3:15, 9). It doesn't get any richer than that!

After reading the book of Zephaniah and other passages about the goodness of God, the honest heart should be more than motivated to repent and seek the Lord!

CONCLUSION

What a blessed privilege the Lord has given to every person—the privilege to repent and seek the Lord! Repenting and seeking the Lord is not just a one-time act that one takes or a one-time decision that one makes in order to become a Christian, and then there's nothing more. No! Repenting and seeking the Lord is a responsibility and privilege in which we must engage every day!

So, brethren, before the day of the Lord comes upon us, let us seek the Lord, seek righteousness and seek humility! For, by the goodness and mercy of God, we may be hidden with Christ in God!

Chapter 27

"Consider Your Ways"
(Haggai 1:5)

Richard Sutton

omeone wrote, "Sometimes everything needs to fall apart to realize who and what is really important." I might add to the quotation, "...and who is in control." God's people spent 70 years in Babylonian captivity learning that lesson. For those who survived the slaughter of Babylon's army, they truly had lost all except their lives. Their names had been changed to reflect the culture they now dwelt in. Their form of worship had changed, for they had no temple, no sacrifice and no need for priests. No wonder the Psalmist lamented as he thought back to the destruction of Jerusalem and their present captivity in Psalm 137:1-6: "By the rivers of Babylon, There we sat down and wept, when we remembered Zion..."

They had lost all. A nation once chosen by God to be a light among the nations had become sinfully arrogant and was now being humbled in captivity. Even their songs had been wrenched from their hearts as they put away their harps rather than be mocked by their captors when they asked them to sing their pitiful songs. But then, even mighty Babylon fell to the Persian king Cyrus, and unlike the Assyrians and Babylonians cruelty and dispersion of the conquered decreed that he was sending the Jews back to their homeland to rebuild what once was -- the temple of God. (cf. 2 Ch. 36:22-23; Ezra 1:1-11) (Roper 414). Zerubbabel, acting as governor, would lead the first expedition of Jews back to Jerusalem (536 B.C.). But only a remnant of 50,000 faithful, who still held "Jerusalem as their greatest joy" (Psa. 137:6; Ezra 2:64-65), would follow. The vast majority had melded in and become comfortable with the pagan culture of Babylon and stayed behind (Laetsch 383-384).

Upon arriving in Jerusalem, they found the city and the once glorious temple in ruins. Ezra records that the Jews immediately went to work to erect and restore the altar of sacrifices to Jehovah; and to lay the foundation of the temple (Ezra 3:12; 5:16). They also began to carry out the mission that Cyrus had sent them back for; rebuilding the temple. But after some years their initial enthusiasm ground to a deafening halt. There are a number of reasons for this, but the end result, regardless of reason, left the temple partially finished and people complacently idle. For 16 years a spirit of indifference, self-indulgence and defeatism caused them to selfishly go about the routine of daily life, complacent to both God and the religious condition of the nation (Hailey 300). They began to focus on rebuilding their own homes, planting crops and vineyards, establishing ranches, and building their own economic stability, while neglecting the Temple of the Lord.

It is this problem that brings the prophet Haggai on the scene. He too has been given a mission by God; to break the selfish self-indulgent and lethargic complacency of the people and get them back working and finishing the temple.

Notice that Haggai's message begins, "Thus says the Lord of hosts, 'This people says, the time has not come, even the time for the house of the Lord to be rebuilt.'" (Hag. 1:2) The first thing that came to my mind was, "Are you kidding me? What do you mean 'the time has not come to rebuild the temple'? You have been in Jerusalem for 16 years. I don't know about you; but when is the right time?" Well, Haggai has a word to God's people that becomes a reoccurring theme that he repeats five times (Hag. 1:5, 7; 2:15, 18). In the NAS and NKJV it is the phrase "consider your ways"; other translations translate the phrase as "look what is happening to you!" or "Give careful thought to your ways." It is a wakeup call! Why haven't the people prospered? They have worked hard, but all their efforts result in dissatisfaction and failure. Why? Their failure is a result of God's displeasure with their priorities. God had been placed on the backburner of their lives. Remember, God said, "I am a jealous God..." (Exo. 20:5) God won't settle for being in second place in anyone's heart much less third, fourth or fifth, etc. to other things. Yet, as you read through the text, the people are going about their business with no thought of God nor the reason they returned to the promised land, to rebuild the temple. How could they be so complacent, so impassionate about God? Haggai's mission is to help the people 'consider their ways' by breaking them out of their complacency and renewing their passion for God.

PASSION

What does the word passion mean? Passion is defined as "an intense, driving, overmastering feeling" (Webster 831). In other words, passion is an overwhelming, all-consuming emotion, conviction or drive for something, someone or some cause. People are passionate about all kinds of things. People are passionate about fashion, politics, books, plants, animals, athletics, education, farming, eating, money; the list is endless. Every person is passionate about something, someone or a cause that drives them. Without passion nothing great ever gets done. Passion is what gets you out of bed in the morning to go to school, work, you name it.

It is my conviction that God's people had lost their passion; they had become distracted by things of far less importance, things that make up the routine of everyday living just like today. Such things as making a living, working hard with their hands, building houses, eating, drinking and shopping for clothes to stay warm; but for what purpose? Maybe they were passionate, but they were passionate about the wrong things. Haggai is going to help them consider their ways, and in doing so, God's people will once again find their real passion for life -- God.

CONSIDER YOUR WAYS – RENEWING YOUR PASSION FOR GOD (HAGGAI 1:2-4)

The key verses that reveal the heart and attitude of the people are verses four and seven which in essence say, "You people are living in your luxurious houses that you have built for yourselves, while my house (the temple) lies desolate in ruin." What is God's issue? Does it anger God for people to build and live in houses? Is God angry because He has no physical temple to dwell in? The universe is His throne! What has God so angry that He withholds His manifold blessings from His people? The answer is this: God, the Lord of hosts had been supplanted by lesser, much lesser things. God no longer sat on the throne of His people's hearts; they had lost their "PASSION" for God and had become complacent about Him. And their complacency was proved by their lack of action in rebuilding God's temple, for if they had been passionate for God, the temple would have been built and in service long before.

Application

Before we are quick to condemn Israel's complacency, we might want to ask ourselves about our own passion for God. Where does God stand on the passion meter of your heart? Is it possible that as a body of God's people (elders, preachers, deacons, teachers, Christians in general we are in need of renewing our passion for God? Have we become settled in the land with our nice church buildings and comfortable pews? Have we become complacent? Are we passionate about God?

Do you know Jesus was passionate? Jesus had three all consuming, overwhelming passions that drove Him in His life and they are found in Matthew's gospel (Matt. 22:37-40).

One day a teacher of the Law came up to Jesus and asked Him a question, "Teacher, what is the greatest commandment in the Bible?" He in essence was asking Jesus, "What is the most important thing in the Scriptures?" (Mt. 22:36) Do you know what Jesus told him? He told the lawyer that the first and most important command is, "You shall love the LORD your God with all your heart, and with all your soul, and with all your mind" (Mat. 22:37). Jesus' love for God consumed Him and drove Him ever more steadily to carry out His mission which would lead Him to the cross because of His Father's love (John. 3:16).

As Christians, His passion should be our passion. Last year I was invited to attend a breakfast banquet sponsored by "Fellowship for Christian Athletes." In attendance that day were about 3,000. The guest speaker that morning was Bobby Bowden, former coach (now retired) for the Florida State University Seminoles from 1976 -2009. Over a period of thirty-three years, Bowden became one of the winningest coaches in NCAA football with a record of 377-129-4, second only to the late coach of Penn State, Joe Paterno. During his time at Florida State, Bowden led FSU to an Associated Press and Coaches Poll National title in 1993 and a BCS National Championship in 1999, as well as 12 Atlantic Coast Conference championships. He has more championship rings than he does fingers. While being interviewed at the banquet he was asked a question by the Master of Ceremonies, "What is your number one priority in life, and what advice would you give to these young athletes?" Now you would think that to Bobby Bowden, football would be his all-consuming, overmastering passion in life; but you would be wrong. He told the audience that morning that life was all about keeping the right priorities in order, that life was like a big wheel with many spokes that had to be kept in balance and at the center of the wheel must be God. He said at the top of the list of priorities in life must be God and then quoted Matthew 6:33. Next he said comes your family, then your church, your education, and your career; he was saying you will be an athlete for only a brief period of your life. Get your education so you can get a job and finally, he said after all this is in order - football. Now he was talking to aspiring high school and college athletes and his message to them was be passionate about God first and foremost – love the Lord your God with all your heart mind and soul and you do so by seeking Him first (FCA Breakfast Bowl)!

Is God our overwhelming, all consuming, overmastering passion? Are we truly seeking Him first or are other things dethroning God from His rightful place in our hearts? Does God fill our thoughts? Is He our motive and reason for being in all that we say, think and do? After all, we too are a temple (1 Co. 6:19).

CONSIDER YOUR WAYS – RENEWING YOUR PASSION FOR THE MISSION (HAGGAI 1:7-11)

When the remnant of Israel returned from captivity, they returned with one clear mission; to rebuild the temple. They had started, but now it had sat unfinished for 16 years. So, Haggai reminded them of their mission, "Thus says the LORD of hosts, Consider your ways! Go up to the mountains, bring wood and rebuild the temple that I may be pleased with it and be glorified." Haggai's message was, "Look what has happened to you; you have become real busy with life, with things you thought were priorities and what has it brought you? Drought, failed crops, vineyards, ranches, all the labor of your hands has come to nothing" (Hag. 1:7-11). What is the remedy? Renew your passion for the mission and build God's temple, then He will be pleased. The implication is, renew your passion for the mission and your fortune will turn around.

Application

Remember I said that Jesus had three all-consuming passions that drove Him? Well, the first was His passion for God, but His second passion was and still is His love for people and their souls (Mat. 22:38). Jesus had a passion for the mission. How many of you saw the movie—"The Passion of Christ"? You see, from the start to the finish of the movie – you know where that movie is heading and what the ending is going to be; Jesus' crucifixion—right? What caused God to send His son into the world to be born in a manger and grow to adulthood? What caused Jesus, who was God in the flesh, to endure all the ugliness of sin and not wash His hands of the whole mess? What caused Jesus to stay faithful and endure the extreme stress in Gethsemane's garden? What intense emotion caused Him to endure the beating on the pavement and then the ridicule? What enabled Him to go to the cross and allow men to drive nails into His hands and feet and endure the insults of the bystanders? What was it that stimulated and stirred His soul to action that He would go through all He went through? The answer to all these questions is His passion. But what was His passion? His passion was not a "WHAT"; it was a "WHO." You see, Jesus' passion was for people. He wasn't excited, invigorated, or exhilarated about the cross. In fact, the Bible says He despised the shame of the cross (Heb. 12:2). Jesus had a passion and His passion was for people, for you and for me. And listen, Jesus wasn't just passionate about his friends; He was also passionate about His enemies. Jesus, you see, was on a RESCUE MISSION. Everything Jesus said and did was centered on His passion for people who were lost, including those who are lost and don't even know it.

What was His mission? "For the Son of man has come to seek and save the lost" (Luke. 19:10). His passion for the mission must be our passion as well. Do we need to consider our ways and remember that we, too, are on a rescue mission? We all know the passages by heart, don't we (Mat. 28:18-20; Mark. 16:15-16)? Are we passionate about the mission, or are we in need of being reminded to go as Haggai told the remnant "Go up to the mountains, bring wood and rebuild the temple..."? Do we need to be reminded to "Go and make disciples...," "Go and preach the gospel to all creation..."? Jesus was able to transfer His passion for people to the early church. How do I know? In the Acts and history of the Apostles (Acts 2:38, 41, 47; 8:1-3; Col. 1:23), they took the mission seriously and not only turned the world upside down; they spread the good news to the then known world in their generation. They got it; they understood they were on a rescue mission.

It was December 7, 1988 – Armenia—they called it the earthquake of 1989. This quake was off the Richter Scale. Altogether 30,000 people died in four minutes. Established businesses lay demolished; dream homes turned into splinters of wood, green parks were blanketed in white rubble. The father of ten year old Armand could not drive to his son's school. Streets were closed. But Armand's father was driven by a passion to find his son—so persistently he finally got to the school. He eventually broke through the crowd, climbed upon a rock pile of rubble to a tree and climbed up high enough to scan the sky line. He studied the layout of the rubble of a once thriving school. He identified where his son's school used to be. He tried to locate where his son's class would be. He finally identified where he believes his son's class was and he began to pull rock after rock, desk after desk; he looked for his lost son and called his name...ten hours has passed, his hands are bleeding, fingernails long since wore and torn loose; his knees were raw from crawling over rubble. But he continued to dig when others told him to give up... Twenty four hours finally passed and Armand's relentless father would not give up. Would you? Hands cracked, knuckles bleeding, heart racing... Twelve hours had turned into 24, then 36. Then, after 38 hours, he pulled a rock back and heard his son's voice. It was a faint cry of "papa, papa, papa ,papa". His passion for what was lost finally paid off.... "Papappppapa, you found me, you found me!"

So why did Armand's dad so persistently pursue his son? It was his *passion* for Armand! Family, to rescue the lost it is going to take a passionate persistence; whether it is a friend, neighbor, relative or a complete stranger, you just can't give up! Don't let others discourage you—don't quit moving the obstacles, don't quit because it takes time. Jesus didn't and hasn't given up on the lost -- nor should you—His Passion must be Our Passion.

Brethren, if we are ever going to make an impact on our world and carry out the one clear mission that Jesus gave to the church, we need to renew our passion for the mission and go!

Maybe it is time we start asking ourselves some hard questions. Why isn't the church today showing a substantial rate of growth numerically? Why are so many of our children falling away after graduation from high school? Why are we struggling today to find and train preachers to fill our empty pulpits? Why do our missionaries have to beg for money to carry out the mission in foreign fields? Could it be that God is blowing all our efforts away because we have become complacent? If the book of Haggai teaches us anything, it teaches "don't do what I say and I will blow your efforts away (Hag.1:9); do what I say and you'll be blessed" (Hag. 2:18b-19).

CONSIDER YOUR WAYS – RENEWING OUR PASSION FOR THE WORD (HAGGAI 1:12-15)

Haggai holds the honor of being one of the few prophets that God's people listened to and obeyed (Hag.1:12). God's Word spoken through one of His prophets renewed a passion in the people that had lain dormant to activity. Would that the people had listened to Isaiah or Jeremiah in the first place. Had they done so they would never have gone into captivity and Solomon's temple would have remained standing. Twenty four days after Haggai spoke to the people, the Lord 'stirred up the Spirit of the people' and they began the work of rebuilding the temple and Haggai, for his part, would live to see it erected. The effort of the people who listened to the Word of God spoken by Haggai, and their obedience to it, pleased the Lord and He promised to be with them and to bless them (Hag.1:13; 2:18-19). It is still my conviction that God's displeasure with the returning Jews really had little to do with the rebuilding of the temple proper; it did have a great deal to do with their complacent lack of honor, respect, reverence and obedience to His Word and Person. God not only deserves, He demands, faithfulness and obedience, and the opposite was demonstrated to God by their lack of effort to rebuild the temple until the prophet Haggai arrived on the scene with a "thus says the Lord of Hosts." Finally, a people listened to God through His messenger; it was about time. They truly did 'consider their ways' and renewed their passion for the one and only God.

Application

Remember I told you Jesus was passionate about three things? Well, the third thing Jesus was passionate about was God's Word (Mat. 22:40). Think back just prior to the beginning of Jesus ministry; Jesus had been baptized by John in the Jordan and then immediately was led to the wilderness where He would go without food for forty days. At the end of the forty days, when He was physically at His weakest moment, the adversary came to tempt Him. He said, "If you are the Son of God, command these stones to become bread." Do you remember what Jesus said at that time? He answered, "Man does not live on bread alone, but from every Word that proceeds from the mouth of God" (Mat. 4:3, 4). What was Jesus' passion?

How passionate are you for God's Word? Let's for a moment reflect on Psalm 119: 103, 105, 127. How many of you are passionate about food? What is your favorite sweet or desert? For the Psalmist it was honey. This is how he viewed God's Word; he goes on to say that God's Word is more desirable than food and more precious than not just gold, but refined pure gold. From God's Word he finds light and wise counsel to navigate through the dark corridors of life that are filled with the obstacles that man continually trips upon. The Psalmist was passionate about God's Word.

Application

Do you have that kind of passion for God's Word that overwhelmingly drives you to hear it preached, or are you more concerned about the clock? Are you passionate to read it, study it and meditate upon its truth in order to put it into daily living in faithful obedience, or are other distractions of more importance?

There are times when I have driven by large denominational buildings where thousands attend and I wonder why the Lord's church can't build such buildings and fill them to capacity like that? It is then that I have to remind myself of the book of Haggai. It is not buildings or large gatherings that impress God; it is passionate faithfulness and obedience to His Word that impresses and pleases God. There was a day when God settled for a small but passionate remnant of faithful and obedient servants (eight in all) who gathered in a large boat as the rest of the world breathed its last. The Lord wants passionate, faithful and obedient people. Are you passionate for His Word?

FINAL THOUGHTS AS WE CONSIDER OUR WAYS AND OUR PASSION

Is your passion for God, the mission and His Word like the very breath you breathe?

When I was a small boy, I learned to swim in a small stream of cold water that fed a trout fish hatchery in the back of the place where I lived in Springville, Utah. It was about twelve feet wide and six feet deep at its deepest point; deep enough to drown in, but shallow enough to dive in, sink to the bottom, and shove off the bottom to make it to the other side. I don't know that such strategy was really called swimming, but after some time I thought I had the hang of it; that is, thought I had learned how to swim. One day a bunch of my buddies all decided to go down to the public swimming pool that was heated and really swim. We all gathered our things and went. Most the guys I hung out with that summer were pretty good swimmers, but not me. Well, upon arriving, the very first thing my friends did was head for the high dive. I thought to myself, "The high dive, are you kidding me?" As we all walked up to the high dive, a life guard asked each of us boys if we knew how to swim, to which they all responded with a yes. When she came to me, how was I to answer? I didn't want to be embarrassed or seem to be a coward. I took a gulp of air and said, "YES!" I just didn't know how big a gulp I was getting ready to take in. Well, I followed and as each boy took his turn at climbing a twelve foot ladder and walking out to the end of the diving board and jumping, it soon became my turn. Gulp, oh boy here goes; I walked to the end of the diving board...do you have any idea how high twelve feet is to a small boy? I could almost swear as I looked down that I saw stars. I gathered my courage, held my nose and jumped. I hit the water and went straight to the bottom. I forgot everything I had learned about swimming! Instead of pushing off from the bottom, which would have shot me to the top, I just started making a swimming stroke, standing dead still on the bottom of that twelve foot pool, thinking it would bring me to the top. But the going up was slow and I began to run out of air; I was getting nowhere fast. Soon, I was completely out of air and strength; I looked toward the surface and said to myself, "you're done." I decided to make two more strokes. If I didn't make it to the surface in two more tries, I had decided I would give up. I made the strokes; one stroke, no surface; but on the second try a couple of my fingers broke the surface. Finding air, I renewed my efforts like I had never done before. I broke the surface, head coming out of the water; I started thrashing around like a mad person and made it to the side of the pool. I pulled myself out of the water, grabbed my towel and immediately left the public swimming pool, friends or no friends! I went back to the comfort of the trout stream for further lessons. Question: while I was below the surface of the water in that swimming pool, out of air and strength, what do you think was the most overwhelming, all consuming, driving force or passion in my life at that moment?

What are you most passionate about at this very moment? Are you passionate about God? Does He consume you? Are you passionate about the mission? What about His Word; do you love reading it, studying and meditating upon its truths? As in the days of Haggai, maybe it is time for us to do some passionate rebuilding ourselves and consider our ways.

WORKS CITED

Hailey, Homer. *A Commentary on the Minor prophets.* Grand Rapids, MI; Baker Book House, 1972. Print.

Roper, Coy D., PhD... *Truth for Today Commentary.* Searcy, AK. Resource Publications, 2013. Print

Laetsch, Theo. *Bible Commentary the Minor Prophets.* Saint Louis, MI. Concordia Publishing House, 1970.

Webster, Mirriam. *Webster's New Collegiate Dictionary.* Springville, MA. G.& C. Merriam Company, 1973

Fellowship of Christian Athletes Breakfast Bowl, Dec. 20, 2013

CHAPTER 28

"Behold Your King Is Coming To You"
(Zechariah 9:9)

Cherie Vestal

Our story opens during the 5th century B.C., a time when Confucius and Buddha were making an impact on the Asian world. It was a time when, by the hand of God, powerful kingdoms had arisen, and conquered the little land of Israel because of their continuing sinful ways. The aggressive Assyrian empire had swept away the northern tribes entirely. The mighty Babylonians had dominated the southern tribes, forcing them into exile. Now, by God's will, the Persian empire had allowed the Israelite people to return to their homeland. They returned to rebuild their nation, literally from the ground up.

It was a time of hope, and yet discouragement. It was a time of hard work and overpowering weariness! It was a time to rebuild their land, and especially to renew their relationship with their God.

Voices were heard: Haggai, and later Ezra and Nehemiah. These men were sent by God to encourage and exhort. Rebuild the Temple! Renew your hearts toward God! Rebuild the wall! So they built. They started the Temple. They built their houses. They faced serious opposition from the surrounding people. And they stopped.

Another voice was heard. God's prophet Zechariah joined the voice of Haggai: Finish the Temple! Work to completion! Don't quit! And then a message of another type was proclaimed by Zechariah, which included these words:

Rejoice greatly, O daughter of Zion!
Shout, O daughter of Jerusalem!
Behold, your King is coming to you;
He is just and having salvation,
Lowly and riding on a donkey,
A colt, the foal of a donkey. (Zechariah 9:9)

These words had a different focus, deeper than the "keep working" exhortation. This message was an invitation to pause for a moment and look up. **Look up from the present, and look to the future.** In the future, a King -- their very own king -- would come to this place, this *exact* place! What a reason for joy, shouting, and exultation!

Their King would be a righteous king, unlike the current empires. His character would be pure and good. Their King would be of humble demeanor, unlike the pomp of the current and recent empires. He would be lowly, even. His appearance would be meek and gentle in nature, not domineering. Their King would make his entrance on a donkey, unlike the warhorses they had no doubt seen. He would come, not charging in, but making an almost understated entrance. A King – their very own king, was coming!

Can you see the glimmer of light in their eyes? Can you feel the spark of hope in their hearts? Can you sense the surge of zeal in their demeanors? Zechariah's message served to bring renewed motivation to God's people of his day, in the 5th century B.C.: "Get ready for the King!"

But not long after Zechariah's message came a silence, a very long silence. 400 years went by without encouragement or exhortation. 400 years passed with no further message from God's prophets. The words, "your King is coming," were echoing down through time, awaiting fulfillment, awaiting realization.

THE FULFILLMENT

Long after Zechariah's words seemed doomed to remain on a dusty scroll (by man's way of thinking), there was a stirring in the now-well-established city of Jerusalem. Something, or more accurately Someone, was causing a commotion. A crowd was approaching from the direction of Bethphage. There was joy! There was shouting!

Another crowd began to form at the entrance to the city of Jerusalem, and soon mingled with the first. There was exultation! At the center of the scene was a Man – humble, not regal in appearance – sitting on a young donkey. He was being treated like a king though, as the crowds laid down their garments and palm branches to form a welcome. He was being lauded and praised, as One coming in the name of the Lord! Little children would even glorify His name!

The Reaction of The Religious Hierarchy

The established religious hierarchy of the day frowned on the procession. Why were these people lauding a nobody, a traveling teacher at best, as though He were

Someone special? If He really was the Messiah, wouldn't it be obvious? Wouldn't He charge in and eradicate the iron grip the Roman empire had on them? To their way of thinking, the crowds' praises were ludicrous, blasphemous! Perhaps these leaders had forgotten Zechariah's words, words which were being fulfilled in their very presence.

The established religious hierarchy loved their religion. They had added some things, and built up themselves as the elite. They had a nice thing going. But Jesus had pointed out their hypocrisy. He had exposed their outward show without the inward purity (Mat. 23). Jesus had drawn their crowds after Himself. Their jealousy would be documented (Mat. 27:18). After this procession, they were more determined than ever to rid themselves of this Jesus!

The Reaction of The Crowds

This moment may have been the apex of the common people's love of Jesus during His earthly life. For this brief moment, it seemed everyone in the streets was lauding His name as One sent by God! They were truly praising! They were joyful! They were living the prediction of Zechariah. But less than one week later, the same crowds would be rallying to the prompting of their leaders, and shouting "Crucify Him!" (Mat. 27:22).

The Reality of Jesus. Jesus knew the hearts of all men (John 2:25). He knew the evil thoughts of the Pharisees and scribes. He even conversed with them in their objection to the crowds' praises (Mat. 21:15-18).

He knew the fickle hearts of the common people, that they would soon be delivering Him up instead of praising Him. But Jesus seemed to understand their sincerity in the moment. And He knew that as He fulfilled this mission, a door of salvation would be opened for all. Even many of those standing here might enter!

The mission was His focus. In this event, Jesus fulfilled Zechariah's prophecy, yes. But His lowly demeanor was perhaps first due to the humbling of Himself to God's will (Phil. 2:5-8, Heb. 5:5-8). He was not here to be crowned in this moment! The crown would come later. Now, He had a job to do. He was quietly bringing salvation to earth. Isaiah in chapters 52 and 53 foretells His quiet, submissive nature as He carried out His Father's mission. Jesus was here, giving His life as a ransom for many (Mark 10:45).

The fulfillment of Zechariah's prophecy was documented by writers of Jesus' day. Four inspired writers -- Matthew, Mark, Luke and John -- recorded the event. Matthew and John even referenced Zechariah's very words! Their living, active, inspired writing became vibrant and available to readers everywhere. Their words, eventually combined in the pages of the New Testament, were passed down from generation to generation to generation. The truth about the lowly King was there, waiting to be realized.

THE REALIZATION

Nearly two-thousand years down the corridor of time, we open on another scene. In a powerful but perhaps waning nation once thought to be "Christian," a small group of ladies have gathered at the 2015 Bear Valley Lectures. These ladies are followers of Jesus, though they have never seen Him (John 20:29). These ladies are considering the powerful prophecy of Zechariah, and its amazing fulfillment. The reality of Jesus' entrance as a humble King can be understood by the record of the succeeding events: it is evident that He humbled Himself to death, even the death on a cross (Phil. 2:8).

Soaking it In. Realizing the truth of what Jesus accomplished in the Triumphal Entry is easy for us in one sense, as we look back. Those in Zechariah's day may have wondered about it. Those in Jesus' day may have missed it. But we can see it more clearly now. It has been explained to us by the gospel writers.

Jesus came, and many missed Him. He wasn't what or who they expected. He had even invited them, saying, "Come to me all who are weary and heavy laden, and I will give you rest. Take my yoke upon you and learn of Me, for I am meek and lowly in heart, and you will find rest unto your souls" Matthew 11:28-29. They missed Him, partly because of the paradox of the King's humility. "Isn't this the carpenter's son?" (Mat. 13:55) "Can any good thing come out of Nazareth?" (John 1:46)

Jesus lived His life as a paradox of God. He was the homeless man who was the Son of God. Jesus was the Savior who was crucified. And here, Jesus was the lowly King. Jesus was the chief cornerstone over which many stumbled (1 Pe. 2:7-8); the paradox was too great for them! And they missed Him.

Living In Its Truth.

God is the master of paradoxes, of two true things which seem to exclude each other. Many in our day trip on God's paradoxes and never really come to Christ. They trip over being saved by faith and by baptism (Eph. 2:8, 1 Pe. 3:21), over needing God's grace, but also needing to live a life of good works (Eph. 2:8, Jas. 2:24), over losing one's life to save it (Luke 17:33). And so they miss Him.

Even as followers of Christ, we struggle with the paradoxes. We struggle with being kind to an enemy (Mat. 5:44), with rejoicing in persecution (Mat. 5:11-12), with forgiving the wrongs of others as part of our own forgiveness (Mat. 6:14). We have a hard time with humbling oneself to be lifted up (Jas. 4:10), with being wise as serpents and harmless as doves (Mat. 10:16), with decaying outwardly while being renewed inwardly (2 Co. 4:16). God's ways are higher than our ways (Isa.

55:9)! And sometimes we miss His ways by thinking too much in human terms. God's paradoxes turn our human reasoning on its head.

Jesus came not only as a lowly King, but in a secondary way to be our example. We are to live in the truth that He demonstrated so perfectly for us. "Deny yourselves, take up your cross daily, and follow Me," He invites (Luke 9:23). How can we better apply Jesus' example of humility in our own present-day circumstances?

To be great in God's eyes, we must be willing to serve – like Jesus was. (Mat 23:11) This means that we are willing to step up, or step down, to the opportunities that God presents us. Sometimes we charge ahead of God, like Moses (Exo. 2:11-12). Sometimes we focus on our own inadequacies, like Gideon (Jud. 6:15). Sometimes we pout, like Jonah (Jon. 4). We need to fine-tune the paradox of great service!

To be pleasing to God, we must turn the other cheek – like Jesus did (1 Pe. 2:21-23, Mat. 5:29). We must let go of the slaps and insults that come our way undeserved. But it's so much easier to harbor a grudge! It is seems right to us; we want to be justified in our wounds. But wasn't Jesus pure and innocent as He received His horrifying, unthinkable wounds? And still He could pray, "Father, forgive them" (Luke 23:34) instead of "Father, give them what they deserve!!" We need to better accept the paradox of persecution.

To be joyful in God we must look past the temporary visible things, and look to the eternal unseen things (2 Co. 4:18) – like Jesus did. But it's so easy to look around! We see others' financial security. We see their earthly comforts and pleasures. And we want that too. Jesus didn't even have a home of his own on this earth (Mat. 8:20). He knew that the physical things wouldn't last. He kindly reminded Martha what was better (Luke 10:41-42). He lovingly begged the rich young ruler to see past his stuff (Mark 10:21). He pleaded, "Don't worry about all these things" (Mat. 6:31-33)! We need to reinforce the paradox of eternal vision, of seeing the invisible.

The realization of Zechariah's prophecy and of Jesus' fulfillment touches our hearts. We soak it in. We take some notes. We hope to do a better job of living the paradox of Jesus' example in our daily lives. We close our Bibles and go out the door to live as humble servants of our Great God. And the clock ticks. And the calendar pages flip. And the world turns. And nations rise and fall. And the words are still there -- the Word of the Lord that lives and abides forever (1 Pe.1:23). The words are still there, waiting for others to take them in and be amazed, inviting others to live in God's paradoxical and profound truth of a humble King.

CONCLUSION

Our story closes in the present day, a time when post-modernism and Islam are making an impact on the world around us. It's a time of hope, and yet discouragement. It's a time of hard work and overpowering weariness! It's a time to rebuild and renew relationships with God. Another prophetic word has survived a dusty scroll, and has been preserved in the pages of the New Testament. After many, many exhortations to persevere and endure, it is a message of another type, a message with a different focus. It's an invitation to pause for a moment and look up. **Look up from the present, and look to the future.** In the future a King, our very own King, will come again –

> And I saw heaven opened, and behold a white horse, and He who sat on it is called Faithful and True, and in righteousness He judges and wages war. His eyes are a flame of fire, and on His head are many diadems;…He is clothed with a robe dipped in blood, and His name is called The Word of God…And on His robe and on His thigh He has a name written, "KING OF KINGS, AND LORD OF LORDS" (Rev. 19:11-16).

Behold, your King is coming to you again! Is there a glimmer of light in your eyes? Is there a spark of hope in your heart? Is there a surge of zeal in your demeanor? For still, as long as mankind continues on the earth, there is a message that serves to bring renewed motivation to God's people: "Get ready for the King!" "The King of kings is coming!"

CHAPTER 29

"Will A Man Rob God?"
(Malachi 3:8)

Corey Sawyers

In a classic episode of The Andy Griffith Show, Sheriff Andy Taylor arrives at the filling station to find Gomer Pyle taking a nap in the garage. Mayberry's head lawman extinguishes a fire of oily rags in the trash can that Gomer was oblivious to in his slumber. The garage attendant feels a great sense of indebtedness to Andy, the man who saved his life. Gomer insists he is Andy's servant for the rest of his days. Instead, Gomer becomes a nuisance for not only Andy, but his entire family. Throughout the episode, Taylor tries to tell Pyle that he has done more than enough. Gomer maintains, "Nothing is too much for the man who saved my life!" Nothing less that his all would do to repay the man to whom he felt he owed everything.

Dim-witted Gomer understood a principle that God's people have struggled with for centuries: an individual owes his or her savior all they have. God's people have forgotten this vital principle. It was true with His people in the Old Testament. It was true with His people in the New Testament. It is true with Christians living under the New Covenant today. His people lose sight of the fact that man owes God everything. Therefore, a faithful child of God must be fully committed and dedicated to Him. This is a subject dealt with by the prophet Malachi.

The book of Malachi was written sometime around 430-400 B.C, making it the last book of the Old Testament chronologically. This is the same time recorded in Nehemiah 13 and Ezra 7 – 10. Zechariah had written his message of returning to the Lord about one hundred years prior, and yet the message was needed again. As with all of the prophets, their names are significant. The name "Malachi" means "my messenger." Malachi was the messenger of God. The priests were also messengers, but they had failed miserably (2:11 NASB).

Despite the fact that the people had been back from captivity and in Judah since 536, they had failed to turn to God as He wanted. While in captivity, all they wanted was to return to their promised land, to restore temple worship, and be able to serve God where and how He had commanded. Now that He had brought them back, they would not fulfill their commitments to Him. They were content where they were, while doing what they liked.

This is seen throughout the book, but it could be argued that it is witnessed nowhere more clearly than in the third chapter of Malachi. There God asks the people, "Will a man rob God? Yet you are robbing Me! But you say, 'How have we robbed You?' In tithes and offerings. You are cursed with a curse, for you are robbing Me, the whole nation of you!" (Malachi 3:8-9). Like the people of Malachi's day, God's people today have a daily choice to make. It is a choice between remaining or returning, contentment or commitment, halfway and whole and disloyalty and dedication. It is a choice between robbing or restoration.

If the child of God today is to make the proper choice - if he or she is to keep from making the mistakes of Malachi's day - one must answer two important questions. These two questions are posed in Malachi 3:8-9. The possibility of robbing God and how exactly that is done are the two questions from the text this lesson will cover. This study will examine how it is possible for a Christian to rob God, and will then give three examples of how a Christian can do so. This study will conclude with an explanation of why one robs from God, and how to correct this mistake. In the process, it will be shown that one must trust God, not rob from Him.

First, how is it possible to rob God? After all, He is God! He is the Creator and Sustainer of all there has been, all there is, and all there ever will be. We cannot break into His home - He is everywhere. We cannot sneak in to steal - He knows all. We cannot deceive Him - He hears and knows our thoughts. He has no billfold to pickpocket, no car to highjack, and no bank accounts from which to embezzle. How is it possible for mortal man to take any thing against the will of and from a God that we cannot even fully explain?

An understanding of the word used in this passage would be helpful. For all of the passages that mention stealing, robbery, or sins of similar nature, the word translated "rob" in Malachi 3 is quite unique. It is a word used only six times in all of the Hebrew scriptures - four of those times are in two verses of Malachi (3:8-9). The other two occurrences are within one verse in Proverbs, which will be dealt with shortly.

This Hebrew word used is a broad word. It can mean to assemble, gather, harvest, withdraw, or remove (Jenni and Westermann 1099-1102). It is used in relation to gathering or collecting grain or money, or in gathering and assembling for battle (Brown, Driver, and Briggs 867). Most interesting is what Gesenius writes concerning the word. He says the basic definition is "to be high and rounded at top, as a mound, the head." He also says the word denotes, "to hide, as the head in a garment, a flower in its calyx." Because of this, the word does not mean simply to rob as in a hold-up. Instead, "it is figuratively to deceive, to defraud any one" (721).

So, what does this mean? The idea is that it is withholding something owed to someone else, of which the person has a completely full cup. It is like telling the beggar on the side of the street, "I have no money," when one has a pocket full of cash. The only other place this Hebrew word for "rob" is found is in Proverbs 22:23. In that verse, that is the exact situation that is explained. When someone "robs" the poor by not giving them what they could, God will "take" the life from that person - and God is the one who has life to give.

In the case of God and the Jews of Malachi's day, they were not giving to God as they should, and yet they had plenty to give. The problem was not they had to hold back or starve. The problem was not that they did not have anything to give. The problem was not that they were lacking in means and thus could not give. They had, and they had in plenty. God has not requires does not, nor ever will, require anything of man that man does not have. They had (as the Hebrew word would indicate) a rounded over, full cup. They just would not give.

This was robbery, in a sense, because it was owed to God. It was the agreement they had made with God beginning at Sinai and had re-committed themselves to in Nehemiah chapter ten and following. God, as always, had kept His end of the bargain. His children had not. They owed God because of their commitment, but also because all they had was His blessing. God not only would not require what man did not have, but He gave man all he needed (and more) to give.

The way Malachi is set up is very unique. "It is known as the didactic-dialectic method. First he makes a charge or an accusation; then he fancies someone raises an objection, which he next proceeds to refute in detail, substantiating the truth of his original proposition" (Robinson 161). Malachi's initial charge in this text is, "Will a man rob God?" The objection he assumes they would have is, "How have we robbed You?" He then explains the answer to that question. That is where this study should now turn also.

So, second, exactly how can one rob God? "In tithes and offerings." He uses this as an example. Remember, this was something they had committed to. This was something they had. This was something that rightly belonged to God. Malachi is going back to the same thing of which they are guilty. God is essentially saying, "I promised and I have given you My best. Then, when the time of offering comes, you give Me less than your best." When this writer took Old Testament VI at Bear Valley, Dave Chamberlin had a humorous way of depicting this that has stuck. He would say that they told God they would give Him only their best, and when time to give arrives, they are saying, "Where is that three-legged lamb?" They had better, but were unwilling to give. Were they giving? Yes! They just were not giving as they should.

The tithe was to be set apart for God (Le 27:30-33). Although God rightfully owns all of creation, it was only these tithes and offerings to which He laid claim. The people were to put it aside first for Him (Hailey 421). It was already supposed to be dedicated to be given to God. While Christians today are not under the Old Testament covenant of tithing, a child of God can be equally guilty of "robbing" God through not giving to Him what is rightfully His. Like the tithe, these are things that are only possessed because He gave them to man, and are things that first and foremost should be committed to Him. While many could be mentioned, at least three examples from Malachi are gifts commonly robbed from God by His children today.

The first gift Christians far too commonly rob from God is homage. This was true in Malachi's day. Their sacrifices consisted of leftovers (1:7-8, 13-14). They did not give as they should (3:8-9). and their worship was heartless (1:13). Today, Christians are guilty of the same wrongdoings. If there have ever been individuals whose cup was overabundantly full, it is the modern child of God. There are more time-saving devices now than in the entire history of mankind. Advances in technology and modern methods have allowed men to have more "free time" than ever before. How many of those extra hours will God receive? There is time for television and movies, but not to show others God's word. There is time for reading newspapers, magazines and novels, but not to read God's word. There is time for talking about sports, the weather, and politics, but not for telling others about Jesus. So, God gets only the leftover time.

The modern American Christian is among the wealthiest people materially in the history of the world. Cars, houses, entertainment, savings, bank accounts, food, clothing, and a multitude of other expenses fill the budgets. So one will spend, save, buy, get, and acquire. Sunday comes and the plate is passed. There is a reach into the pocket and whatever is leftover is given to God.

Talents are used to make more money, to advance in careers, to climb the corporate ladder. One will use whatever talents he or she may have to entertain, to please and to posture to gain social status. Yet, when are those talents used for God? Are they bound behind the excuse of, "I am not comfortable doing _____" until nothing gets done? Doing only what we care to do, God only gets the leftovers of our talents.

The time, the treasure, and the talents one has, he or she only has because they were given to them by God. The cup is full. These things should be dedicated and committed to Him from whom they came. Yet, through a lack of giving to God talent, time and treasure first - solely to give Him honor, glory, and praise, God is robbed. "How have we robbed you?" In holding back the homage He deserves.

The second gift Christians far too commonly rob from God is homes. This was also true in Malachi's day. They had abandoned God's plan for what marriage should be (2:10-16). The permanency of marriage had been ignored through unjust divorce. The preeminence of marriage had been ignored through polygamy. The purpose for their marriages had been forgotten in choosing spouses outside of a relationship with God.

Today's Christian also robs God when he or she does not take seriously what the home should be about. When marriages are not dedicated to God, a husband and wife have failed to see to whom they made vows - not only to each other, but also to Jehovah. The marriage relationship was given by God to man. A spouse is a blessing from God. That home that is begun when that covenant is entered into must be taken seriously, and must be devoted to the God who established the home. When that is not the case, marriages can be easily thrown away, relationships will not be as cherished, and roles will not be fulfilled as they should be.

When parents fail to see children as the blessing from God they are, they are less likely to dedicate their raising to the God who gave them. The Psalmist reminds parents that not only did their sons and daughters come from God, but they should be sent back to Him (127:3-5). In comparing them to arrows in a quiver, the point is clearly seen: a parent's job is to aim those blessings back to Him who gave them. When that is not seen, children are taken for granted, easily disposed of, and are not trained to know God through word and example.

Homes, and the relationships had in them, are only had because they were given by God. The cup is full. The home should be dedicated and committed to Him from Whom it came. Yet, through a lack of giving to God Christian homes, God is robbed. "How have we robbed you?" In holding back the homes He deserves.

The third gift Christians far too commonly rob from God is hearts. This was also true in Malachi's day. The first argument propositioned by Malachi is found in the first five verses of chapter one. The people supposed God did not love them. In turn, they refused to give God what He deserved - and what He wanted most - their love. In fact, it could be argued this breaking of relationship was the foundational problem in all of Malachi (Baldwin 216-7).

What is that God wants more than anything else? He wants the hearts of men. What is it that God cannot do? He cannot make man love Him. That is why He is pictured over and over as this Father longing for the day when His children will return to Him by choice, as in Jesus's parable of the Prodigal Son. That is why John tells us of how much God loves man in what is perhaps the most well-known verse of the Bible (John 3:16). God can command (Mal. 4:4). God can remind (Mal. 3:16-18). God can threaten (Mal. 3:9) and He keeps those negative promises as well. However, God cannot make man love Him.

How many children who grew up in the pre-internet world loved getting the "Sears Christmas Wishbook." It would arrive in October or November and officially would signal the holiday season. Every year, this writer (and his brother) would write initials by all the presents that Momma and Daddy were supposed to buy. The number of initials in the book always outnumbered the presents under the tree, yet what made Christmas fun was the receiving. As a husband and father, those priorities change. A wife's smile at the perfect present and a son's laughter at wishes fulfilled bring greater joy than anything that could be received.

What made the difference in that priority change? Two words are the answer: heart and love. When one loves as he or she should they do not hide, they do not hold back, and they do not rob! They give! The same principle holds true with one's relationship to God.

One's heart and love are only possible because they were given by God. The cup is full. The heart of man should be dedicated and committed to Him from Whom all blessings came. Yet, through a lack of giving our love to God, God is robbed. "How have we robbed you?" In holding back the hearts He deserves.

How is it possible to rob God? God is robbed when one does not give to Him what he has that God deserves. How exactly does one rob God? God is robbed when one does not give Him his homage, his home, or his heart. So, what needs to be done? It seems so simple. The Christian must not rob God. He must give God homage through the way time, treasure, and talents are prioritized. He must dedicate his home to God. He must love Him with all his heart. But honestly, how many Christians do not know that is what God demands and deserves? So, why do Christians keep robbing God?

The problem is faith - it is trust. Why was it that Moses struck the rock rather than doing it God's way? He did not believe (Num. 20:12). Why did kings of Israel and Judah make foreign alliances they were forbidden to make? They did not trust in the Lord (2 Ch. 16:7). Why was the church at Laodicea lukewarm? They did not think they needed God (Rev. 3:17). Why was it that the children of Israel turned from a God that had saved them? He told them beforehand it would be because they did not trust in Him (Deut. 31:20).

Trust must be with all the heart (Pro. 3:5). Trust means to not be ashamed (Psa. 25:1-2). Trust means to not be afraid (Psa. 56:11). So, how is it done? How does one cultivate trust? It gets back to that love. One must truly believe God loves him, that God wants the best for him and will take care of him. That is known in a "factual way" when the gospel is obeyed. Then, when one gives to Him (a little at first), he or she sees God's care and love. They trust to give Him a little more, and the cycle continues. Christians must just start the cycle.

Former Pennsylvania Senator and Presidential candidate Rick Santorum tells a story that happened after his wife, Karen, gave birth to their youngest daughter, Bella. Bella was born with a rare chromosomal disorder. A majority (over 99%) of those diagnosed with this particular condition do not live past a couple weeks. A very religious family, they did all they could do. They prayed. One day, Senator Santorum and his eldest daughter, Elizabeth, were putting together the crib they had bought for Bella. The father told his daughter to be sure and keep the box. After all, he explained, we may not ever use it. Elizabeth broke down crying. She said, "How could you not believe?" Immediately, she began tearing up the box (Santorum).

For far too many Christians, God is just the emergency "9-1-1" number to call when something is wrong. Even at that, many want to hold on to the box and trust in self and stuff. A Christian must have faith and tear up the box. He must learn to trust in God. He must quit robbing Him of what He so rightfully deserves - homage, homes and hearts.

Why was Abel willing to give God his very best? He tore up the box and trusted. Why was Abraham willing to offer his son's life to God? He tore up the box and trusted. Why was Joseph willing to give up his position and do what was right to honor God? He tore up the box and trusted. Why was Moses willing to give up the benefits of being in the house of Pharaoh for being a nomad? He tore up the box and trusted. Why was Paul willing to give up his former life as a Pharisee (with all the honor and wealth it afforded) to be beaten, stoned, imprisoned, and persecuted constantly for the cause of Christ? He tore up the box and trusted.

Each Christian must ask, "What box am I hanging on to?" Tear it up and trust. Only when one trusts Him as he should will that Christian give as he should. There must be a willingness to give God one's self first, realizing giving is man's portion of grace (2 Co. 8:5-7). One should get into the book of Hebrews and see how God always rewards trust. A dedication should be made to giving God more. God wants all of His children to get outside of themselves, tear up the box, and trust in Him. That is the challenge God gave His people in Malachi 3:10. He challenged them to "test" Him. God is saying, "Put me to the test and watch Me bless you!"

God has richly blessed. The cups are full. One can rob God if he or she does not give back to Him what rightly belongs to Him: homage, homes and hearts. Instead, each Christian should trust Him with their time, treasure, and talents. When Christians richly give to Him from their full cup, He will pour out a flood of blessings that all the containers on earth could not hold. So, tear up that box. You do not need it. You only need to trust in Him and give yourself to Him.

WORKS CITED

Baldwin, Joyce G. *Haggai, Zechariah, Malachi: An Introduction and Commentary.* London: The Tyndale Press, 1972. Print.

Brown, Francis, S.R. Driver, and Charles Briggs. "עבק." The Abridged Brown-Driver-Briggs Hebrew and English Lexicon. Trans. Edward Robinson. Oxford: Clarendon Press, 2000. Print.

Gesenius, Wilhelm. "עָבַק." Gesenius' Hebrew-Chaldee Lexicon to the Old Testament Scriptures. Trans. Samuel Prideaux Tregelles. Rome: n.p., 1846. Print.

Hailey, Homer. *A Commentary On The Minor Prophets.* Grand Rapids, MI: Baker Book House, 1972. Print.

Jenni, Ernst, and Claus Westermann. "עבק." *Theological lexicon of the Old Testament.* Trans. Mark E. Biddle. Peabody, MA: Hendrickson Publishers, 1997. Print.

Robinson, George L. *The Twelve Minor Prophets.* Grand Rapids, MI: Baker Book House, 1965. Print.

Santorum, Rick. Interview by Sean Hannity. *The Sean Hannity Show.* Premiere Networks. 10 Feb. 2015. Radio.